Experimental Phonology

Experimental Phonology

Edited by

John J. Ohala
Department of Linguistics
University of California
Berkeley, California

Jeri J. Jaeger
Linguistics Program
University of California
Davis, California

1986

ACADEMIC PRESS, INC.
Harcourt Brace Jovanovich, Publishers
Orlando   San Diego   New York   Austin
London   Montreal   Sydney   Tokyo   Toronto

ACADEMIC PRESS, INC.
Orlando, Florida 32887

United Kingdom Edition published by
ACADEMIC PRESS INC. (LONDON) LTD.
24–28 Oval Road, London NW1 7DX

LIBRARY OF CONGRESS CATALOGING-IN-PUBLICATION DATA

Main entry under title:

Experimental phonology

    Includes bibliographies and index.
    1. Grammar, Comparative and general—Phonology.
2. Phonetics, Experimental.   I. Ohala, John J.
II. Jaeger, Jeri J.
P217.3.E96   1986   414   85-15682
ISBN 0-12-524940-3 (alk. paper)
ISBN 0-12-524941-1 (paperback)

PRINTED IN THE UNITED STATES OF AMERICA

86 87 88 89   9 8 7 6 5 4 3 2 1

Contents

Contributors   ix

Preface   xi

1. Introduction
John J. Ohala and Jeri J. Jaeger

Why Experiments?   1
Introduction to the Chapters in the Present Volume   6
Conclusion   11
References   11

2. Phonetic Universals in Vowel Systems
Björn Lindblom

Introduction   13
Some Facts about Vowel Systems   14
Present Approach to the Theory of Vowel Systems   16
Implementation of the Framework   20
Extensions and Limitations   36
References   42

3. The Behavior of Nasalized Vowels in the Perceptual Vowel Space
James T. Wright

Introduction   45
The Experiment   50
Perception of the Quality of Nasalized Vowels   57
Conclusions   64
References   65

4. On Describing Vowel Quality
Sandra Ferrari Disner

Introduction   69
ANOVA   71
Conclusion   77
References   79

5. Phonetic Explanation for Phonological Universals:
The Case of Distinctive Vowel Nasalization
Haruko Kawasaki

Introduction   81
Phonological Universals in Nasals and Nasalization   82
Experiment 1   87
Experiment 2   89
Discussion   94
Appendix: References to the Languages Cited in the Text   96
References   98

6. The Size and Structure of Phonological Inventories:
Analysis of UPSID
Ian Maddieson

Introduction   105
Design of the Database   106
Variations in Inventory Size   107
Relationship between Size and Structure   109
Phonetic Salience and the Structure of Inventories   113
Compensation in Inventory Structure   116
Segments and Suprasegmentals   118
Segment Inventories and Syllable Inventories   120
Conclusions   121
References   122

7. Quichean (Mayan) Glottalized and Nonglottalized Stops:
A Phonetic Study with Implications
for Phonological Universals
Sandra Pinkerton

Introduction   125
Method   127
Results and Analysis   130
Discussion   136
References   139

8. **Phonological Contrast in Experimental Phonetics: Relating Distributions of Production Data to Perceptual Categorization Curves**

Terrance M. Nearey and John T. Hogan

Phonological Units of Perception	141
Relating Distributions of Natural Speech Production to Perceptual Categorizations	143
Further Applications of the NAPP Model	158
Conclusion	160
References	160

9. **Testing Phonology in the Field**

Lyle Campbell

Introduction	163
The GP Program	163
External Evidence	165
Recommendations	169
Questions	171
Conclusion	172
References	173

10. **Word Games: Some Implications for Analysis of Tone and Other Phonological Constructs**

Jean-Marie Hombert

Introduction	175
Word Games and the Analysis of Segments and Syllabicity	176
Tone	178
Level of Application of Word Game Rules	183
Conclusion	184
References	185

11. **Experimental Phonology at the University of Alberta**

Bruce L. Derwing and Terrance M. Nearey

Introduction	187
Early Studies on Rule Productivity	188
Morpheme Recognition Studies	191
Studies on the Psychological Reality of the Phoneme	197
Further Attempts to Test Phonemic Analyses	200
Experiments on Phonological Rules	205
Conclusion	207
References	208

12. Concept Formation as a Tool for Linguistic Research

Jeri J. Jaeger

Introduction   211
The Concept-Formation Technique   214
Experiment 1: Automated Concept Formation   221
Experiment 2: Verbal Response Concept Formation   225
Conclusions   234
References   235

13. Testing Hypotheses Regarding the Psychological Manifestation of Morpheme Structure Constraints

John J. Ohala and Manjari Ohala

Introduction   239
Prior Hypotheses   240
The Conflict between the Hypotheses   242
Experiment 1: G&J versus EGP   244
Experiment 2: G&J versus C&H   246
Experiment 3: Judgments on Paired Stimuli   247
Discussion   248
Conclusion   251
References   251

14. Sound Change in Perception: An Experiment

Tore Janson

Introduction   253
Methods   254
Results and Discussion   255
Conclusions   259
References   260

Subject Index   261
Language Index   264

Contributors

Numbers in parentheses indicate the pages on which the authors' contributions begin.

Lyle Campbell (163), Department of Anthropology, State University of New York, Albany, New York 12222

Bruce L. Derwing (187), Department of Linguistics, University of Alberta, Edmonton, Canada T6G 2H1

Sandra Ferrari Disner (69), Phonetics Laboratory, Department of Linguistics, University of California, Los Angeles, California 90024

John T. Hogan (141), Department of Linguistics, University of Alberta, Edmonton, Canada T6G 2H1

Jean-Marie Hombert (175), Université de Lyon II, U.E.R. des Sciences du Langage, 69500 Bron-Parilly, France

Jeri J. Jaeger (1, 211), Linguistics Program, University of California, Davis, California 95616

Tore Janson (253), Department of Linguistics, Stockholm University, S-106-91 Stockholm, Sweden

Haruko Kawasaki (81), Voice Processing Corporation, Cambridge, Massachusetts 02142

Björn Lindblom (13), Department of Linguistics, Stockholm University, S-106-91 Stockholm, Sweden

Ian Maddieson (105), Phonetics Laboratory, Department of Linguistics, University of California, Los Angeles, California 90024

Terrance M. Nearey (141, 187), Department of Linguistics, University of Alberta, Edmonton, Canada T6G 2H1

John J. Ohala (1, 239), Department of Linguistics, University of California, Berkeley, California 94720

Manjari Ohala (239), Linguistics Program, San Jose State University, San Jose, California 95192

Sandra Pinkerton* (125), Department of Linguistics, University of Minnesota, Minneapolis, Minnesota 55455

James T. Wright (45), Speech Plus Inc., Mountain View, California 94043

*Present address: Hewlett-Packard Laboratories, Speech Recognition Group, Palo Alto, California 94304.

Preface

There are three characteristic features of this book we would call readers' attention to. It is, first, a collection of chapters which attempt to give answers to traditional *phonological* questions. Second, it is a collection of chapters which approach their topic using *experimental* means. Neither of these first two characteristics is remarkable by themselves. Rather, it is the third property of this book, that it is the intersection of the first two, which makes it noteworthy: It is the first collection of chapters which approach phonological questions using experimental methods. These chapters are offered as original contributions to the various questions they address, but even more, they have been put together in one volume so that they might constitute a critical mass which demonstrates the viability of experimentation in phonology.

The questions addressed in the chapters are those that phonologists have always asked: questions about the mechanisms of sound change, the causes of phonological universals, what speakers know about the sound patterns of their language, and how this knowledge is used. The experimental means used to approach these questions include phonetic studies (articulatory, acoustic, or perceptual in nature), traditional techniques of field linguists (e.g., word games), and methods adapted from experimental psychology. Statistical analysis and the development of formal mathematical models which can account for or predict a wide range of phonological data are also important aspects of some chapters.

Although the book is intended primarily for the linguist, particularly the phonologist, actively engaged in research on the structure and behavior of speech sounds, there are two other groups of readers that may find the book of interest. Supplemented by other readings, especially many of those referred to in the individual chapters, this book could serve as the nucleus for graduate or undergraduate courses on experimental phonology. Many of the experimental methods utilized in the essays (e.g., word games and concept formation) do not require elaborate equipment or resources not usually found in any linguistics department. Other experimental techniques (e.g., some of those used in the perceptual phonetic studies) could be easily adapted to require nothing more complicated than tape-splicing facilities. In addition, we hope this book will be read by nonlinguists, especially those in sister disciplines (e.g., psychology, communication engineering, speech pathology, language and teaching, philosophy), as well as by the informed layman, in order to obtain some idea of what types of questions occupy phonologists and what means they are currently using to get answers to those questions.

The chapters have been arranged according to the general topic they cover: The first six deal with problems of phonological universals, the next one considers how the structure of a particular language biases the way a native speaker perceives speech, the next five explore the psychological representation of phonological constructs, and the last considers the detection of ongoing sound change. Some readers may find the following groupings also useful for their purposes:

Development of mathematical models: Lindblom (Chapter 2), Wright (Chapter 3), and Nearey and Hogan (Chapter 8)

Techniques appropriate to fieldwork: Pinkerton (Chapter 7), Campbell (Chapter 9), Hombert (Chapter 10), Derwing and Nearey (Chapter 11), Jaeger (Chapter 12), and Ohala and Ohala (Chapter 13)

Studies concerned with speech perception: Lindblom (Chapter 2), Wright (Chapter 3), Disner (Chapter 4), Kawasaki (Chapter 5), Nearey and Hogan (Chapter 8), and Janson (Chapter 14)

Studies relevant to theories about sound change: Lindblom (Chapter 2), Wright (Chapter 3), Kawasaki (Chapter 5), Pinkerton (Chapter 7), and Janson (Chapter 14)

Studies concerning vowels: Lindblom (Chapter 2), Wright (Chapter 3), Disner (Chapter 4), Kawasaki (Chapter 5), and Janson (Chapter 14)

Studies concerning consonants: Maddieson (Chapter 6), Pinkerton (Chapter 7), Nearey and Hogan (Chapter 8), Derwing and Nearey (Chapter 11), and Jaeger (Chapter 12)

Constraints on sound sequences: Kawasaki (Chapter 5) and Ohala and Ohala (Chapter 13)

Studies addressing issues of the units of speech (syllable, phoneme, feature): Nearey and Hogan (Chapter 8), Hombert (Chapter 10), Derwing and Nearey (Chapter 11), and Jaeger (Chapter 12)

In the editing of this book we have benefited from the critical comments of many of our colleagues and associates, especially Manjari Ohala and Richard Janda, and from the clerical assistance of Wendy Wiener.

Introduction

JOHN J. OHALA
JERI J. JAEGER

WHY EXPERIMENTS?

The evolution of a scientific discipline is probably similar to that of human economic evolution. Originally the food and clothing needed for survival were obtained by hunting and gathering; later it was discovered that these necessities could be obtained in greater abundance—and virtually on demand—by raising livestock and cultivating plants. That is, rather than rely on chance opportunities for obtaining sustenance, humans found that they could create and control these opportunities themselves. Likewise, one can generally identify a "hunting and gathering" stage in the history of most scientific disciplines, where the evidence needed to sustain a hypothesis is obtained by chance observations. Gradually the discipline's practitioners discover how to create and control the opportunities they need in order to make those crucial observations, that is, they learn how to conduct experiments.[1]

We would like to believe that phonology is on the verge of developing into an experimental discipline. We could be wrong. There have been many prior calls for phonologists to turn to experimental studies of speech behavior, and in some isolated cases this call has been answered by practice (e.g., Osthoff & Brugmann 1878/1967; Rousselot 1891; Thumb & Marbe 1901;

[1]Ohala (1974) differentiates between 'nature-made experiments' and 'man-made experiments.' For the purposes of this introduction and the sense intended by the title of this book, the term 'experiment' used here refers to the latter.

1

EXPERIMENTAL PHONOLOGY

Verner 1913; Esper 1925; Grammont 1933; Haden 1938; Fry 1960; Lisker, Cooper, & Liberman 1962), but these have not triggered a self-sustaining tradition of experimental phonological studies.

Physiology has a similar history. Although there are isolated examples of physiological questions being answered or explored experimentally before the nineteenth century (e.g., by Harvey, Haller, Priestley), it was not until the mid-nineteenth century that the experimental approach was firmly established in the field through the efforts of Claude Bernard and those of like mind (e.g., Helmholtz, Pasteur, Purkyně). To a large extent their struggle was to demonstrate the unity of all scientific endeavor, that is, that there is fundamentally only one method in science. This method does not belong exclusively to physics, which was the first discipline in history to firmly establish what is known as the scientific method; rather, there is no bar to the application of knowledge derived from other disciplines to questions in one's own field. (This view should not be confused with naive reductionism, the notion that the ultimate understanding of all aspects of the universe *requires* that they be interpreted or reduced in terms of some common set of fundamental physical entities, for example, subatomic particles. All that can be asked is to *allow* such interpretation where it enhances our understanding.)

The experimental method is based on the recognition that our knowledge of the world is subject to many distortions, in other words, that the world is not as it may seem. We must take special pains, then, to make as carefully as we can the observations that our knowledge is based on; we must refine these observations and structure them in such a way that we can eliminate or attenuate the factors which might distort them or render them ambiguous (with respect to the light they shed on the object of our study). An experiment, then, is simply the creation—contrivance, if one prefers—of a situation in which crucial observations, those relevant to a given question, may be made in such a way that they will be free from as many anticipated distorting influences as possible.

The primary purpose of experimentation is not to create knowledge, although by chance it often happens that completely new, unexpected things are observed during experimentation. It is, rather, a way of refining our knowledge. Following Popper (1959), one might even say that in a sense experiments actually destroy knowledge; at least they help to show which of our beliefs about the workings of the world do not agree with observations and hence should be discarded.

There is a popular misconception that experimentation always involves instrumentation or complex procedures of some sort—at the very least, statistical analysis. This, of course, is not true. The research reported in this volume in the papers by Hombert and Campbell, for example, which involve word games, illustrates this. However, it is easy to identify the origin of the misconception: A great many of the experiments in the mature disciplines *do* involve instruments and complex procedures. But it is important to emphasize that the complexities are simply a reflection of the advances made in those fields, that is, the accumulated wisdom about what steps are necessary to make observations of phenomena in a way that is free from distortion. Naturally, as experimentation proceeds, the discipline gains experience in recognizing previously overlooked sources of error and in finding ways to compensate for them. Several of the authors in this volume criticize their initial experimental results and conduct new experiments designed to overcome what are perceived as potential sources of error; see, for example, the chapters by Lindblom, Derwing and Nearey, Kawasaki, Ohala and Ohala, Wright, and Janson. The instrumentation or complex procedures, however, are not the essence of experimentation; the level of complexity is dictated solely by the level of sophistication attained in previous investigations of the given question. What is common to all experiments is *taking as much care as possible to refine one's beliefs*. It may be asked—and has been (Chomsky 1964, p. 81, 1965, p. 20)—whether such care in making observations of the universe should be the primary concern of scientists or whether the search for insight into the nature of the universe should be the principal goal. Of course, the desire to understand the workings of the universe has driven all scientific work since the time of the early Greek philosophers. But, as was demonstrated by Galileo and other fomenters of the Scientific Revolution, little progress can be made toward achieving this goal *unless* care is taken in observing the universe. To build a bridge it is not enough to just have the intention of getting to the other side; one must have some experience with how various materials—wood, stone, steel—behave when a load is applied to them and then how to correct any behavior which interferes with the main purpose of the structure.

Although conceptually one may regard making theories[2] as distinct from making experiments, in practice the distinction is blurred. First, experiments, in the sense used here, have no meaning unless motivated by theory. Theory dictates which observations, of the infinite observations that *could* be made, *should* be made. Without theory there would be no indication of what to observe and how to interpret it once observed. Aimless data gathering, therefore, does not constitute doing experiments. On the other hand, theory construction (when this is correctly considered not as a static thing but as

[2]Traditionally, a distinction was made between the terms 'hypothesis' or 'speculation' on the one hand and 'theory' on the other, in that the latter term was reserved for hypotheses that had been subjected to a substantial body of experiments and supported by their results. In current linguistic usage, however, 'theory' has been used in the sense of the original term 'hypothesis', that is, a guess or speculation that often has little or no empirical support. In the discussion here we follow, with some misgivings, the usage current in linguistics.

something that develops and evolves) that is not checked and guided by experiment is equally useless, as numerous cases in the history of science reveal to us, for example, the fantasy of Cartesian cosmology.

Second, experiments often require that a theory be refined, sometimes so extensively that the result differs greatly from the original, casually offered, theory. When trying to find an observable consequence of the theory, it is frequently necessary to make quite explicit what the theory would predict in specific situations. Especially when theories are first tested, as is the case in our field, as much or more effort may go into a careful, explicit, (re)formulation of them as into the data gathering itself (the data in some cases may already have been gathered for some other purpose). It is in this type of situation that *models* are important. A model is, ideally, simply a theory that is so explicit in its formulation that it eliminates all ambiguity as to what it would predict. It should be able to stand on its own without being propped up, or fudged, by its maker. The model, once wound up and made to "go," either behaves in a way that accords with observations of the thing it represents or is judged wanting. In the present book, the chapters by Lindblom, Nearey and Hogan, Wright, and Derwing and Nearey report efforts to refine a model sufficiently to bring it into alignment with empirical observations.

This discussion of models, then, also provides a clear answer to an issue that is currently debated in phonology: the role of *formalism*. Formalism makes theories explicit. Formally stated theories are easier to test than informally stated ones. Beyond this, formalism has no further function. The formal statement of the theory is the *first* step of the many needed to properly test a theory. Perhaps it is unnecessary to repeat this in a book on phonology, since it is over a century since phonologists were warned about putting too much reliance on the

> method of investigation according to which people observe language only on paper and resolve everything into terminology, systems of rules, and grammatical formalism and believe they have then fathomed the essence of the phenomenon when they have devised a name for the thing . . . for on paper almost everything is possible. (Osthoff & Brugmann 1878/1967:202, 198)

Of course, there is no sure path to the truth—with the exception of divine revelation—and the results of any experiment will always be subject to criticism of some sort and possible rejection. The same is true of the non-experimental or non-empirical methods used to evaluate theories, for example, the authority, prestige, or eloquence of the person or group espousing the theory or the perceived elegance or simplicity of the theory. It may seem, then, that in comparison with the latter methods, experimental methods come out the loser: non-empirical methods involve much less effort but the result is the same, only tentative, temporary "truths." In the short term, especially during that period when a field is just beginning to employ experimental methods, this may indeed seem to be the case. But in the long term, the result is not the same. Changes in the direction of current theory which come about due to debating methods or the rise and fall of the prestige of theory makers show little or no coherence. Such is evident, for example, in the periodic replacement of one dominant school by another in Greek (and subsequent European) philosophy, as well as in other fields such as political science, literary criticism, and theology with little or no experimental base. On the other hand, changes of theory which are motivated by examination of experimental or empirical results exhibit the property of *convergence*. We may judge an experiment (others' or our own) to have been misguided or deficient in one way or another. With the experimental tradition, though, the proper response to a "bad" experiment is a better experiment. As a consequence, as history demonstrates, the experimental results get progressively better in the sense of giving us power over the world, that is, allowing us to predict events with more accuracy. Dalton's atomic model had to be revised given the experimental results of Rutherford and Thompson, and their conceptions in turn had to be revised given the findings of Bohr, Heisenberg, and others. But at each stage of refinement some aspect of the old theory is retained or, at the very least, is recognized as a necessary conceptual precursor to later theories, as, for example, many historians of science regard the early, now superseded, "fluid" theories of heat and electricity. The same convergence, the same ultimate usefulness, of theories in a non-experimental tradition is not found. It is not the rationalist construction of Cartesian cosmology which forms the basis of current space guidance systems. It is not the *a priori* model of human physiology based on the four humors that forms the basis of the medical tradition which today has been able to eradicate such diseases as smallpox and poliomyelitis. Aside from applications which exploit phonology's quite successful conquest of the linguistic past and its taxonomy of elements of speech, the discipline has relatively little to show in the practical domain for the theoretical turmoil that has absorbed the energies of phonologists over the last century or so. This is not because, like literary criticism, society makes no practical demands of our field. If phonology were making any progress in finding out how speech sounds behave (in their physical and psychological form), confident recommendations on methods of second-language instruction, methods of correcting pathological speech, ways to synthesize high-quality speech, and ways to do automatic recognition of speech would be possible. It might be expecting too much to look so soon for solutions to these very difficult problems, but one cannot help wonder if phonology's apparent lack of progress in these and other areas is due to its weak empirical base.

The characterization of the nature of experimentation given here may be accepted, but many would still maintain that the experimental method is not appropriate to phonology or any aspect of linguistics (Itkonen, 1978). Among the reasons for this view might be the quite correct assessment that linguistic behavior, unlike the behavior of physical systems such as pendula, the orbits of electrons, and chemical reactions, is dependent on so many factors that it is virtually impossible to control them all in contrived, experimental settings. But this situation only tells us—trivially—that it is more difficult to do experiments in linguistics (or any behavioral science), not that it is any less necessary. Bernard, who wanted to understand the workings of the human body, faced the same problem and the same objections to experimentation, but answered:

> Experimentation is undeniably harder in medicine than in any other science; but for that very reason, it was never so necessary, and indeed so indispensable. The more complex the science, the more essential it is, in fact, to establish a good experimental standard, so as to secure comparable facts, free from sources of error. (Bernard 1865/1957, pp. 2-3.

The issues of whether phonology should adopt accepted scientific methods of validating theories or whether it should isolate itself from the scientific mainstream, as in earlier days physiology tried to do, is such a fundamental one, on which phonologists hold such strong opinions, that probably no amount of argumentation will change anyone's mind on the matter. The ultimate form of persuasion, if any would succeed, though, should be "existence proofs": There is no more convincing way to show that experiments can help to answer questions in phonology than by answering phonological questions through experiments. Ultimately, it was the success of the experimental method in physiology rather than Bernard's eloquent persuasion which finally transformed that field. We hope the papers in this volume will add to the growing body of literature which constitutes this existence proof.

INTRODUCTION TO THE CHAPTERS
IN THE PRESENT VOLUME

The chapters in this volume span a wide range of subareas in phonology: the first six deal with phonological universals, the next with the way language-specific structure influences native speakers' perception of speech, the next five with the psychological mechanisms underlying speakers' mastery of the sound system of their language, and the last chapter with the detection of ongoing sound change.

Studies on Phonological Universals

Phonetic and phonological universals—whether absolute universals of the sort 'all languages utilize stops in their sound inventory' or statistical universals like 'sequences of labial consonant plus [w] tend to be avoided in syllable onsets'—give us important clues to the fundamental mechanisms underlying speech. They may serve a function comparable to that of Mendeleyev's periodic table of elements in the development of chemistry.

Björn Lindblom, in his chapter "Phonetic Universals in Vowel Systems," offers a further refinement of the model presented in Liljencrants and Lindblom (1972) which attempts to predict, on the basis of articulatory, acoustic, and perceptual constraints, the spacing of the vowels in the vowel space for languages with a given number of vowels. He elaborates the perceptual components of the model with current findings from psychophysical models of auditory processing, achieving a significant improvement in the agreement of the model's predictions with data on the vowel inventories of languages. Lindblom argues persuasively for the elimination, where possible, of *axiomatically postulated* constructs in phonology, for example, distinctive features and natural processes, and their replacement with comparable *deductively derived* constructs.

A test of a hypothesis about how nasalization affects vowel quality, which was offered to account for certain sound changes, is reported in the paper by James T. Wright, "The Behavior of Nasalized Vowels in the Perceptual Vowel Space." His study, which uses the method of multidimensional scaling of perceptual judgments, attempts with considerable success to reconcile phonological facts and phonetic predictions, the latter from the articulatory, acoustic, and perceptual domains. Wright's results are particularly important in that they illustrate the role of the listener in the implementation of sound change and, like Janson's and Kawasaki's chapters (discussed below), that these things can be studied in the laboratory.

Investigations of phonological universals require cross-language comparisons of phonetic and phonological data. There are many areas where it is not very clear exactly how to make these comparisons. Vowel quality is one such case. The measured acoustic properties of vowels are influenced to a major extent by the dimensions of the speaker's vocal tract as well as by the language- or dialect-specific vowel norms. Modern theories of the forces that shape vowel spaces have now become sufficiently detailed that it is important to be able to know if it is true, for example, that, as claimed, the Danish /i/ is higher than the English /i/. Sandra F. Disner, in her chapter "On Describing Vowel Quality," offers a solution to this problem by showing the advantages of an analysis of variance of acoustic measures of vowel quality and applies her results in an evaluation of current theoretical work on universals of vowel systems.

Haruko Kawasaki, in her chapter "Phonetic Explanation for Phonological Universals: The Case of Distinctive Vowel Nasalization," presents the results of a perception experiment which helps to explain universal (cross-language) tendencies between distinctively nasalized vowels and nasal consonants, specifically, the fact that the two tend not to appear adjacent to each other. She shows that listeners hearing the same nasalized vowel in the context of a nasal versus non-nasal consonant "discount" some amount of the nasalization when a nasal consonant is nearby, because it can be "blamed" for some of the nasalization. They thus fail to hear the vowel as having as much nasalization as it actually does. This finding has significant implications for a wide range of other universal constraints on the sequencing of sounds as well as for mechanisms of sound change.

In a chapter using a quite different technique from the others, Ian Maddieson demonstrates in "The Size and Structure of Phonological Inventories: Analysis of UPSID" how a statistical analysis of the phonemic inventories of a balanced sample of hundreds of languages (as derived from the linguistic literature) can be used to test certain claims about phonological universals. He looks at a number of hypotheses about phonemic inventories, including questions of whether there is an optimal number of segments in a phonemic inventory, the relation between the size of an inventory and its segmental content or structure, and the familiar hypothesis that complexity in one area of the phonology of a language (e.g., vowels) is compensated for by simplicity in another (e.g., consonants or suprasegmentals); on this last question he finds that, contrary to the common belief, "complexity of different kinds goes hand in hand."

The revolution in electronic and digital technology offers phonology unprecedented opportunities to acquire high-quality data with considerably less difficulty than was possible in the past. Sandra Pinkerton, in her chapter "Quichean (Mayan) Glottalized and Nonglottalized Stops: A Phonetic Study with Implications for Phonological Universals," describes how she was able to travel through Guatemala with a miniature phonetics lab and collect aerodynamic data from several speakers of various Mayan languages. The results help clarify phonetic descriptions of the stops in these languages which figure as exceptions to certain claims about universal correlations between voicing, place of articulation, and the ingressive–eggressive character of glottalized series of stops. In addition, she discovered a glottalized stop with an unusual biphasic oral pressure impulse that might be the link between the ejectives and implosives, which are found to alternate in certain Mayan dialects.

The Influence of Language Structure Upon Perception

The idea that the way people perceive speech is biased by the sound system of their native language, particularly by its phonemes, was explicitly stated, on the basis of empirical evidence, by Sapir in the 1930s. Although modern perceptual phonetic studies have provided more convincing empirical evidence of this phenomenon, it is not yet possible to predict precisely, given the phonological inventory of the speaker's language, what form this "warping" of the perceptual space will take. Terrance M. Nearey and John T. Hogan, in their chapter "Phonological Contrast in Experimental Phonetics: Relating Distributions of Production Data to Perceptual Categorization Curves," apply to this problem two mathematical models originally developed for general-purpose pattern recognition or categorization of input signals. They demonstrate the potential of these models for the categorization of stops, fricatives, and vowels. To the extent that these are useful models of the native speaker's perceptual processes, they may be applicable as well to automatic speech recognition.

Psycholinguistic Studies of Phonological Issues

The chapters by Lyle Campbell ("Testing Phonology in the Field") and Jean-Marie Hombert ("Word Games: Some Implications for Analysis of Tone and Other Phonological Constructs") show how word games can be used to shed light on a variety of phonological issues: the psychological reality of certain phonological rules; whether phonotactic rules or sequential constraints require reference to purely phonological units such as syllables or whether morphological information is needed as well; whether tone (and other phonetic properties of words) can be analyzed in a segmental way or as prosodies that "float" on the word, that is, which need not always be temporally tied to the segments of the word. On the latter point, Hombert presents evidence that African and Asian tone languages behave somewhat differently. Both chapters illustrate how a technique that has long been used by some fieldworkers to clarify points of phonological analysis can, with the introduction of certain controls, become a valuable experimental technique.

In "Experimental Phonology at the University of Alberta," Bruce L. Derwing and Terrance M. Nearey give an account of a wide range of pioneering psycholinguistic phonological studies they and their co-workers have undertaken since the early 1970s. These range from the problem of trying to discover the form of the rule by which native speakers of English generate the phonetic shape of the plural suffix, to the basis of subjects' judgments of phonetic similarity or dissimilarity between two phoneme strings, to the psychological reality or accessibility of various phonological rules. Their work illustrates the advantages of having a continuing program of experimental studies in order to be able to refine data and techniques and thereby converge on a common result.

The power of the concept-formation experimental paradigm for psycholinguistic studies in phonology is demonstrated by Jeri J. Jaeger in her chapter, "Concept Formation as a Tool for Linguistic Research." The technique, which involves, in essence, teaching subjects linguistic concepts or categories by induction and then giving them an opportunity to apply these concepts to phonological entities whose categorization is controversial, is appropriate for both laboratory and field work. She reports the results of several concept-formation experiments that clarify the psychological reality for English speakers of the phonemic membership of the phone [k] in word-initial [sk] sequences, the status of [tʃ] and [dʒ] as unit phonemes versus clusters, and the phonetic feature [voice].

Language-specific morpheme structure constraints (MSCs) represent a construct that has survived the many overhauls in phonological theory since the 1950s. Investigations of the psychological representation of MSCs are presented by John J. Ohala and Manjari Ohala in "Testing Hypotheses Regarding the Psychological Manifestation of Morpheme Structure Constraints." Using experimental techniques previously applied to studies of MSCs by Greenberg and Jenkins (1964) and Zimmer (1969), they pit the Greenberg and Jenkins model for MSCs against those proposed in early generative phonology and in *The Sound Pattern of English* (Chomsky & Halle 1968). The Greenberg and Jenkins model, which is based on a general method for comparison of candidate words with words stored in the mental lexicon, is more in accord with the experimental results.

The Detection of Ongoing Sound Change

Sound change—the steps by which distinct daughter languages arise from a common parent language—was the first topic that phonologists succeeded in analyzing in what may be called a scientific way, that is, with a clear understanding of the possible sources of error in such an undertaking and the development of rigorous procedures to compensate for those errors (Rask 1818; Grimm 1822; Schleicher 1861–1862). In part, though, the comparative method relies on an intuitive sense of what kinds of sound changes are likely to occur and which direction they might take, for example, that /ki/→/tʃi/ is more common than the reverse. It remains to put this aspect of the comparative method on as firm a basis as the other components. It is in this context that Tore Janson's paper, "Sound Change in Perception: An Experiment," is particularly important. He demonstrates that sound change can be studied in the laboratory. He finds a difference between older and younger speakers of Stockholm Swedish for the perceptual norms of the vowels /a:/ and /o:/, a difference that can be attributed to an ongoing sound change. In addition, his results help resolve the issue of whether sound changes are phonetically gradual or abrupt; he shows that the sound change he studied must be counted as phonetically gradual since it is doubtful that listeners of either generation would ever have a chance to exhibit a clear category shift on the vowel continuum in a way that would be detectably different from the other generation.

CONCLUSION

In every discipline the number of questions asked always exceeds the number of questions successfully answered. In phonology there have really been only two kinds of questions that have received answers that have demonstrated, time-tested validity: (1) What is the physical nature of speech sounds? Panini, some 2300 years ago, gave initial answers to this question, and phonetics research up to the present time continues to refine this knowledge; (2) What is the history of languages and language families? In the nineteenth century the classical grammarians, using and refining the comparative method, successfully reconstructed the linguistic past. These questions bore fruit because they were married to suitable *methods* of investigation. Currently phonologists have given much attention to many other questions: What psychological structures underlie language use? How and why does sound change take place? What forces shape segment inventories? To obtain answers to these questions it is necessary to develop appropriate methods to study them. This volume represents a collection of studies that employ candidates for these needed methods and at the same time offer candidate answers to some of these important questions. We hope that phonologists will find these papers stimulating—whether they agree with the conclusions reached or not—and go out and do some experiments of their own.

REFERENCES

Bernard, C. 1957. *An introduction to the study of experimental medicine* H. C. Green, trans. New York: Dover. (Originally published as *Introduction à l'ètude de la mèdecine experimental.* Paris: J. B. Bailliere et Fils, 1865).

Chomsky, N. 1964. Current issues in linguistic theory. In J. A. Fodor & J. J. Katz, eds., *The structure of language*, 50-116. Englewood Cliffs, NJ: Prentice-Hall.

Chomsky, N. 1965. *Aspects of the theory of syntax.* Cambridge: MIT Press.

Chomsky, N., & M. Halle. 1968. *The sound pattern of English.* New York: Harper & Row.

Esper, E. A. 1925. *A technique for the experimental investigation of associative interference in artificial linguistic material.* Language Monographs No. 1.

Fry, D. B. 1960. Linguistic theory and experimental research. *Transactions of the Philological Society of London*, 1960: 13-39.

Grammont, M. 1933. *Traité de phonétique.* Paris: Librairie Delagrave.

Greenberg, J. H., & J. J. Jenkins. 1964. Studies in the psychological correlates of the sound system of American English. *Word* 20: 157-177.

Grimm, J. 1822. *Deutsche Grammatik.* (Vol. 1, 2nd ed.). Göttingen: Dieterichschen Buchhandlung.

Haden, E. F. 1938. The physiology of French consonant changes. *Language Dissertations* No. 26.

Itkonen, E. 1978. Linguistics: Nonempirical and empirical. In W. U. Dressler & W. Meid (eds.), *Proceedings of the 12th International Congress of Linguists*, Vienna, 1977, 157-158. Innsbruck: Universität Innsbruck.

Liljencrants, J., & B. Lindblom. 1972. Numerical simulation of vowel quality systems: The role of perceptual contrast. *Language* 48: 839-862.

Lisker, L., F. S. Cooper, & A. Liberman. 1962. The uses of experiment in language description. *Word* 18: 82-106.

Ohala, J. J. 1974. Experimental historical phonology. In J. M. Anderson & C. Jones, eds., *Historical linguistics II. Theory and description in phonology*, 353-389. Amsterdam: North Holland Publishing Co.

Osthoff, H., & K. Brugmann. 1967. Preface to *Morphological investigations in the sphere of the Indo-European Languages I*. In W. P. Lehmann, ed. and trans., *A reader in nineteenth century historical Indo-European Linguistics*, 197-209. Bloomington: Indiana University Press. (Originally published as Preface. *Morphologische Untersuchungen auf dem Gebiete der indogermanischen Sprachen I*. iii-xx. Leipzig: S. Hirzel, 1878.)

Popper, K. R. 1959. *The logic of scientific discovery*. London: Hutchinson and Co.

Rask, R. 1818. *Undersøgelse om det Gamle Nordiske eller Islandske Sprogs Oprindelse*. Copenhagen.

Rousselot, L'abbè. 1891. *Les modifications phonétiques du langage*. Paris: H. Welter.

Schleicher, A. 1861-1862. *Compendium der vergleichenden Grammatik der indogermanischen Sprachen*. Weimar.

Thumb, A., & K. Marbe. 1901. *Experimentelle Untersuchungen über die Psychologischen grundlagen der Sprachlichen Analogiebildung*. Leibzig: Verlag von Wilhelm Englemann.

Verner, K. 1913. To breve fra Karl Verner udgivne af Vilh. Thomsen og J. P. Gram. *Oversigt over det Kongelige Danske Videnskabernes Selskabs, Forhandlinger*, 161-190. (French translation pp. 191-211).

Zimmer, K. 1969. Psychological correlates of some Turkish morpheme structure conditions. *Language* 45: 309-321.

2

Phonetic Universals
in Vowel Systems

BJÖRN LINDBLOM

INTRODUCTION

Phonetic Explanation of Language Universals

From an evolutionary point of view, it does not appear unnatural to assume that language form is forged by the sociobiological conditions of its use. Thus spoken language tends to evolve sound systems and grammars that can be explained, at least in part, with reference to the fact that it is spoken. It uses the vocal-auditory channel and ought therefore to exhibit adaptations to the developmental and adult mechanisms of speech production and speech perception. This point of view implies furthermore that the structuring of sign language should similarly reflect the constraints of its transmission medium, the gestural-visual channel, and that comparative study of speech and sign would be capable of offering important insights into the mechanisms of language (Bellugi & Studdert-Kennedy 1980).

The present chapter is a contribution to the paradigm aiming at the phonetic explanation of language universals (Ohala, forthcoming), and thus it exemplifies the functional perspective described above. It investigates the extent to which certain universal aspects of vowel systems can be said to be consequences of similarly universal properties of speech production, human hearing, and speech perception.

13

EXPERIMENTAL PHONOLOGY

Table 2.1

Vowel Categories[a]

Front		Central		Back		
i	ü	i̇	u̇	ɯ	u	high
I	Ü	ɨ	U̇	Ï	U	lower-high
e	ö	ė	ȯ	ë	o	higher-mid
E	Ö	ə	Ȯ	Ė	O	mid
ɛ	ɔ̈	ė̩		ʌ	ɔ	lower-mid
æ		ǽ			ɒ	higher-low
ä		a	ȧ	ɑ	α	low

[a]From Crothers (1978).

SOME FACTS ABOUT VOWEL SYSTEMS

The source of the data on vowel systems used in this paper is Crothers (1978), who presents a typology based on an "areally and genetically representative" sample of 209 languages taken from the Phonology Archive of the Stanford Project on Language Universals. Crothers (henceforth C; in addition, data, tables, and appendices from C are referred to as C-data, C-appendix, etc.) uses the "classical phonemic method," adding a distinction between marginal phonemes and full phonemes. His analyses are based principally on the fully phonemic vowels and their major phonetic realization (i.e., a fairly narrow transcription of the primary member of the phoneme, see C-Appendix III). Vowel quality is quantized in terms of 37 categories, as shown in Table 2.1.

Figure 2.1 demonstrates some gross trends in the C-data (unnormalized, C-Appendix III). It shows as a proportion of all systems examined how often a given phonetic symbol occurs (observations below 5% excluded). The data pertain to all vowel systems containing three through nine vowels and have been arranged in Table 2.1 in the form of a quasiacoustic vowel chart. We note that [i], [a], and [u] are particularly favored. Peripheral qualities, notably [e], [ɛ], [o], and [ɔ], are next in rank. In third place we find two central vowels, [ɨ] and [ə]; two front rounded vowels, [ü] and [ø]; one back unrounded vowel, [ɯ] (we use C's vowel symbols in this chapter, supplemented by standard IPA symbols, some of which are defined acoustically in Table 2.3). Why Figure 2.1 should look the way it does can be understood in light of the following information. These remarks are based entirely on C's work.

Table 2.2 lists the vowel system types most frequently observed in the C-corpus. The symbols indicate broad transcriptions, since this count was apparently made after applying normalization, that is, turning [I], [ɯ], and [ü] into /i/, /u/, and /ɨ/, respectively.

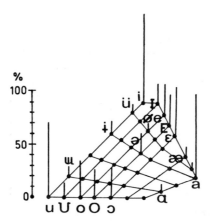

Figure 2.1 Occurrence of phonetic symbols expressed as a proportion of the total number of languages examined (about 200). The data are based on systems containing three through nine vowels (adapted from Crothers, 1978, Appendix III). The phonetic qualities of the unlabeled points are left out for clarity (scores below 5%) but can be inferred with the aid of Table 2.1.

Except for a few cases of two-vowel systems, all languages have /i/a/u/. As systems containing more than these basic three are examined, we first encounter /ɨ/, /ɛ/, or /ɔ/. The vowels /e/ and /o/ occur in larger systems (≥ 7 vowels). A pattern of five basic vowel qualities appears to be the norm, the most common systems being those with close to that number of basic vowels. C further notes that (1) the number of height distinctions is typically equal to or greater than the number of front–back distinctions, (2) the number of interior vowels (e.g., /ü ɨ ə/) cannot exceed the number in the front or back columns, and (3) the number of height distinctions in front vowels is equal to or greater than the number of back vowels. Although Figure 2.1 was constructed without regard to cooccurrence dependencies among the units, the generation of groups of vowels by applying a criterion of highest rank will result in systems that share some of the characteristics that C lists as universals.

Some Previous Attempts to Predict Vowel Systems

Among the first attempts to systematize vowel-system data are those of Troubetzkoy (1929) and Hockett (1955). These studies present typological data and discuss various regularities. The implicational laws of Jakobson (1941) make statements about possible contrasts in the phonological systems of children and in the languages of the world. The gradual unfolding of the vowel contrasts (and other oppositions) is said to obey a rule which we shall here use predictively, namely, the principle of maximal contrast.

In their discussion of the concept of 'markedness', Chomsky and Halle

Table 2.2

Common Vowel Systems Types[a]

Number of vowels in system	Frequency of occurrence in corpus	Vowel qualities (normalized)
3	23	i a u
4	13	i ɛ a u
	9	i ɨ a u
5	55	i ɛ a u ɔ
	5	i ɛ ɨ a o
6	29	i ɛ ɨ a u ɔ
	7	i e ɛ u o ɔ
7	14	i e ɨ ə a u o
	11	i e ɛ a u o ɔ
9	7	i e ɛ ɨ ə a u o ɔ

[a]From Crothers (1978 p. 105).

(1968;409–411) explore how the complexity of a given vowel system can be measured in terms of the marking conventions and the marked–unmarked status of the vowels in the lexicon on the one hand and certain system conditions on the other. Donegan (1978; Donegan-Miller 1972) presents an account of vowel inventories developed within the framework of natural phonology (Stampe 1973). The regularities of such inventories are seen as "manifestations of phonetically-motivated natural processes." Systems are generated (and evaluated with respect to complexity) by applying context-free and hierarchically organized processes (raising, bleaching, lowering, coloring, and so on) in various patterns of interaction.

PRESENT APPROACH TO THE THEORY OF VOWEL SYSTEMS

Axiomatic and Deductive Definitions of Phonological Constructs

The present approach differs from the above-mentioned accounts in a number of respects. We share with Donegan the belief that phonetically motivated natural processes may underlie many vowel-system regularities. Likewise, we do not deny that bleaching, coloring, and so on sometimes have a certain intuitive appeal in natural vowel phonology when seen as 'fortition' and 'lenition' processes (i.e., processes facilitating perception and production, respectively). Nevertheless we find that, although in many respects insightful, Donegan's framework—like Jackobson's implicational rules and the Chomsky and Halle markedness theory—leaves largely unresolved the theoretically fundamental questions of specifying more precisely the nature of these processes, their independent motivation, and their consequences for linguistic form. Central issues are what causes these dimensions of contrast to arise and what causes bleaching, coloring, and other such processes. It may be objected that these questions are premature, that the prospects of replacing many *axiomatically postulated* constructs in current phonology (such as distinctive features, processes, and rules) by derived concepts rigorously and *deductively obtained* and explicitly anchored in speech behavior appear utterly remote at present. However, since in any scientific field the question of independent motivation is the crucial one in the search for explanations, research priorities seem quite clear. The prospects of such a program scoring rapid and easy success may indeed appear remote, but this circumstance should lead to an intensification of efforts rather than a deferral of action and a search for shortcuts (Lindblom 1980, Ohala 1978).

Hypothetical Universals Shaping Vowel Systems

Several hypotheses about universals that influence the shape of vowel systems are presented below and are developed in three steps and deal with the following topics: (1) the definition of the notion of 'possible vowel,' (2) the processes of normal speech perception, and (3) evolutionary constraints on vowel systems.

NOTION OF 'POSSIBLE VOWEL'

'Possible vowel' is defined articulatorily, acoustically, and perceptually. This is done by capturing "possibilities" in terms of the notion of space and by applying this notion in turn to articulation, acoustics, and perception.

A physiologically oriented model, Lindblom and Sundberg (1971) (hereafter L&S), is used to provide a definition of *possible vowel articulation*. In the L&S model, the parameters that control the shape of the vocal tract are as follows: labial width and labial height, mandible position, tongue body (front-back position and deviation from neutral position), tongue blade (elevation and front-back position), and larynx position. A first intermediate representation is constructed from specifications of these parameters in the form of an articulatory profile similar to a tracing of a lateral X ray of the midsagittal outline of the vocal tract. The class of all such profiles defines the space hypothesized to be the universal articulatory space for vowels.

The L&S model can also be used to define the corresponding *acoustic space* (Figure 2.2). The steps involved in its derivation are as follows: A second intermediate representation is generated from the profile. It represents the

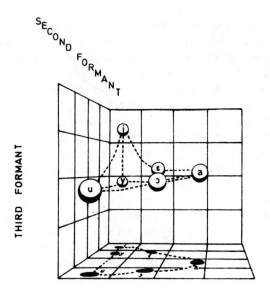

Figure 2.2　Three-dimensional illustration of a hypothetic universal: the acoustic vowel space.

cross-sectional areas along the tract, the so-called vocal tract area function. This is a quantification of the cavity shapes. It is used to derive the end product, the formant frequencies associated with the input articulatory configuration. The class of all formant patterns defines the acoustic vowel space.

The perceptual vowel space is obtained by mapping acoustic onto auditory representations. This has been done in two ways. In a preliminary implementation of the present framework (Liljencrants & Lindblom 1972), henceforth L&L) we substituted the physical frequency scale used in formant specifications for a perceptually more satisfactory dimension, namely, the quasilogarithmic mel scale (Fant 1973).

In the current version we go several steps farther and incorporate a numerical model of the human hearing system that is due to Schroeder, Atal, and Hall (1979). This acoustic-to-auditory transformation is described below.

NORMAL SPEECH PERCEPTION

Human listeners appear capable of making at least the following two types of judgment when listening to a native speaker of their own language: they are able to determine *what* was said (to judge the structure and meaning of an utterance) and to say something about *how* it was said (to judge speech-quality features such as a foreign accent or the phonetic symptoms of patho-

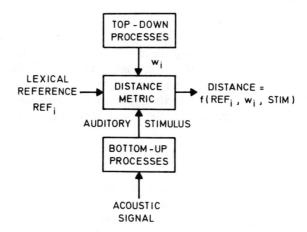

Figure 2.3 Conceptualization of speech perception. An identification depends on the relative distance between stimulus and reference patterns weighted by the grammatical-semantic plausibility of the reference patterns.

logical speech). One approach to the conceptualization of these aspects of a listener's behavior is illustrated in Figure 2.3. Stimulus-controlled (bottom-up) processes refer to the series of transformations that the acoustic signal undergoes in the auditory periphery. These processes are universal in that by definition they are independent of language and cognitive conditions. Some examples are the frequency analysis and the spatio-temporal coding of neural impulses that the peripheral stages of the auditory system pass on to the brain for conceptual analysis (see the auditory model described below). There are also conceptually determined (top-down) processes that delimit a range of alternative candidates for identification in a given context as defined by grammatical structure, "expectations," presuppositions about the speaker, and so on.

How can these phenomena be modeled? Assume that a listener matches the auditory-neural representation of a given speech signal against reference patterns that he retrieves from lexical storage and derives on-line under the influence of grammatical, conceptual, and pragmatic constraints. His judgment of what was said is based on that reference pattern which best fulfills a combination of two criteria: phonetic similarity and grammatical-conceptual plausibility. This matching presupposes a perceptual *distance metric*: phonetic similarity is quantified in terms of the "distance" between the auditory stimulus (STIM in Figure 2.3) and a given reference pattern (REF). This distance is weighted by a coefficient, w_i reflecting grammatical-conceptual-pragmatic plausibility. It is this weighting that introduces top-down effects and aims at describing phenomena such as phonemic restorations and our ability to listen non-physically—that is, our ability occasionally to hear only what we "want" to hear.

A listener's judgment of how something was said is possible because the concept of distance accounts for the identification of an utterance not in terms of a perfect match but in terms of the match that is best relatively speaking. Thus, the highest scoring interpretation may quite commonly be achieved by a distance which is greater than zero or might occur when a listener understands what is being said but furthermore notices that, for instance, the speaker has a heavy accent or exhibits symptoms of dysarthria.

EVOLUTIONARY CONSTRAINTS

We hypothesize that vowel systems tend to evolve so as to make the process of speech understanding efficient and to ensure speech intelligibility under a variety of conditions and disturbances. Such efficiency depends in part on vowel identification, which can be assumed to be facilitated by the ontogenetic and diachronic development of perceptual difference among the targets of a vowel system that are maximally, or, perhaps, sufficiently large (see Jakobson 1941). Our work explores measures of both maximal and sufficient perceptual contrast.

Since the notion of perceptual distance used here depends not only on stimulus-related but also on conceptual factors, it must be pointed out that all calculations reported below were undertaken on the assumption of equal top-down probabilities of vowel-system members. We strongly suggest that such an assumption would be at variance with the facts of everyday speech communication. We know that in individual languages certain vowel contrasts are found more frequently than others, a notion explored under the concept of 'functional load.' However, within the present framework, computational experiments incorporating non-uniform functional load can easily be accommodated. To test the model more fully against data from individual languages it will indeed be necessary to undertake such studies. The trouble appears to be how to define functional load quantitatively (see Wang 1967; King 1967). Nevertheless, since assumptions about unequal top-down probabilities must necessarily introduce language-specific conditions, they have been left aside in the present attempt to explore the influence of universal conditions.

IMPLEMENTATION OF THE FRAMEWORK

A Phonetic-Phonological Paradox:
The Lesson of the L&L Model

An early attempt to implement some of the ideas presented above was made in L&L. That study differs from the present one primarily in the following three respects. First, the three-dimensional acoustic space of Figure 2.2 was represented by a two-dimensional approximation. Second, the perceptual space was obtained by translating the two dimensions of the acoustic representation—that is, the first formant frequency, F_1, and an effective upper formant frequency, F_2', both calibrated in Hz—into the perceptual parameters M1 and M2' specified in auditorily relevant units, mels. Third, the perceptual distance between two arbitrary vowels i and j was defined as the Euclidean distance between the points representing their location in the perceptual plane. Thus perceptual distance, D_{ij}, was defined as

$$D_{ij} = [(M1_i - M1_j)^2 + (M2_i' - M2_j')^2]^{1/2} \qquad (1)$$

Vowel systems were then derived according to a criterion of maximal perceptual contrast which was defined in terms of all the possible vowel pairs of an n-vowel system. Thus Equation 1 is applied to all pairs. After the inversion and squaring of D_{ij}, summation occurs across all cells of the triangular vowel-by-vowel matrix. We have

$$\sum_{i=2}^{n} \sum_{j=1}^{i-1} 1/(D_{ij})^2 \rightarrow \text{minimized} \qquad (2)$$

For a given number of vowels, n, a computer algorithm was used to find that combination of formant patterns (that system of vowel qualities) for which intervocalic distances were maximized according to Equation 2.

The results are presented in Figure 2.4, which shows the wedge-shaped vowel plane in terms of linear frequency scales for systems ranging in size from three through twelve vowels. The horizontal and vertical lines correspond to divisions of F_1 at every 200 Hz from 200 to 800 Hz and of F_2 at every 500 Hz from 500 to 2500 Hz. In the top row the rightmost figure shows a superposition of the results for all systems.

For a detailed discussion the reader is referred to the original study (Liljencrants & Lindblom 1972). The predicted systems containing three through six vowels show reasonable agreement with observed facts. The favoring of peripheral vowels is similarly a positive result. However, systems with seven or more vowels turn out to have too many high vowels compared with natural systems. The seven- and eight-vowel systems lack interior mid vowels such as [ø] and exhibit four rather than three or two degrees of backness in the high vowels. The nine-, ten-, eleven-, and twelve-vowel systems have five degrees of backness in the high vowels, which is at least one too many. How do we account for this discrepancy?

In Lindblom (1975), the mel distances between the extreme corners of the vowel space of Figure 2.2 were found to be 850 (i/u), 675 (i/a), and 550 (u/a) using Equation 1. This finding lies at the bottom of the less successful L&L predictions. It is hard to reconcile with data from a typological survey of 150 vowel systems (Sedlak 1969) showing that for about 70% of the languages the preferred number of vowels between /i/ and /u/ is zero and one between

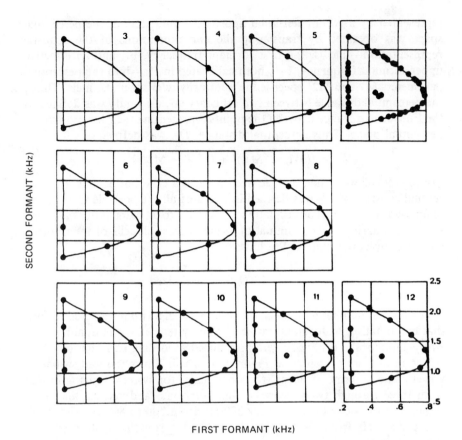

Figure 2.4 Results of vowel system predictions plotted on an F_2/F_1 plane (from Liljencrants & Lindblom 1972).

/a/ and /u/ as well as between /a/ and /i/. This trend is clearly borne out also in the C-data. (See Figure 2.1).

Expressed in acoustic terms, these facts indicate that the dimension of F_1 (a major correlate of articulatory opening and vowel height) is favored in vowel contrasts over higher formants (related mainly to front–back and rounding). Lindblom (1975) argues that if vowel systems had developed security margins guaranteeing a certain amount of perceptual differentiation in communication under noisy conditions, they would be expected to exploit F_1 (height or sonority) more than other formants, since, according to acoustic theory, F_1 is more intense and thus statistically more resistant to noise. Lindblom (1975) contains some revised and more successful predictions obtained by weighting F_1 differences in the distance computations so as to make them a much more important determinant of computed distance than the contribution from higher formants.

Crothers obtains a revision of the L&L model by defining the vowels as circular areas on a two-dimensional vowel chart and by letting the optimal arrangement be "that which allows the maximum diameter for a given number of vowels in the vowel space" (p. 126). He notes that F_1 is much more important perceptually than higher formants and adjusts his vowel space accordingly. Predictions for seven-, eight-, and nine-vowel systems are clearly improved.

A Revised Model and Some New Results

TOWARDS PERCEPTUALLY REALISTIC DISTANCE MEASURES

The L&L study can be criticized on a number of grounds. One decision that we question is the adoption of the formant-based distance measure, Equation 1. While it seems reasonable to suppose that spectral peaks, or their temporal equivalents, play a rather special role as determinants of vowel quality, there is in fact little evidence to suggest that the ear literally tracks formants and discards all other information. Such an idea appears particularly implausible in view of the following two circumstances. First, formants defined as poles in the complex frequency domain are highly elusive in acoustic representations and lack unambiguous spectral correlates owing to the complex interactions associated with voice-source characteristics, aspiration, nasalization, or simply because of a high F_0. Second, there are several studies showing that, along with the formant pattern, the F_0 and local relations among formant levels contribute toward determining phonetic quality. If we intend to apply distance measures not only to ideal zero-free oral vowels but to voiced and voiceless consonants and to nasalized and aspirated segments as well, formant-based, or pole/zero-based, distance measures promise to become rather unwieldly tools, especially if we want to project onto such measures the characteristics of the auditory system.

Bernstein (1976) developed a quantitative representation of vowel perception in order to predict the patterning of vowel systems. Although his study was limited to steady-state synthetic vowels, he concluded that it was not possible to describe his experimental results on subjective vowel dissimilarities solely in terms of the lowest three formant frequencies. Formant levels were found to contribute significantly.

We use Bernstein's finding to further support our conviction that perceptual distance functions defined on acoustic parameters should be abandoned and replaced by distance functions defined in terms of dimensions more directly related to the processes of the *auditory* system.

At this point let us return to describing our current procedure for mapping acoustic onto auditory representations. As pointed out, we do so by means of the mathematical model proposed by Schroeder *et al.* (1979). The input to the model is the harmonic power spectrum of an arbitrary (but possible) vowel. This spectrum is then passed through an auditory filter whose shape is given by psychoacoustical data on pure tone masking. The result of this analysis is a sort of spectrum, an auditory spectrum, that represents theoretically the effect of masking on a pure tone by that vowel. This broadband spectral analysis simulates certain well-known universal aspects of human hearing:

1. *Frequency resolution.* The auditory filters, or critical bands, increase in width as a function of frequency. Formants forming a part of a high-frequency formant complex may therefore not always be individually resolved in the auditory representation. These bandwidth variations are modeled by choosing a single auditory filter shape and an auditory frequency scale that is calibrated in Bark units (each of them one critical band wide) and brings about a quasi-logarithmic transformation of the physical frequency scale.

2. *Asymmetrical masking characteristics.* Lower frequencies tend to mask higher frequencies more than conversely (this is known as 'upward spread of masking'). This effect is introduced by the use of an asymmetrical filter shape.

Other features of the model are

3. *Nonlinear frequency response.* The intensity of sound pressure level (SPL) of a pure tone that is just audible varies as a function of frequency. This measurement defines the threshold of hearing. The SPL of two tones of different frequencies that appear to sound equally loud (or equivalently stated, to have the same loudness level—a quantity measured in phons) may differ considerably depending on the frequency separation. These facts, the equal loudness level contours and the threshold of hearing (which is the zero loudness-level curve), give what is known as the Fletcher-Munson curves when plotted on an SPL versus frequency diagram and are nonlinear functions of frequency. When corrections for such nonlinearities are applied to the output of the auditory filter, their main effect on a vowel is to reduce the contribution of the low-frequency components.

4. *Loudness.* We suggested previously that spectral peaks may be more conspicuous than spectral valleys in the perceptual analysis of vowel quality and should therefore undergo special processing in simulations. Psycho-

acoustics does in fact offer a scale that relates physical intensity of a sound to its subjective strength. That is the loudness scale. It should be clear that the loudness of a tone must depend on its intensity; however, this would not be its absolute sound pressure level because the relevant measure is the number of dB above hearing threshold. It is also dependent on its frequency since, as we saw in the preceding section, the ear's sensitivity to different frequencies is rather nonuniform. We also mentioned that if the intensity value is expressed in terms of phons, the tone is described in a way that takes the ear's nonlinear frequency response into consideration. Consequently psychoacousticians use numbers calibrated in phons to calculate loudness, which is given in 'sones.' The relation is $S = 2^{(L-40)/10}$, which says that, at 40 phons or above, loudness (S, in sones) is doubled by every increase of ten phons (L). It follows indirectly also that between 0 and 40 phons (a range calling for another formula), loudness grows slowly from zero to one. We conclude that a difference of 10 phons in a spectral valley is going to be reflected by a much smaller loudness difference than the corresponding difference in two pronounced peaks. Thus by incorporating loudness calculation into the model, we take some steps toward formally representing the idea that peaks should carry greater weight perceptually than valleys. The present algorithm is a somewhat modified version of the model proposed by Schroeder *et al.* (1979). It is described in greater detail in Bladon and Lindblom (1981, henceforth B&L).

We can now summarize the steps involved in deriving the auditory representation of a steady-state vowel (steps 5 through 8, below) from its acoustic specification (steps 1 through 4).

1. Specification of formant frequencies.
2. Computation of formant bandwidths (Fant 1972).
3. Derivation of the harmonic spectrum using standard assumptions about voice source, radiation, and higher-pole correction (Fant 1960).
4. Absolute calibration: specification of SPL and dB.
5. Conversion of Hz into Bark (B&L).
6. Auditory filtering: Schroeder's equation for the 'smearing' induced by basilar membrane mechanics and neural processing is used. The input power spectrum is convolved with the filter function to produce an excitation pattern calibrated in dB/Bark versus Bark.
7. Correction for nonlinear frequency response. Calibration of auditory spectrum in phon/Bark versus Bark.
8. Derivation of the loudness density plot. Calibration in sones/Bark versus Bark.

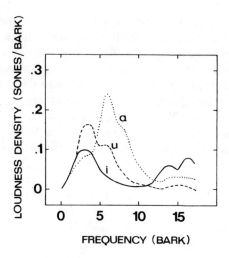

Figure 2.5 Loudness density plots (auditory spectra) of [i, u, ɑ].

Examples of this type of representation are shown in Figure 2.5
As a point of departure in developing distance metrics, we begin by considering a measure adapted from Plomp (1970):

$$D_{ij} = [c \int_0^{24.5} |E_i(x) - E_j(x)|^p dx]^{1/p} \tag{3}$$

where $E(x)$ stands for the auditory representation of a vowel (calibrated in
sones/Bark (E) versus Bark (x)), indices refer to the members of a given vowel
pair, c is a constant, and 0–24.5 Bark is the interval of integration (i.e., the
audio range). When this measure is computed and compared with perceptual dissimilarity judgments, fairly high correlations ($r \geq .85$) have been
observed (B&L; Carlson & Granström 1979; Nord & Sventelius 1979). These
results are encouraging, although they also indicate that a number of problems
in devising perceptually realistic distance metrics still await their final solution.
    Our first application of the distance notion is a comparison of data obtained
from Equations 1 and 3 for a given set of vowels (Table 2.3). Equation 1
was modified to accommodate M3 also. These vowels were obtained by quan-
tizing a mel-scale version of the three-dimensional acoustic spaces of Figure
2..2. Roughly equal quantization steps were chosen individually for M1, M2,
and M3. Table 2.3 lists the corresponding Hz values and gives approximate
phonetic labels for this set of quasi-cardinal vowels.

Table 2.3

Formant Frequencies of Quasi-Cardinal Vowels
Used in Vowel System Simulations[a]

	F_1	F_2	F_3	F_4
[i]	255	2191	3112	3594
[y]	263	2191	2482	3594
[ü]	269	1693	2331	3594
[ʉ]	276	1256	2331	3594
[ɯ]	283	897	2331	3594
[u]	290	625	2331	3594
[e][a]	364	2260	2811	3594
[ø]	371	1860	2413	3594
[ə]	377	1400	2413	3594
[ɤ]	384	1014	2413	3594
[o]	392	690	2413	3594
[ɛ]	481	1979	2681	3594
[œ]	489	1514	2593	3594
[ʌ]	495	1121	2506	3594
[ɔ]	502	790	2425	3594
[æ]	610	1732	2568	3594
[ɶ]	616	1293	2553	3594
[ɑ]	621	924	2538	3594
[a]	750	1250	2521	3594

[a] [e] is an empirically motivated modification of the
model-based vowel space (Fant 1973).

Figure 2.6 shows the results of the computations. To enable the reader
to replicate our results we need to add that the SPL of [a] is set at 70 db,
the vowels have their inherent intensities, $F_0 = 100$ Hz, and $p = 2$ in Equation 3. Formant-based distances are given along the abscissa and auditory
spectrum distances along the ordinate. The presentation has been limited to
distances from the vowel [i]. We can see that the largest distance computed
according to Equation 1 is the [i]/[u] distance, D_{iu}, which is several hundred
mels larger than D_{ia} and $D_{iɔ}$. For the auditory model measure plotted along
the ordinate the results are different: D_{iu} is nearly half as great as D_{ia} and
$D_{iɔ}$. What do these results mean?

They imply that as we substitute the spectrum-based for the formant-based
measure we achieve a warping of the perceptual space that can be visualized
in terms of the two-dimensional projection of the vowel space. We bring about
a compression of the two-dimensional plane in what corresponds to the
front–back dimension. In other words, height, or sonority, is caused to span
a wider relative range than backness. How does this come about?

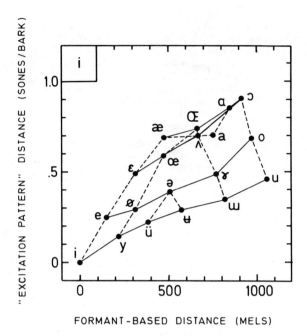

FORMANT-BASED DISTANCE (MELS)

Figure 2.6   Comparison of formant-based (abscissa) and spectrum-based (ordinate) distances computed for a given set of vowels (Table 2.3). All values represent distances in relation to [i].

To suggest an answer, let us examine once more the auditory spectra of Figure 2.5. Comparing $E_i(x)$, $E_u(x)$, and $E_a(x)$ and making an informal visual judgment, we obtain the answer to the preceding question: There is a closer resemblance between the curves of [i] and [u] than between those of [i] and [ɑ]. This impression is captured by Equation 3, which for $p = 1$ equates D_{ij} with the area enclosed between the curves. (For $p \neq 1$, D_{ij} will correspond only indirectly to this area; see B&L).

We also note that the peak corresponding to F_1 dominates these spectra. The reason for this is partly acoustic (F_1 is already strong in the harmonic spectra), partly psychoacoustic (the transformation into sones/Bark enhances this effect).

In conclusion, we find that by adopting an auditorily somewhat more realistic distance measure we derive a perceptual vowel space that appears to have precisely those properties that were lacking in the L&L model. Now what do predictions based on this new space look like?

DERIVED SYSTEMS: MAXIMAL AND SUFFICIENT CONTRAST

From a more detailed exploration of the present algorithm and of a more approximate model based on a set of $\frac{1}{3}$-octave filters (Plomp 1970), we have learned that the relative reduction of D_{iu} is brought about by a combination of conditions: (1) vowel spectra should retain their inherent intensity variations; (2) filtering and a spectrum-based distance measure must be adopted. The conversion into loudness density is thus not the primary cause of the reduction of D_{iu}. For this reason we decided to include two interpretations of $E(x)$ in Equation 3: (1) $E(x)$ = loudness density pattern in sones/Bark versus Bark (the Schroeder representation), and (2) $E(x)$ = output of the auditory filter in dB/Bark (relative to threshold) versus Bark (the Plomp approximation).

The question arises which of these two interpretations represents a better approximation of the neural excitation pattern. It is by no means an established fact that timbre (vowel quality) and loudness judgments use identical inputs. They might tap partly parallel and partly different processes (Møller 1978). However, assuming that they do use the same input, we choose hypothesis (1), which implies that the auditory cues of vowel quality are those present in a loudness density plot. Assuming that they do not, we adopt hypothesis (2), which means that the auditory cues of vowel quality are better represented in the (pure-tone, simultaneous) masking curve generated by a vowel masker. The present results do not provide evidence for the resolution of this issue. Still more sophisticated auditory models are required to simulate truly realistic neural excitation patterns. For our present purposes, however, we regard hypotheses (1) and (2) as approximations of such patterns.

In the style of L&L (see Figure 2.4), Figures 2.7 and 2.8 show the results of computations based on Equations 3 and 2. In the calculations for Figure 2.7, $E(x)$ of Equation 3 is defined as the loudness density pattern of the vowel (step 8, above). In those for Figure 2.8, it is interpreted as the output of the auditory filter (step 6) defined relative to the threshold of hearing. As described above, the former definition has the effect of enhancing formant peaks somewhat, particularly F_1. The diagrams show optimal vowel systems, that is, given the vowel inventory of Table 2.3, the computer program made an exhaustive search and identified that combination of vowels for which the criterion of *maximal system contrast*, Equation 2, was met. Table 2.4 presents the results in terms of the vowel symbols of Table 2.3. (In this table we repeat for ease of comparison the C-data from Table 2.2; where C listed two vowel inventories for a system of a given size, both are listed and labeled C-1 for the more frequently occurring system and C-2 for the less common system. For eight vowels per system C observed only a few cases.)

Comparing the results of Figure 2.7 with those of L&L (Figure 2.4), we note that the revised interpretation of perceptual vowel representation (= loudness density plot) does indeed reduce the number of high vowels in systems with large numbers of vowels. Moreover, while it was true for L&L that all systems had [i] and [u] but not always [a], the reverse is the case in Figure 2.7. The back-vowel series now appears favored (possibly because of an F_1-F_2 proximity and a concomitant enhancement along the loudness

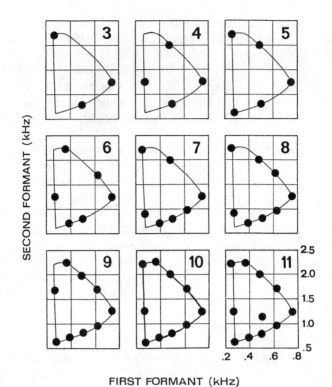

Figure 2.7 Revised predictions analogous to those of Figure 2.4. Auditory representation of vowel = loudness density plot.

scale). Figures 2.4 and 2.7 are similar in that a mid-central vowel appears only for the very largest systems.

Turning to a comparison between Figures 2.4 and 2.8, we can make the observation that in the latter the second revision of the perceptual vowel representation (output of the auditory filter) also reduces the number of high vowels in large systems, although not so drastically as the first. All systems have [i], [a], and [u]. A mid central vowel appears somewhat earlier than in Figures 2.4 and 2.7. Regretably we are unable to present a comparison between predictions and facts in terms of acoustic measurements. In any case, had formant frequency data been available for the languages of the C-data, in spite of many recent contributions, we would have had trouble selecting a linguistically and perceptually valid normalization procedure capable of separating language-specific from speaker-idiosyncratic determinants of such data (Disner 1980). We accordingly make the comparison in terms of pho-

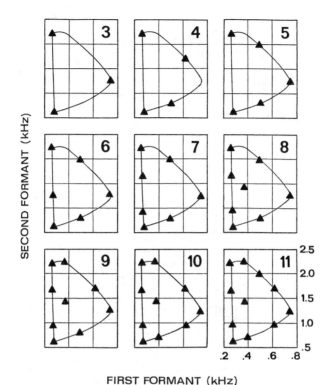

SECOND FORMANT (kHz)

FIRST FORMANT (kHz)

Figure 2.8 Revised predictions analogous to those of Figure 2.4. Auditory representation of vowel = output of auditory filter.

netic symbols. The following observations refer to Figures 2.7 and 2.8 and Table 2.4.

Three vowels: Facts and predictions are in agreement. Systems containing [i, a, o], as suggested in Figure 2.7, have been reported.

Four vowels: The L-prediction (loudness density) is more similar to C-2. Closest match: [ɪ a ɯ o] (Amahuaca) and [e a ʌ o] (Squamish). The F-prediction (auditory filter) is more similar to C-1. Closest match: [i æ u ɑ] (Chamorro).

Five vowels: Both the L- and F-predictions are in good agreement with C-1.

Six vowels: F-prediction is in good agreement with C-1. L-prediction yields a pattern very atypical owing to the lack of [i] and [u].

Seven vowels: Mid, central vowel of C-1 is missing in the patterns predicted

Table 2.4

C-data of Table 2.2 Compared with
Derived Optimal Systems

No. of vowels	System type	Vowel qualities
	C	i a u
3	L[a]	i a ɔ
	F[b]	i a u
	C₁	i ɛ a u
4	C₂	i ɨ a u
	L	ɛ ʉ a ɔ
	F	i æ ɔ u
	C₁	i ɛ a ɔ u
5	C₂	i ɛ ɨ a o
	L	i ɛ a ɔ u
	F	i ɛ a ɔ u
	C₁	i ɛ ɨ a ɔ u
6	C₂	i e ɛ u o ɔ
	L	e æ ʉ a ɔ o
	F	i ɛ ʉ a ɔ u
	C₁	i e ɨ ə a u o
7	C₂	i e ɛ a u o ɔ
	L	i ɛ ɯ a ɑ ɔ o
	F	i ü ɛ a u ɯ ɔ
	C	i e ɛ ɨ ə a u o ɔ
9	L	e ɛ æ ü a ɑ u o ɔ
	F	i e æ ü ə a u ɯ ɔ

[a]Loudness density patterns.
[b]Output spectra of an auditory filter.

by both F and L. Closest match (L): [i ɛ ɯ ʌ u ɔ ɑ] (Dafla). Criterion of sufficient contrast (see below) applied to F gives good agreement with C-1.

Eight vowels: Closest match (L): [i e ɛ a ə u o ɔ] (Javanese, Mianka). Closest match (F): [i ɛ ü ɔ̈ a ɯ u O] (Turkish).

Nine vowels: The pattern predicted by L is atypical owing to the lack of [i]. Closest match (F): [i y u e ʉ o ɛ ø ɑ] (Norwegian).

By and large, the revised sets of predictions give somewhat more satisfactory results than L&L, but certain systematic discrepancies remain. The L-predictions are not obviously superior to the F-predictions although they do incorporate additional psychoacoustic facts and ought, therefore, currently at least, to be a better representation of the auditory spectrum. Languages offer a rich variety of phonetic realizations for a given size and type of vowel system (C-Appendix III). This quality variation suggests that predictions should not be restricted to the criterion of *maximal* perceptual contrast which gives one unique configuration per system of size n. The C-data clearly show that for a given n there can be several types of systems (see the classification with respect to number of interior vowels, for example, 7:0, 7:2, where the number to the left of the colon indicates the total number of vowels and that to the right, the number of this total which are interior vowels) as well as phonetic variations in the implementation of a given type. The question then arises whether some of these effects could also be deduced within the present framework.

To investigate this question we introduce the criterion of *sufficient contrast*. One way of defining this notion is to have the algorithm enumerate, say, the best m systems for each value of n. Another approach which seems preferable is to make a quantitative estimate of sufficient system contrast, keep it independent of system size, and study its effect on the predictions. We chose the former method, letting $m = 50$. We have studied the structure of the best 50 systems with respect to both phonetic variation and type. The results were obtained by means of the F model.

Suppose that sufficient contrast does operate in real systems and that it tends to be invariant across languages and system sizes. It follows from this assumption that the phonetic values of vowel phonemes should exhibit more variation in small than in large systems. We find this expectation supported by the C-data when we examine how C transcribes the vowels that function as /i/, /a/, and /u/ in systems varying in size. For instance, in the three-vowel systems we find [i ɪ e] for /i/, [u o ʊ ɯ] for /u/, and [a ɛ ä æ ǣ] for /a/. In the nine-vowel systems, on the other hand, /u/ is [u] or [ʊ]. Figure 2.9 shows the percentage of occurrences of the extreme [i], [u], and [a] qualities as a function of n. Also shown is the percentage of occurrence of the corresponding vowels in the best 50 simulated systems. For [i] and [u] the C-data support the notion of sufficient contrast. In the computed results the frequency of the corner vowels increases with system size.

How well do predictions match the C-data with respect to favored system types? Table 2.5 compares the distributions of interior vowels (indicated by the number following the colon). In the C-data, an interior vowel is defined as a vowel that is nonperipheral, that is, is not found in the leftmost or rightmost columns or in the bottom row of Table 2.1. In the computer simulations this concept was similarly defined. With reference to Table 2.3, the following vowels are interior: 2–5, 8–10, 13–14, 17. (Exception: in the absence of the vowels numbered 1, 6, or 19, the vowels numbered 2, 5, or 17, respectively, were not classified as interior.)

In the C-data, the eight- and nine-vowel systems are particularly small samples. Caution is also advisable in the use of Table 2.5, since the criterion

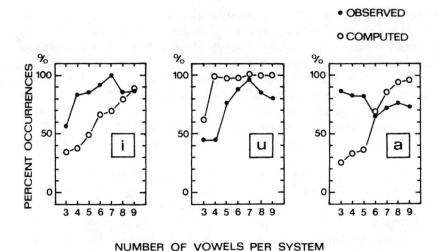

NUMBER OF VOWELS PER SYSTEM

Figure 2.9   Occurrences of [i], [u], and [a]. Filled circles show the extreme vowels [i], [u], and [a] as realizations of /i/, /u/, and /a/ in Crothers' data (1978, Appendix III); open circles show the same vowels, based on simulations.

of sufficient contrast is interpreted in a rather ad hoc fashion. The major point is rather that predictions of system type can be made.

Figure 2.10 shows the distribution of predicted vowel systems belonging to the 7:2 type. The dots indicate the optimal system as given in Figure 2.7. The majority of the 50 predicted systems have [ɨ] and [ə] as the favored interior vowels this is shown by the centrally located peaks in the distributional profiles. This is a case where the optimal system differs from the most common among those meeting the condition of sufficient contrast. Figure 2.10 underlines the necessity to consider a wider range of solutions to the problem of optimizing system contrast.

In concluding this section, we find that the present framework generates vowel systems sharing a number of essential characteristics with natural systems. If the frequency of occurrence in the simulations was investigated for each individual vowel category, it would be possible to construct a diagram analogous to Figure 2.1. These figures would be highly similar.

However, we must also draw attention to one of the more conspicuous negative findings. Although the current predictions are much more satisfactory than those of L&L with regard to high vowels in large systems, it is somewhat problematic that the fairly popular 7:0 system (e.g., that of Italian and Bengali) is still absent. By setting the criterion of system contrast so generously that 7:0 instances *are* produced, we also generate many cases of 7:2

Table 2.5

Comparison of Observed (C) and Predicted (F) Vowel System Types

System type	3:0	3:1	4:0	4:1	5:0	5:1	6:0	6:1	6:2	7:0	7:1	7:2	8:0	8:1	8:2	8:3	9:2	9:3
C(%)	100	0	59	41	87	13	22	73	5	39	11	50	0	44	22	33	73	36
F(%)	76	24	38	62	10	80	0	68	32	0	12	82	0	4	50	44	16	76

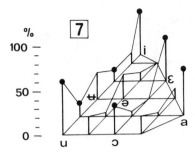

Figure 2.10   Distribution of predicted qualities in the best 50 seven-vowel systems. Dots refer to the optimal predicted system.

systems where, unfortunately, according to the data, the "2" represents two high vowels (e.g., [ü/ɯ], rather than a high/mid pair (e.g., [ɨ/ə]). Thus we see that to some extent there are still too many high vowels and that we must look for still further ways of constraining the space of vowel contrasts.

EXTENSIONS AND LIMITATIONS

Diphthongs

Would it be possible to apply the present framework also to diphthongs? Edström (1971) examined diphthongs of over 80 languages reported to have diphthongs. In view of the secondhand and heterogeneous nature of the data, few generalizations can be made. However, one trend that ought to survive further diphthong typologies is presented in Table 2.6, which indicates that diphthongs like [aj] and [aw] are favored over [ej] and [ow], which are in turn used more often than [uj] and [iw]. We can restate this and say that diphthongs are favored according to the degree of sonority of their nuclei. Alternatively, visualizing the diphthongs as trajectories in acoustic space, we see that their frequency of occurrence is positively correlated with the extent of the diphthong trajectory in the *revised* F_1-dominated space.

Quantal Aspects of the Vowel Space

One of the more striking features of language, including its phonological aspect, is its structuring in terms of *discrete* and hierarchically organized units. We have nevertheless made the present predictions with the aid of a *continuous* space. This is deliberate, since explanatory phonology ought to aim at

Table 2.6

Percentage of Languages for which the Indicated Vowel is the Nucleus of a Nucleus + Glide (Palatal or Velar) Sequence (N = 83)[a]

a/ɑ	o/ɔ	e/ɛ	u	i
83%	34%	25%	18%	7%

[a]From Edström (1971).

giving a deductive account of the quantal nature of speech. There are no doubt numerous reasons for speech being quantal (Stevens 1972; Studdert-Kennedy & Lane 1980). The present work bears on this issue by demonstrating a possible origin of universally favored vowel quality categories such as [i], [a], [u], [ɛ], and [ɔ]. In our results these vowels recur in a stable manner and practically independently of system size. Thus, even though based on a continuous space, the procedure favors certain vowel qualities more than others. Given such a distribution rather than a uniform one, the phonetic space will appear quantal.

Acquired Similarity and the Language Dependence of the Vowel Space

By definition, our vowel space is a hypothetical universal. It remains fixed. 'Similarity' is a function defined in terms of the space. Let us briefly examine this assumption critically.

Everyday experience shows that things that at first looked very similar may after a while cease to look so. It is also rich in situations where we find ourselves in disagreement over similarity judgments, sometimes because we tend to limit our perception of a person or an object to certain features rather than the whole, and our selective samplings may differ more than hypothetical Gestalt impressions.

Similar considerations can also be made in the case of speech-sound perception. Does the strategy of feature extractions occur in normal speech perception? Are vowel similarities partly acquired? If we say "yes," it may be because we believe that different languages require listeners to attend to and learn different cues whose similarity relations may be subjectively different from those of the wholes.

These remarks have implications both for the predictions of vowel systems and for the empirical verification of the vowel space by perceptual experiments. It would seem that if the space is to a large extent malleable during acquisition, we would perhaps expect social and cultural rather than universal factors to shape vowel systems. Furthermore, such elasticity would make it very hard to observe the space experimentally in its language-innocent state (see Terbeek & Harshman 1972).

Figure 2.11 is based on perceptual data on Swedish from Hanson (1967: Table 9.1), and our calculations derived from Hanson's stimulus specifications (Table 10.1). The results are presented for nine vowels in a three-by-three matrix, each cell comparing a given vowel (insert) with all the remaining vowels. There are thus eight dots in each diagram. (In the [o:] plot there are nine, since it includes a comparison between [o:] and [ɔ], a reference point assigned a dissimilarity of 5.) Each such dot represents a given vowel pair and a comparison between computed and observed dissimilarity values. The point is that, if we assume that listeners' similarity judgments are language-independent and describable by a unique function of the acoustic stimulus attributes, we would expect to be able to fit this unique function, that is, a *single line*, to the nine individual vowel plots of Figure 2.11. Clearly, we cannot. What we have done is to use three best-fitting lines, one for each column of graphs. There is, significantly, a larger intercept and a less-steep slope for the front vowels.

What does this difference between front and back lines tell us? It says that for a vowel pair with a small spectral distance, the predicted perceptual dissimiliarity must be made dependent on whether the vowels are front or back. For instance, although [y:] and [ø:] may have a spectral distance similar to that for [u:] and [o:], the front pair is heard as more dissimilar. It is as if listeners make their space more spacious at the point where the universal perceptual space seems most crowded.

The lesson appears to be that the more language-dependent plasticity the subjective vowel space possesses, the greater we should expect the discrepancies to be between natural systems and systems derived from a theoretical universal baseline.

Universal Phonetic Space = Articulatory Space * Perceptual Space

We have tried to justify the present framework primarily with reference to the criterion of perceptual contrast. What about production? Having introduced the concept of sufficient contrast, we have in principle invited the interaction of other processes, for example, mechanisms of memory and speech motor control that might contribute systematic effects under the heading of sufficient perceptual differentiation.

It makes sense, in fact, to talk about sufficient contrast also in the contexts of memory retrieval operations and the feedback control of speech gestures (perhaps particularly with regard to speech development). If we were to look at the optimization of vowel systems from this broader perspective, an optimal system might be one that meets not only perceptual but also

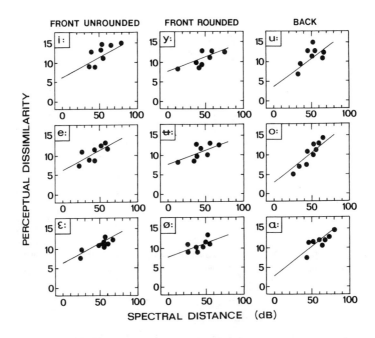

Figure 2.11 Perceptual dissimilarity estimates (Hanson 1967) plotted against computed distances for the nine long Swedish vowels.

memory-based and sensori-motor conditions of distinctiveness. For instance, how, in that case, could the detailed geometry of the articulatory (= sensori-motor) space influence the design of sound inventories?

Let us draw attention to three sets of matching facts: (1) Articulators have greater mobility at the front of the mouth (e.g., lips, tongue tip). (2) There appears to be a richer supply of structures for sensory control at anterior vocal tract locations (Hardcastle 1970). (3) Acoustic-perceptual effects are greater at the front than at the back, given geometrically comparable articulatory perturbations and conditions typical of, for example, voiceless consonants (Stevens 1968). Is there a fourth set of matching facts, namely, the data on consonant inventories that indicate (by Hardcastle's hypothesis) that languages exhibit a richer variety of front than back consonants (see also Figure 2.12)? If so, does the asymmetry of vocal tract sensori-motor representation also manifest itself in vowel systems? Does it contribute to the primacy of height (sonority or F_1) over front–back (chromaticity or F_2) distinctions and the favoring of vowel contrasts produced in anterior articulatory regions that have expanded sensory representations? Hopefully, these are empirical questions.

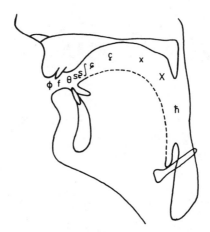

Figure 2.12   The set of IPA symbols used to describe voiceless fricatives shown on a vocal tract profile to illustrate an asymmetry with respect to how languages exploit the articulatory space (Hardcastle 1970).

Role of Sequential Constraints: [iᶻ] and [ɚ]

It is clear that the present definition of 'possible vowel' is too restricted and should at least be extended to include also dimensions such as nasalization, retroflexion, apicalization, length, phonation type, and so on. Let us briefly comment on [iᶻ] (the apicalized or coronal vowel of Chinese and certain Swedish dialects) and retroflex [ɚ]. Formant patterns for these qualities might be those given below:

	F_1	F_2	F_3
[iᶻ]	310	1610	2775
[ɚ]	500	1350	1700

A revision of Figure 2.2 modified to include these vowels would show two peaks in high-vowel territory: one for [i] and one for [iᶻ]. Owing to the extreme low F_3 value of [ɚ], it would also have a marked minimum hanging down from the center. By the present definitions of perceptual contrast, these vowels are highly distinctive. Exploratory work on predicting systems from inventories containing also these qualities indicates that they tend to be favored and are often capable of ousting many dorsal competitors.

This result appears to weaken the force of the present conclusions since, in fact, these vowels are quite rare in the languages of the world. On the other hand, it brings out an observation that parallels a principle noted previously in studies of consonant clusters (Elert 1970): differentiation of articulatory place. The parallel is the fact that vowels tend to be primarily dorsal, whereas the typical consonant system (Nartey 1979) exploits the anterior articulators more fully.

It does not seem unreasonable to suggest that in the disfavoring of [i^Z] and [ə˞]—which often seem to originate as contextual variants when they do occur—we see the operation of a dynamic articulatory constraint having to do with the facilitation of the coarticulatory integration of successive gestures. The implication of this is that vowel systems tend to become *syntagmatically* as well as *paradigmatically* optimized, that is, as different as possible not only with respect to other vowels but also with respect to the consonants they appear next to.

"Maximal Utilization of Available Features"

Ohala (1980) applies the notion of space and the principle of maximum perceptual contrast to consonant systems. He convincingly argues that this principle would predict systems with rather preposterous and counterfactual properties. As an alternative principle he suggests 'maximum utilization of the available distinctive features,' which would make many consonants perceptually very similar and would create minimal rather than maximal differences with respect to number of distinctive features. His reasoning leads him to ask whether consonant inventories are structured according to different principles from those which apply to vowel inventories.

His point is well taken. We do not try to respond to it fully here but simply offer a tentative and methodologically motivated "no." It is not hard to believe that the discovery of features and the generalization of such features to yield new phonemes may play an important role in the acquisition of phonology and that such processes apply also to the development of vowel systems. Given, say [i ɛ a ɔ u], by perceptual criteria and some abstract and discrete recoding of the associated component articulations (i.e., into features), a child might discover and conquer new contrasts by recombining the articulatory gestures mastered so far. This strategy supported and elaborated with the aid of empirical observations would be worth exploring along with other constraints (sufficient perceptual contrast) in the predictions of future vowel systems. A major difficulty, though, is to give a substantive, *deductive account* of the features.

In response to Ohala's query, then, our comment is that, insofar as the integration of several speech behavior constraints can be achieved within the present framework for describing vowels, it may well be that the principles underlying consonant systems on the one hand and vowel inventories on the other might turn out to be more similar than Ohala, for the sake of argument, wanted to imply.

The Distance Metric

It would be misleading to conclude this discussion section without making a few critical comments on the above presentation of the distance metric. Implicit in our model of speech perception is the idea that it would in principle be possible to formulate a complete and realistic theory of vowel perception in terms of the notion of distance. Upon further reflection we realize that this represents a rather strong claim about the power of such a metric. It must account for, among other things, formant-frequency-difference limen data, the effect of F_0, level, and spectral tilt, and duration on vowel quality across speakers having different vocal tract geometries. We do not at present have a unified theory that explains these and other systematic phenomena (Ainsworth 1980) and there are accordingly no distance measures and auditory models capable of comprehensively imitating natural vowel perception.

Much work remains to be done on breaking in distance measures and constructing auditory models. Therefore the present results are preliminary and serve the primary purpose of illustrating the possibility of a substance-based, deductive approach to phonological questions.

ACKNOWLEDGMENTS

The author is grateful to Peter Ladefoged and John Ohala for many helpful comments on the manuscript of this chapter.

REFERENCES

Ainsworth, W. (1980). *Summary of the session on Vowel perceeption, Gotland Workshop* (Quarterly Progress and Status Report 1/1980), 8–12. Stockholm: Speech Transmission Laboratory, Royal Institute of Technology, Stockholm.

Bellugi, U., & M. Studdert-Kennedy, eds. 1980. *Sign language and spoken language: Biological constraints on linguistic form.* Dahlem Workshop, Weinheim: Verlag Chemie.

Bernstein, J. C. 1976. *Vocoid psychoacoustics, articulation and vowel phonology* (Natural Language Studies No. 23). Ann Arbor: Phonetics Laboratory, University of Michigan.

Bladon, R. A. W., & B. Lindblom. (1981). Modeling the judgment of vowel quality differences. *Journal of the Acoustical Society of America* 69:1414–1422.

Carlson, R., & B. Granström. (1979). Model predictions of vowel dissimilarity. (Quarterly Progress and Status Report 3-4/1979), 84–104. (Stockholm: Speech Transmission Laboratory, Royal Institute of Technology.)

Chomsky, N., & M. Halle. 1968. *The sound pattern of English.* New York: Harper & Row.

Crothers, J. 1978. Typology and universals of vowel systems. In J. H. Greenberg, C. A. Ferguson, & E. A. Moravcsik, eds., *Universals of human language. Vol. 2: Phonology,* 93–152. Stanford: Stanford University Press.

Disner, S. F. 1980. Evaluation of vowel normalization procedures. *Journal of the Acoustical Society of America* 67:253–261.

Donegan, P. J. 1978. *The natural phonology of vowels* Dissertation, (Working Papers in Linguistics 28). Columbus: Ohio State University.

Donegan-Miller, P. J. 1972. Some context-free processes affecting vowels (Working Papers in Linguistics 23). Columbus: Ohio State University.

Edström, B. 1971. Diphthong systems. Stockholm University. Unpublished paper.

Elert, C.-C. 1970. *Ljud och Ord i Svenskan:.* Stockholm, Almqvist & Wiksell.

Fant, G. 1960. *Acoustic theory of speech production.* The Hague: Mouton.

Fant, G. 1972. Vocal tract wall effects, losses and resonance bandwidths. (Quarterly Progress and Status Reports 2-3/1972), 28–52. Stockholm: Speech Transmission Laboratory, Royal Institute of Technology.

Fant, G. 1973. *Speech sounds and features.* Cambridge, MA: MIT Press.

Hanson, G. 1967. *Dimensions in speech sound perception.* Ericsson Technics 23.

Hardcastle, W. J. 1970. The role of tactile and proprioceptive feedback in speech production (Work in progress 4), 100–112. Department of Linguistics, Edinburgh University.

Hockett, C. 1955. A manual of phonology. *International Journal of American Linguistics,* Memoir 11.

Jakobson, R. 1941. *Kindersprache, Aphasie und allgemeine Lautgesetze.* (*Språkvetenskapliga Sällskapets i Uppsala Förhandlingar 1940-1942*) Uppsala: Almqvist & Wiksell. (Reprinted in R. Jakobson. 1962. *Selected writings I,* 328–401. The Hague: Mouton.

King, R. D. (1967). Functional load and sound change. *Language* 43:831–852.

Liljencrants, J., & B. Lindblom. (1972). Numerical simulation of vowel quality systems: The role of perceptual contrast. *Language* 48:839–862.

Lindblom, B. 1975. Experiments in sound structure. Plenary address, 8th International Congress of Phonetic Sciences, Leeds. (Also in *Revue de Phonétique Appliquée* 51:155–189. Université de l'Etat Mons, Belgique.

Lindblom, B. 1980. The goal of phonetics, its unification and application. In *Proceedings of the Ninth International Congress of Phonetic Sciences.* (Vol. 3) 3–18. Copenhagen: Institute of Phonetics.

Lindblom, B., & J. Sundberg. 1971. Acoustic consequences of lip, tongue, jaw and larynx movement. *Journal of the Acoustical Society of America* 50: 1166–1179.

Møller, A. R. 1978. Neurophysiological basis of discrimination of speech sounds. *Audiology* 17:1–9.

Nartey, J. N. A. 1979. A study in phonemic universals—especially concerning fricatives and stops 46. (Working papers in phonetics University of California at Los Angeles).

Nord, L., and E. Sventelius. 1979. Analysis and prediction of difference limen data for formant frequencies (Quarterly Progress and Status Report 3-4/1979), 60–72. Stockholm: Speech Transmission Laboratory, Royal Institute of Technology.

Ohala, J. J. 1978. Phonological notations as models. In W. U. Dressler & W. Meid, eds., *Proceedings of the 12th International Congress of Linguists* (Vienna, Aug. 28–Sept. 2, 1977), 811–816. Innsbruck: Innsbrucker Beiträge zur Sprachwissenschaft.

Ohala, J. J. 1980. Moderator's introduction to Symposium on Phonetic Universals in Phonological Systems and their Explanation. *Proceedings of the Ninth International Congress of Phonetic Sciences (Vol. 3)* 181–185. Copenhagen: Institute of Phonetics.

Ohala, J. J. Forthcoming. *The origin of sound patterns in language.*

Plomp, R. 1970. Timbre as a multidimensional attribute of complex tones. In R. Plomp & G. F. Smoorenburg, eds., *Frequency analysis and periodicity detection in hearing*, 397–414. Leiden: Sijthoff.

Schroeder, M. R., B. S. Atal, & J. L. Hall. 1979. Objective measure of certain speech signal degradations based on masking properties of human auditory perception. In B. Lindblom & S. Öhman, eds., *Frontiers of speech communication research*, 217–229. London: Academic Press.

Sedlak, P. 1969. Typological considerations of vowel quality systems. (Working Papers in Language Universals 1) 1–40. Stanford: Stanford University.

Stampe, D. 1973. A dissertation on natural phonology. Ph.D. diss., University of Chicago.

Stevens, K. N. 1968. Acoustic correlates of place of articulation for stop and fricative consonants (Quarterly Progress Report 89), 199–205. Cambridge, MA: MIT.

Stevens, K. N. 1972. The quantal nature of speech: Evidence from articulatory-acoustic data. In P. B. Denes & E. E. David Jr., eds., *Human communication: A unified view*, 51–66. New York: McGraw-Hill.

Studdert-Kennedy, M., & H. Lane. 1980. Clues from the differences between signed and spoken language. In U. Bellugi and M. Studdert-Kennedy, eds., *Signed language and spoken language: Biological constraints on linguistic form* Dahlem Workshop, 29–39. Weinheim: Verlag Chemie.

Terbeek, D., & R. Harshman. 1972. Is vowel perception non-Euclidean? (Working Papers in Phonetics 22) 13–29. University of California at Los Angeles.

Troubetzkoy, N. S. 1929. Zur allgemeinen Theorie der phonologischen Vokalsysteme. *Travaux du Cercle Linguistique de Prague* 1:39–67.

Wang, W. S-Y. 1967. The measurement of functional load. *Phonetica* 16:36–54.

3

The Behavior of Nasalized Vowels in the Perceptual Vowel Space

JAMES T. WRIGHT

INTRODUCTION

Phonetic research has not played as central a role in phonological theory as it should. Its function has been assumed to be essentially interpretive rather than predictive, mapping the physical aspects of speech production onto the underlying features adopted a priori from phonological theory. But phonetic research can help us discover a substratum of physiological and perceptual constraints which can predict or determine the structure of phonological systems. Evidence for a phonetic substratum should be drawn from two sources. First, phonological patterns found cross-linguistically seem to owe their existence to universal physiological or perceptual constraints shared by all language users. Second, empirical phonetic evidence for the presence of these constraints in populations of individual speakers can be taken as evidence of their existence in all speakers. However, neither of these kinds of evidence is of itself sufficient to establish the link between the characteristics of a language and the behavior of individual speakers. What are further required are models that mediate between the experimental data and the systemic properties of a language. In this chapter an experimentally supported model of the perceptual vowel space is used to explain a well-established synchronic pattern in nasal vowel systems.

EXPERIMENTAL PHONOLOGY

Phonological Universals of Nasal Vowel Systems

Cross-linguistic surveys of vowel systems (Ruhlen 1973, 1975; Sedlak 1969) have found that nasal vowels bear a systematic relationship to their oral counterparts: There are never more nasal vowels than oral vowels in the segmental inventory. Most commonly there are an equal number, as is the case in Beembe (Figure 3.1). It is about equally common for the nasal vowel system to have fewer segments. Generally, when there is an imbalance, one or more of the mid vowel contrasts is missing; Dakota, for example, lacks the nasal mid vowel series, while in Portuguese the lower-mid vowels are missing. Rather less frequent are cases in which the high vowels are not present, such as in Ebrie and French.

Claims about positional differences between corresponding elements in the oral and nasal vowel systems are more controversial. Low nasal vowels may have a tendency to be higher than cognate oral vowels, but systematic differences in high and mid vowels are problematic (Bhat 1975; Beddor 1982).[1] Related claims have been made about nasalization as a diachronic process, specifically that it promotes a lowering of high and mid vowels. Chen (1973) motivates this as an areal feature of Chinese, and it has been proposed as well by Lightner (1970) and Foley (1975), who provide Indo-European examples. French is often taken as the archetypal example. Synchronic morphophonemic alternations such as French *finir/fin*—exhibiting an [i] ~ [æ̃] alternation—have been produced by successive mergers to a lower vowel, first of oral mid front vowels before nasal consonants and later by the merger of high and mid nasal vowels, as shown in Figure 3.2. The resulting synchronic state of French is somewhat atypical in the lack of high and mid nasal vowels, although the loss of the height contrast by itself is typical.

The synchronic patterning of nasal vowels systems and the diachronic processes that give rise to them must be related. Distinctively nasal vowels are commonly believed to result from allophonic nasalization of vowels in the environment of tautosyllabic nasal consonants accompanied by the loss of the conditioning consonant. On the face of it, this diachronic process seems sufficient to account for the skewing of vowel systems such that there may be more oral vowels than nasal vowels but not the converse. Simply, the input to the diachronic rule $VN \rightarrow \tilde{V}$ is at least limited to the original set of oral vowels and may be even further restricted by fairly common phonotactic restrictions on the occurrence of certain vowels before nasals. However, this

---

[1]Beddor (1982) reviews the major proposals concerning the direction of changes in vowel height due to nasalization. Examining synchronic phonological processes in 75 languages, she found significant cross-language regularities in height differences for allophonic nasalization and in morphophonemic alternations. High vowels systematically lower, low vowels raise, and mid vowels show regularities if vowel backness and context are taken into account.

Beembe (Congo)   Dakota (Yankton-Teton)

i	u	ĩ	ũ	i	u	ĩ	ũ
e	o	ẽ	õ	e	o		
	a		ã		a		ã

Portuguese (Continental)   Ebrie (Niger-Congo)

i	u	ĩ	ũ	i	u		
e	o	ẽ	õ	e	o	ẽ	õ
ɛ	ɔ						
	a		ã		a		ã

Figure 3.1   Examples of oral and nasal vowel systems.

account glosses over a more interesting question: Why is it that subsequent evolution of the nasal vowels through, for example, splits, still fails to lead to increases in the number of distinctively nasal vowels such that occasionally there might be more nasal vowels in the system than oral vowels? The answer has to be that vowel nasalization somehow tends to prevent an increase in the number of distinctively nasal vowels. If this is the case, it suggests that some acoustic characteristics of vowel nasalization give rise to language-independent perceptual effects.

Two Proposals for Phonetic Substratum Effects

Two proposals have been made to link the acoustic consequences of nasalization to the patterning of vowel systems. It is clear from a review of these proposals that both rely heavily on models which seek to predict perpceptual properties from acoustic data.

LOSS OF CONTRAST

Lindblom (1975) attempts to extend his notion of the maximization of contrast in vowel systems to nasal vowels by trying to show that the spectra of nasalized vowels are acoustically less distinct. He builds his model on a spectral measure of acoustic distance motivated by Plomp's investigation of critical-band phenomena (Plomp 1964, 1975; Plomp & Mimpen 1968). Plomp finds high correlations between listeners' dissimilarity judgments and a Euclidean distance measure derived from a 1/3-octave simulation of critical-band

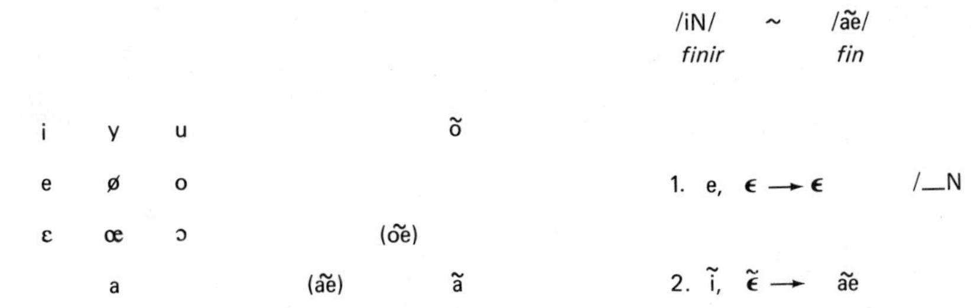

/iN/   ~   /ãe̴/
finir   fin

i   y   u   õ

e   ø   o   1. e, ɛ ⟶ ɛ   /__N

ɛ   œ   ɔ   (õe̴)

a   (ãe̴)   ã   2. ĩ, ɛ̃ ⟶ ãe̴

Figure 3.2   The French vowel system and some of the mergers which resulted in fewer nasal than oral vowels.

filtering for complex acoustic stimuli. Lindblom demonstrates that Plomp's metric is lawfully related to confusion data for oral vowels by an inverse square relation. He then makes the assumption that it can be used to predict perceptual distance between nasal vowels as well. When applied to synthetic vowels produced by House and Stevens' (1956) electrical analog of the oral and nasal tracts and to vowels produced by a cleft palate patient (with and without obdurator), pairs of nasalized vowels are found to be acoustically closer than the corresponding oral pairs. Given Lindblom's assumptions, they should also be perceptually closer. The significance of this loss of contrast becomes clear when a model of the behavior of vowel systems is taken into account. Liljencrants and Lindblom (1972) argue that vowel systems attempt to maximize the degree of acoustic contrast between vowels. Lindblom (1975) further proposes that there is also a minimum level of contrast that the vowel system must maintain; dipping below the threshold tends to promote a self-correcting reduction in the number of vowels in the system. Hence an acoustic loss of contrast would account for the asymmetry in the number of oral and nasal vowels that appear cross-linguistically.

To what extent does direct testing of perceived similarity support the proposal that nasalized vowels are perceptually closer than oral vowels? Mohr and Wang (1968) had speakers of American English make similarity judgments between [i, a, u, ĩ, ã, ũ] and found that nasalized stimuli are judged to be closer. Bond (1975) excised vowels from /N__N/ and other contexts and found that the greatest number of confusions in an identification task occur on the vowels from the nasal contexts. Butcher (1976) presents results which may be interpreted as showing that French and German adults judge nasalized vowels as being more similar than oral vowels.[2] All three studies appear to support the predictions of Lindblom's spectral distance model,

[2]However, in the Butcher study children aged 10 to 12 years did not judge nasalized vowels as being more similar than oral vowels.

but it should be noted that none of them could guarantee that the oral and nasal vowels in their studies were articulatorily comparable. That is, could the nasal vowels have appeared closer to each other not because of the effect of nasalization per se but because they were articulatorily similar?

MOVEMENTS OF F_1

Lindblom's model makes no predictions as to whether nasalization should cause any shifts in vowel quality within the vowel space, although it does imply that information from the whole spectrum, rather than just formant-peak information, is important in determining acoustic distance. A second proposal, (Ohala 1974, 1975), on the other hand, claims that perceptible quality shifts occur as a function of the type of perturbation in the formant structure created by nasalization. Ohala cites data from electrical analogs of the oral and nasal tracts (House & Stevens 1956; House 1957; Hecker 1962; Fant 1960) as a basis for predicting that nasalization tends to raise the frequency of the first formant of mid and high vowels. The analytic study by Fujimura (1960) similarly predicts that the poles in the transfer function related to the first oral formant will move upwards in frequency as coupling increases between the oral and nasal tracts. This conclusion is supported by Fujimura's and Lindqvist's (1971) sweep-tone measurements of the transfer function of human vocal tracts. With low vowels, however, it appears that the main spectral prominence could shift to a lower frequency (due to complex interaction of the pole-zero structure in the vicinity of the first formant). Since vowel height is inversely related to first-formant frequency, it would be expected that vowel nasalization would cause high and mid vowels to lower auditorily and the low vowels either to lower or to raise depending on the speaker and vowel. Thus there should be predictable quality changes associated with nasalization, notably changes in vowel height.

Again, it should be asked to what extent perceptual evidence supports this hypothesis. A further analysis of Bond's confusion data (Wilson & Bond 1976) indicates that the greater confusability of the nasalized vowels was largely due to confusions along a dimension correlating with vowel height and that these confusions were more prevalent for the /N__N/ contexts than for the others. High nasalized vowels were misidentified as lower vowels, while the reverse was true for low vowels. A direct test of this hypothesis (Wright 1975) also found that phonetically trained subjects judged high and mid nasalized vowels as lower, but the low vowels as higher.

Both experiments apparently support the predicted perceptual consequences of the acoustic model. Nevertheless, ironically, examination of the formant structure of the vowels used by Wright and Bond in these experiments casts doubt on the validity of the model. In neither case did the measured shift in the first formant (averaged values in the Bond study) necessarily accompany the perceived differences in vowel height. Further, acoustic analysis of natural speech fails to provide convincing evidence that the direction of perturbation of the first formant for high vowels is as consistent as the analog studies suggest (Fujimura 1961; Coleman 1963; Mrayati 1975; Beddor 1982; Beddor & Hawkins 1984). The spectra of naturally nasalized vowels are more complex than the spectra produced by the analogs, probably due to details of the structure of the nasal cavity not modeled by the electrical analogs (Lindqvist & Sundberg 1972; Takeuchi, Kasuya & Kido 1974a, 1974b).

It should be noted that both the "loss of contrast hypothesis" and the "shifting first formant hypothesis" are based on extrapolations from acoustic data to predictions about perceptual effects. While some perceptual evidence is available which supports these predictions, they should be tested with pairs of oral and nasal vowels that are established by an independent measure to be articulatorily equivalent (except for velic lowering).

THE EXPERIMENT

Experimental Design

Given the complexity of the acoustic signal of nasalized vowels, it may be most efficient to simply bypass this stage of the speech chain and look for the predicted effects of physiological nasalization chiefly in the perceptual domain. The method chosen, then, to test these hypotheses was the multidimensional scaling of all possible pairings of a variety of vowels, each produced oral and nasalized, where care was taken to ensure articulatory equivalence of related oral–nasal pairs. Multidimensional scaling supplies a means of constructing a spatial representation in which the stimuli are specified as points in an N-dimensional space. Distances between each pair of points in the space reflect distances established experimentally using a measure of proximity, that is, some measure of similarity , affinity, or confusability between the vowels in the set. Procedures for recovering these spatial models have been widely used for studies of vowel perception (Hanson 1967; Pols, van der Kamp, & Plomp 1969; Klein, Plomp, & Pols 1970; Singh & Woods 1971; Terbeek & Harshman 1971, 1972; Terbeek & Fox 1975; Butcher 1976; Terbeek 1977). The scaling may be viewed as merely a data-reduction device, but the possibility that the scaling may also reflect a parameterization of the signal at some level of auditory processing is also considered. In this case each parameter (or dimension) is considered to be independent and is represented in the perceptual space by an axis in the space. The analysis problem in recovering this space is twofold. First, it is necessary to determine the number of dimensions that most nearly matches the number of parameters used by subjects in the task from which the proximity measure is derived. Second, it is necessary to have some means to locate the direction of the axes through the space that best represents these assumed underlying parameters.

INDSCAL

INDSCAL, the multidimensional scaling of individual differences (Carroll & Chang 1970), was chosen in preference to other procedures because it is the most constrained in its criteria for determining the maximum number of dimensions, because the projections of the dimensions through the space are non-arbitrary, and because individual variation in subjects may be examined in terms of the analysis. Jennrich (1972) offers a proof that the minimum number of dimensions appropriate to the analysis is determined by the largest number of dimensions at which a unique solution is found when beginning from different initial configurations of the solution matrix. With real (hence noisy) experimental data, the criterion of uniqueness is not infallible, but it does effectively set an upper limit on the dimensionality of solutions to be considered. The second advantage of INDSCAL is that it determines the projection of the axes through the space. It assumes that different individuals perceive the stimuli in terms of a common set of dimensions which may be differentially weighted for each individual. The differential "stretch" for each subject is utilized to specify the projections of the axes in the space, given the correct number of dimensions. This has two consequences: First, the projections of axes (along which this differential stretch is found) is unique—axes cannot be rotated—and second, these dimensions may directly reflect a parameterization of vowel quality if the assumptions concerning the individual weighting of dimensions are valid. The final advantage of INDSCAL is that individual differences between subjects may be evaluated by considering the weighting of each subject on each dimension.

EXPERIMENTAL PROCEDURE

Stimuli consisted of eight oral vowels corresponding to the American English vowels [i, e, ɛ, æ, ɑ, o, ʊ, u] and their nasalized counterparts. Because both hypotheses argue that the perceptual effects of nasalization are due to spectral changes caused solely by oral–nasal coupling, it was necessary to make sure that any given oral–nasal vowel pair did not involve any other articulatory difference. The single most important parameter is that of tongue configuration, which reflects not only tongue shape but movement of the tongue body and mandible as well. The dynamic optical palatograph (Chuang & Wang 1975; Wright 1967a) was used to measure tongue configuration during the production of vowels. Four infrared emitter-sensor pairs were implanted along the midsagittal line of an artificial palate. The four emitters were sequentially pulsed in a 5 msec cycle and the light reflected from the tongue surface was sampled, measured, and used to determine the distance between the sensor and the reflecting portion of the tongue. Given the known optical axis of each emitter–sensor pair and the distance, tongue configuration can be reconstructed.

Recording of the stimuli was carried out in a sound-treated room. The author, fitted with the artificial palate, articulated a steady-state vowel and lowered the velum partway through its production, thereby nasalizing the latter half. Each production was monitored continuously by optical palatography, giving the time-versus-distance measure for the four points along the tongue blade and dorsum. From a total of about 80 productions, one was selected for each vowel in which tongue position was most closely matched within target segments of the oral and nasalized portions. A single period was excised from the corresponding segment of the recording, digitized, and stored on a magnetic tape unit. Tongue configuration beneath the artificial palate for each of the vowels is shown in Figures 3.3 and 3.4.

Proximity data were derived from direct magnitude estimation of similarities on a 100-point scale. All possible pairs from an $N \times N$ matrix of the stimuli excluding the diagonal were presented to subjects in a randomized list. The presentation was self-paced so that the subject could listen to members of each pair in either order for as many repetitions as desired before scoring a response, which was done by turning a knob. Sixteen speakers of American English heard 240 pairs. For each subject, the stimuli were presented in a single session over headphones in a sound-treated room. Five of the subjects had no training in linguistics. Duration of the stimuli, iterations of the single vowel periods, was 250 msec with a 15-msec amplitude onset and offset controlled by a hardware gater to eliminate objectionable transients.

Experiment Results and Discussion

THE PERCEPTUAL SPACE

The upper bound on the dimensionality for the INDSCAL analysis is determined by the largest number of dimensions for which a unique solution is found. Repeated analyses with different starting configurations clearly showed that solutions of five or more dimensions had to be rejected. This criterion

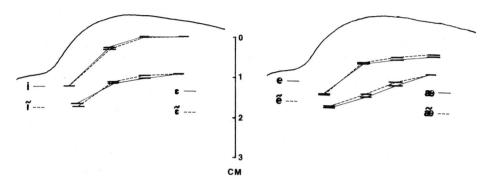

Figure 3.3   Tongue configuration for the front vowels used as stimuli for the perception test.

was more equivocal in the case of the four-dimensional spaces. These differed in detail, although the violations of uniqueness were slight and principally affected the weightings of the stimuli along the fourth dimension. The fourth dimension was difficult to interpret. It correlated weakly with pitch differences in the stimuli, which did not exceed 1 Hz for the same vowel in seven of the eight oral–nasal pairs, but was not controlled for across vowels. Because this fourth dimension appeared to violate the uniqueness condition and did not appear to be readily interpretable, the four-dimensional analysis was rejected. The three-dimensional analysis was taken to best represent the data, but all comments in the discussion which follows are equally applicable to the first three dimensions of the four-dimensional analysis.

Subject weightings provide criteria by which the validity of the analysis may be checked. For example, negative subject weightings indicate viola-

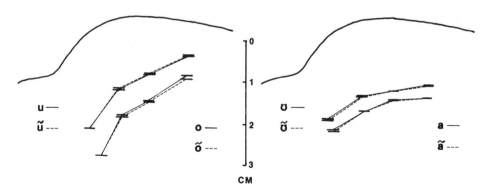

Figure 3.4   Tongue configuration for the back vowels used as stimuli for the perception test.

tions of the assumptions underlying INDSCAL; in the present case, all subject weightings were positive. Subject weightings also give a measure of individual differences. Here again, examination of the subject space, by both visual inspection and a clustering algorithm (Johnson 1967) failed to find any clustering of the weightings suggestive of separate populations within the test group. In particular, there was no clustering of the five linguistically naive subjects vis-a-vis linguistically sophisticated subjects.

The first two dimensions of the three-dimensional analysis are shown in Figure 3.5. Dimension I (DI), along the vertical axis, distinguishes among vowels roughly in terms of vowel height, while Dimension II (D II) separates front from back vowels. The orientation of the axes representing these dimensions is determined by INDSCAL, and the resulting tilt with respect to the traditional vowel space is characteristic of analyses made by procedures related to INDSCAL, such as Harshman's PARAFAC, and to perceptual spaces derived from other multidimensional procedures which are subsequently rotated to account for the greatest variance (see Pols *et al.* 1969; Terbeek & Harshman 1971; Fox 1974; Butcher 1976). The traditional relations of height and front–back have a ready interpretation in this space and are retained in the discussion for descriptive purposes.

Within the plane defined by the first two dimensions, the nasalized vowels (connected by the dashed line) and the oral vowels (connected by the solid line) show systematic differences with respect to vowel height. High and mid vowels, when nasalized, lower with respect to their oral counterparts. The low vowels, on the other hand, raise. As mentioned previously, a similar direction of movement was found by Wright (1975), and it appears to be consistent with the pattern of confusions for vowels taken from nasalizing contexts in the Wilson and Bond study. An additional tendency is also observable: There is some centralization, although it is rather small except in the cases of [ɪ̃] and [õ]. The major effect of nasalization on vowels, then, appears to be a contraction of the perceptual vowel space in the height dimension.

The third dimension found by the analysis appears to reflect a component in listener judgments of perceived nasality. Figure 3.6 represents the height and front–back dimension in the lower plane, while the third dimension is projected along the vertical axis. Open circles represent oral vowels; closed circles represent the nasalized stimuli. For each pair, the nasalized vowel is farther along this projection that the corresponding oral stimulus. A plane may be projected through the space which cleanly separates both sets (with the exception of [u, ũ], suggesting that listeners use a perceptual dimension corresponding to nasality in making similarity judgments.

A final point concerns the relative distance between pairs of oral and nasalized vowels in the set. In Figure 3.7 the Euclidean distance between a given

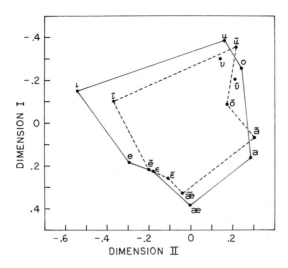

Figure 3.5 The first two dimensions in the perceptual space as determined by INDSCAL analysis.

pair of oral vowels in the three-dimensional space (along the ordinate) is plotted against the distance between the corresponding nasalized pair (along the abscissa). All of the points fall to the right of the diagonal, indicating that the distance between members of the nasalized pair is less than that for the matching oral pair. Perceptually, nasalization has led to a loss of contrast within the set.

THE ACOUSTIC SPACE

I have outlined three perceptual consequences of nasalization in this study: (1) changes in vowel height, (2) the separation of the oral and nasal vowels along an independent dimension, and (3) loss of contrast among members of the nasalized set. While I have noted a number of other studies which support these conclusions, the degree to which these results may be generalized depends, in part, on being able to account for the effects noted by reference to the spectral changes induced by nasalization.

Insofar as changes in vowel height are concerned, the formant structure of the stimuli suggests that changes in vowel height due to nasalization are not simply a function of first-formant movement. Acoustic analysis of the oral vowels was carried out with a spectrum analyzer, and formant peaks were estimated using conventional techniques. As the oral and nasal vowels were articulatorily equivalent, a graphic technique (Fant 1960; Fujimura 1960)

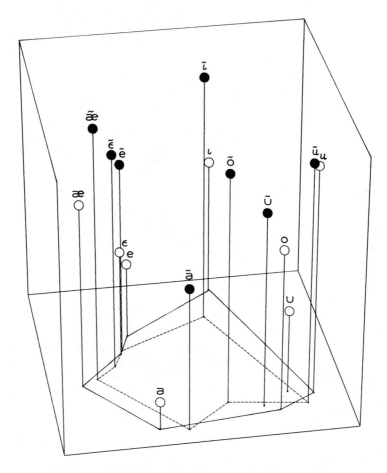

Figure 3.6   The three dimensions of the INDSCAL-derived space.

could be applied to predict the order of the poles and zeroes of the transfer function. Spectral prominences in the nasalized vowels were identified with the predicted poles and used to estimate the frequencies of the first two oral formants and the first nasal formant. Figure 3.8 displays the mel values (technical mel scale) of the first two formants of the stimuli used in the experiment. For the mid vowels, the perceived lowering of the nasalized vowel matches, as would be predicted, a raising of the first-formant frequency. Nevertheless, the auditory lowering of the high vowels does not appear to have been caused by a raising of the frequency of F1; the F1 of [ĩ] does not shift with respect to [i], and [ũ] lowers only slightly. More striking is that the shift of F_1 for the low vowels [æ̃] and [ã] is in the wrong direction for the auditory raising found by INDSCAL analysis. Within the limitations of the method of acoustic analysis used, the spectral prominence associated

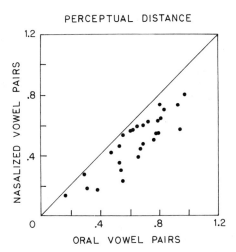

Figure 3.7 Comparison of distances in the perceptual space between oral vowels and between nasal vowels. Abscissa: perceived distance between a given pair of oral vowels; ordinate: perceived distance between the same pair of vowels when nasalized. The fact that the data points lie below the diagonal indicates that nasalization reduces the distinctiveness of vowels.

with the first oral formant did not prove a good predictor of perceived changes in vowel height between oral and nasal conditions.

It is noted in passing by Fant (1960) that the addition of nasal formants in synthesis influences vowel quality in respects other than simply adding nasalization. His observation suggests that the relation of the first nasal formant to F_1 be examined. Figure 3.9 plots the frequency of the first nasal formant (abscissa) against F_1 (ordinate). The diagonal line partitions the space into an area in which the first nasal resonance is lower in frequency than F_1 and into a second area in which it is higher. This partition happens to separate the nasalized vowels into [æ̃, ã], which were perceived as higher when nasalized, and into the high and mid vowels which lowered. It is possible that the position of the first nasal formant with respect to F_1 influences perceived vowel height, but it is not immediately clear how this interaction might take place.

PERCEPTION OF THE QUALITY
OF NASALIZED VOWELS

Given the complexity of nasalized vowels, especially with respect to the complication of formant structure, it is difficult to see how theories of vowel perception that depend on the correct identification of formant peaks can explain the perception of timbre in these vowels. Peak-picking would appear

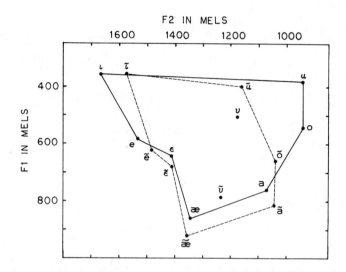

Figure 3.8 F_1 versus F_2 plot of the mel values of the stimuli.

to be highly susceptible to error given the addition of spectral prominences (due to the additional poles in the transfer function) and given the possible attenuation of oral formants (due to zeroes). Part of the attraction of spectrum-based theories of vowel perception is that they would be relatively robust with respect to perturbations in the spectrum that obscure the location of formant peaks. Relatively little attention has been given to whether spectrum-based and formant-peak-picking models can be discriminated experimentally (although see Karnickaya, Mushnikov, Slepokurova, & Zhukov 1975), but nasalized vowels may provide a test case with important implications for phonology.

Spectrum-based Model of Vowel Perception

How, exactly, might a spectrum-based model of vowel perception account for the loss of contrast in nasalized vowels? A series of experiments with Dutch vowels (Klein *et al.* 1970; Pols *et al.* , 1969) shows that the spectral output of a 1/3-octave simulation of critical bands may be reduced from the original 18-dimensional critical-band space to a lower-dimensional representation using a principal-components analysis. Applied to vowel spectra, a principal-components analysis is a data-reduction technique which seeks new directions through the original space (factors); these new directions are linear combinations of the original dimensions and account for as much of

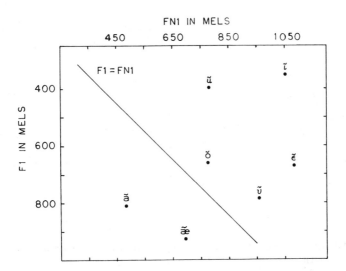

Figure 3.9 Relation between the first oral formant and the first nasal formant of the vowel stimuli.

the variance between vowels as possible. What is interesting is that this procedure produces an acoustic space that is quite similar to spaces with the same number of dimensions that were generated by a parallel set of multidimensional scaling experiments using the same vowels. The implication is that the principal-components analysis captures dependencies between different parts of the critical-band representation of the spectrum that also have perceptual significance for the listeners.

These dependencies are given by the eigenvectors for each factor which may be interpreted as a weighting function on the spectrum. In Figure 3.10 are shown the first two eigenvectors of a principal-components analysis for 15 Dutch vowels produced by 20 speakers (Klein *et al.* 1970) after a speaker-dependent correction by translation. Following Pols (1975), the factor score y_j^k may be found by taking the sum of the product x_j^k (the normalized dB level for the kth vowel in the jth 1/3-octave band) times e_{ij}, the value of the ith eigenvector for the jth band:

$$y_j^k = \sum_{i=1}^{18} X_j^k e_{ij}$$

In the factor space, the first eigenvector will make a distinction among vowels according to the relative predominance of low-frequency versus high-frequency energy in the spectrum, similar to the traditional grave–acute fea-

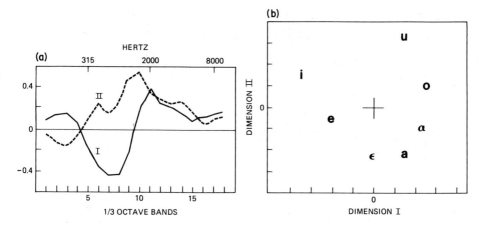

Figure 3.10 (a) First two eigenvectors from a principal components analysis (Klein *et al.*, 1970) for 600 Dutch vowels and (b) the I–II plane of the factor space derived from it.

ture. The second eigenvector separates vowels with energy in the high and low bands from those in the mid bands, much like the compact–diffuse feature distinction (Jakobson, Fant, & Halle 1951). Averaged values for seven of the Dutch vowels shows this factor space to resemble the DI–DII plane in the INDSCAL analysis presented above. If vowel nasalization can be expected to distribute energy more evenly through the spectrum by lowering the amplitude of the oral formants (through greater damping and through interaction with nasal zeroes) and by introducing additional spectral prominences, the factor scores should shift towards zero, thereby centralizing the nasalized vowels and reducing contrast.

This prediction may be tested qualitatively by examining the spectrum of articulatorily equivalent oral and nasal vowels synthesized by a computer simulation of a transmission line analog of the oral and nasal tracts (Wright 1976b). The analog predicts that the acoustic consequence of increasing coupling to the nasal tract is a reduction in the intensity of F_1, while an additional nasal formant will appear at about 1000 Hz, as shown in Figure 3.11, which shows such results for the vowel /i/. The spectra of such synthesized vowels are similar to the spectra of naturally produced vowels. Using the Klein *et al.* eigenvectors, it is possible to predict independently the shape of the spectral 1/3-octave envelope given a change in the factor scores paralleling the perceived movement in the DI–DII plane of the perceptual space. This is done in Figure 3.12. The resulting shift of the 1/3-octave envelope is consistent with the acoustic effects of nasalization in both the natural and synthesized [i], suggesting that it may be possible to account for the loss of

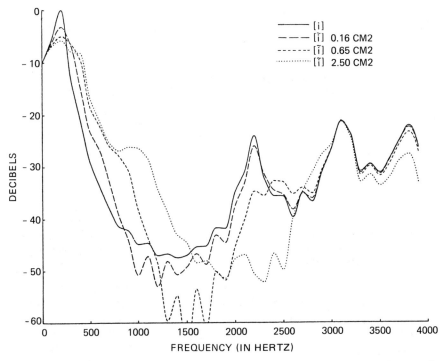

Figure 3.11   The spectral envelope of simulated oral [i] and [ĩ] with three degrees of velopharyngeal coupling.

contrast by means of a mapping operation from the 1/3-octave spectra to the perceptual space. It should be noted, however, that this use of the factor space is not necessarily a claim that the perception of vowel quality is governed by analogous transforms. All we may say at this point is that the equivalence of the empirical-factor spaces and the multidimensional-scaling spaces merely permits a qualitative prediction from the spectral domain to perception.

Nasalization and the Maximization of Contrast

It is now possible to return to the original question: To what extent do the perceptual characteristics of nasalization relate to the patterning of vowel systems? In particular, why are vowel systems skewed such that there may be more oral vowels than nasal vowels but not the converse? Work by Lindblom and his colleagues may provide some answers to this question.

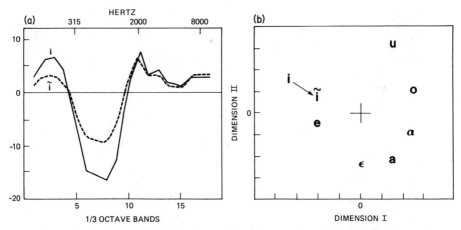

Figure 3.12   (a) Modification in the spectral envelope predicted by the first two eigenvectors (Klein *et al.* 1970) for 600 Dutch vowels and (b) change in factor score for [i] paralleling the shift in the DI-DII plane of the factor space.

Liljencrants and Lindblom (1972) attempt to assess the explanatory value of the principle of the maximization of contrast (in the construction of vowel inventories) by quantitative simulation. By examining the natural degrees of freedom of the lips, tongue, and jaw, they determined the extreme ranges of the first three formants. When graphed in a two-dimensional figure, F_1 versus F_2' (derived from F_2 and F_3), the articulatory constraints effectively define the limits of the acoustic space. Maximizing the acoustic distance between a given number of elements in this space (which can be thought of as candidate vowels) result in their being located on the space in regions that coincide very closely with well-known inventories when the number of such vowels is less than or equal to six. For more than six, however, the vowel configurations tend to have too many high vowels, especially high central vowels, indicating that the model incorporates too great an acoustic distance between [i] and [u]. Subsequent refinements of the acoustic space in terms of a spectrum-based measure appears to correct this problem (Lindblom 1975; see also Bladon & Lindblom 1981; Lindblom, this volume).

This model, then, provides a framework in which the articulatory limits of vowel production, their acoustic characteristics, and recurring patterns in language vowel inventories may be shown to be related. It should nevertheless be recognized that there are problems in directly extending Lindblom's model to nasalized vowels. While Plomp's acoustic measure of spectral distance appears to predict correctly that nasalization reduces contrast, it is difficult to see how it can account for the additional nasality dimension in the perceptual space. At issue is whether there is evidence for coding properties for nasality which are distinct from those which determine oral vowel quality.

Hawkins and Stevens (1985) examine the question of which acoustic properties lead to the perception of vowel nasality for Gujarati, Hindi, Bengali, and English listeners. They presented five oral-nasal vowel continua created by increasing the separation of a pole-zero pair near the first formant. All language groups showed similar crossover points in the identification functions, leading Hawkins and Stevens to argue that the percept of vowel nasality is primarily related to the degree of prominence of the major spectral peak in the vincinity of F_1. The addition of the pole-zero pair near F_1 reduces the prominence of this spectral peak. However, the location of the pole and zero is vowel dependent, which leads Hawkins and Stevens to suggest that it is the pattern of responses at the auditory nerve to the local structure of this prominence that encodes the presence of nasalization. Thus, the primary acoustic property of nasalization may be detected by a perceptual mechanism different from those which decode the general spectral attributes that determine characteristics of vowel quality common to both oral and nasal vowels.

Evidence for a language-independent primary acoustic property of nasality provides motivation for extending Lindblom's principle of the maximization of contrast to include vowel systems which include phonemically nasal vowels.

The Truncated Cone Hypothesis

The overall morphology of the plane defined by DI and DII of the IND-SCAL analysis resembles that of Liljencrants and Lindblom's original acoustic space if only the oral vowels are considered. Without a doubt, articulatory constraints will delimit a bounded region in this plane paralleling that of the F_1 versus F_2' plane in the Lindblom model. At the same time, it is necessary to account for an additional degree of freedom along which articulatorily equivalent oral and nasal vowels separate, projecting this space along this third dimension as shown in Figure 3.13. Loss of contrast attendant on nasalization suggests that the part of this perceptual space occupied by nasalized vowels is more tightly bounded, resulting in a conelike contraction of the boundary along the third dimension.

This perceptual model has two implications for the patterning of vowel systems. First, nasalization could be interpreted as an optional direction in which to expand the vowel space in order to increase the number of elements while maintaining as high a level of perceptual contrast as possible. Second, when nasal vowels are created, the lesser contrast between the nasal mem-

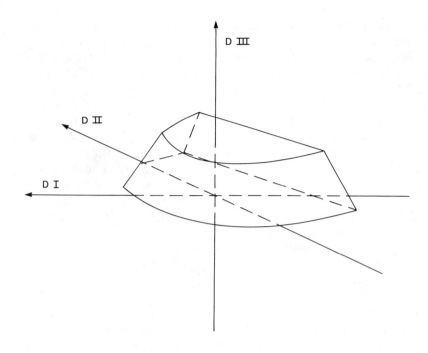

Figure 3.13   The shape of the perceptual vowel space according to the truncated cone hypothesis.

bers of the set would tend to inhibit the development of further nasal vowels, while there would be nothing preventing the development of further oral vowels (through, for example, splits, or monophthongization of diphthongs). A corollary to this prediction would be that diachronic processes which favor mergers, say, of back vowels in the environment of grave consonants would tend to result in mergers among nasal vowels first (as apparently is the case in Yoruba, according to Ward 1952). Both processes together would explain the asymmetry of oral and nasal vowel systems. The perceptual characteristics of nasalization would thereby constitute part of a substratum of constraints that condition the structuring of vowel systems.

CONCLUSIONS

Evidence has been presented that the spectral changes which accompany vowel nasalization lead to a loss of contrast within the set of nasalized vowels while increasing the contrast of these vowels with respect to the oral vowels.

If vowel systems tend to be structured such that some minimal level of contrast is maintained, these results would predict that (1) nasalization of vowels is an effective way to enlarge the number of structurally contrasting vowels, but (2) the development of new vowels ("new" in the sense of having qualities not already represented by preexisting oral or nasal vowels) should occur preferentially among the oral vowels. These predictions seem to be borne out, so far as we can tell, from the synchronic patterning of languages' vowel systems.

REFERENCES

Beddor, P. S. 1982. Phonological and phonetic effects of nasalization on vowel height. Ph.D. diss. University of Minnesota

Beddor, P. S, & S. Hawkins. 1984. The "center of gravity" and perceived vowel height. *Journal of the Acoustical Society of America* 75:S86.

Bhat, D. N. S. 1975. Two studies on nasalization. In C. A. Ferguson, L. M. Hyman, & J. J. Ohala, eds., *Nasalfest. Papers from a symposium on nasals and nasalization,* Language Universals Project, Stanford University. 27–48.

Bladon, R. A. W. and B. Lindblom. 1981. Modeling the judgment of vowel quality differences. *Journal of the Acoustical Society of America* 69:1414–1422.

Bond, Z. S. 1975. Identification of vowels excerpted from context. *Journal of the Acoustical Society of America* 57:S24.

Butcher, A. 1976. The influence of the native language on the perception of vowel quality. *Arbeitsberichte* (Kiel) 6:1–137.

Carroll, J. D., & J. Chang. 1970. Analysis of individual differences in multidimensional scaling via an *n*-way generalization of Eckart-Young decomposition. *Psychometrika* 35:283–319.

Chen, M. 1973. Nasals and nasalization in the history of Chinese. Ph.D. diss. University of California, Berkeley.

Chuang, C. K., & W. S.-Y. Wang. 1975. A distance-sensing device for tracking tongue configuration. *Journal of the Acoustical Society of America* 59:S11.

Coleman, R. O. 1963. The effect of changes in width of velopharyngeal aperture on acoustic and perceptual properties of nasalized vowels. Ph.d. Diss. Northwestern University.

Fant, G. 1960. *Acoustic theory of speech production.* The Hague: Mouton.

Foley, J. 1975. Nasalization as universal phonological process. In C. A. Ferguson, L. M. Hyman, & J. J. Ohala, eds., *Nasalfest. Papers from a symposium on nasals and nasalization,* 197–212. Language Universals Project, Stanford University. 197–212.

Fox, R. A. 1974. An experiment in cross-dialect vowel perception. *Papers from the regional meeting, Chicago Linguistic Society* 10:178–185.

Fujimura, O. 1960. Spectra of nasalized vowels (Quarterly Progress Report 58), 214–218. Research Laboratory of Electronics, MIT.

Fujimura, O. 1961. Analysis of nasalized vowels (Quarterly Progress Report 62), 191–192. Research Laboratory of Electronics, MIT.

Fujimura, O., & Lindqvist, J. 1971. Sweep-tone measurements of vocal-tract characteristics. *Journal of the Acoustical Society of America* 49:541–558.

Hanson, G. 1967. Dimensions in speech sound perception. *Ericsson Technics* 23.

Hawkins, S. & K. N. Stevens. 1985. Acoustic and perceptual correlates of the non-nasal–nasal distinction for vowels. *Journal of the Acoustical Society of America* 77:1560–1575.

Hecker, M. H. L. 1962. Studies of nasal consonants with an articulatory speech synthesizer. *Journal of the Acoustical Society of America* 34:179-188.

House, A. S. 1957. Analog studies of nasal consonants. *Journal of Speech & Hearing Disorders* 22:190-204.

House, A. S., & K. N. Stevens. 1956. Analog studies of the nasalization of vowels. *Journal of Speech & Hearing Disorders* 21:218-232.

Jakobson, R., G. Fant, & M. Halle. 1951. *Preliminaries to speech analysis; The distinctive features and their correlates.* Cambridge, MA: MIT Press.

Jennrich, R. 1972. A generalization of the multidimensional scaling model of Carroll and Chang (Working Papers in Phonetics 22), 45-47. University of California at Los Angeles.

Johnson, S. C. 1967. Hierarchical clustering schemes. *Psychometrika* 32:241-254.

Karnickaya, E. G., V. N. Mushnikov, N. A. Slepokurova, & S. Ja. Zhukov. 1975. Auditory processing of steady-state vowels. In G. Fant & M. A. A. Tatham, eds., Auditory analysis and perception of speech, 37-53. London: Academic Press.

Klein, W., R. Plomp, & L. C. W. Pols. 1970. Vowel spectra, vowel spaces and vowel identification. *Journal of the Acoustical Society of America* 48:1000-1009.

Lightner, T. M. 1970. Why and how does vowel nasalization take place? *Papers in Linguistics* 2:179-226.

Liljencrants, J., & B. Lindblom. 1972. Numerical simulation of vowel quality systems: The role of perceptual contrast. *Language* 48:839-862.

Lindblom, B. 1975. Experiments in sound structure. Plenary address, 8th International Congress of Phonetic Sciences, Leeds.

Lindqvist, J., & J. Sundberg. 1972. Acoustic properties of the nasal tract. (Quarterly Progress and Status Report 1/1972), 13-17. Speech Transmission Laboratory, Royal Institute of Technology, Stockholm.

Mohr, B., & W. S.-Y. Wang. 1968. Perceptual distance and the specification of phonological features. *Phonetica* 18:31-45.

Mrayati, M. 1975. Etudes des voyelles nasales françaises. *Bulletin de l'Institute de phonétique de Grenoble* 4:1-26.

Ohala, J. J. 1974. Experimental historical phonology. In J. M. Anderson & C. Jones, eds., *Historical linguistics II. Theory and description in phonology*, 353-389. Amsterdam: North Holland.

Ohala, J. J. 1975. Phonetic explanation for nasal sound patterns. In C. A. Ferguson, L. M. Hyman, & J. J. Ohala, eds., *Nasalfest. Papers from a symposium on nasals and nasalization*, 289-316. Language Universals Project, Stanford University.

Plomp, R. 1964. The ear as a frequency analyzer. *Journal of the Acoustical Society of America* 36:1628-1636.

Plomp, R. 1975. Auditory analysis and timbre perception. In G. Fant & M. A. A. Tatham, eds., *Auditory analysis and perception of speech*, 7-22. London: Academic Press.

Plomp, R., & A. M. Mimpen. 1968. The ear as frequency analyzer II. *Journal of the Acoustical Society of America* 43:764-767.

Pols, L. C. W. 1975. Analysis and synthesis of speech using a broad-band spectral representation. In G. Fant & M. A. A. Tatham, eds., *Auditory analysis and perception of speech*, 23-36. London: Academic Press.

Pols, L. C. W., L. J. Th. van der Kamp, & R. Plomp. 1969. Perceptual and physical space of vowel sounds. *Journal of the Acoustical Society of America* 46:458-467.

Ruhlen, M. 1973. *Nasal vowels.* (Working Papers in Language Universals 12), 1-36. Stanford University.

Ruhlen, M. 1975. Patterning of nasal vowels. In C. A. Ferguson, L. M. Hyman, & J. J. Ohala, eds., *Nasalfest. Papers from a symposium on nasals and nasalization*, 333-352. Language Universals Project, Stanford University.

Sedlak, P. 1969. *Typological considerations of vowel quality systems.* (Working Papers in Language Universals 1), 1-40. Stanford University.

Singh, S., & D. R. Woods. 1971. Perceptual structure of 12 American vowels. *Journal of the Acoustical Society of America* 49:1861-1886.

Takeuchi, S., H. Kasuya, & K. Kido. 1974a. An active model for extraction of nasality and its perceptual evaluation. *Preprints of the Speech Communication Seminar. Vol. 3: Speech Perception and Automatic Recognition*, 141-148. Stockholm: Speech Transmission Laboratory, Royal Institute of Technology.

Takeuchi, S., H. Kasuya, & K. Kido. 1974b. Effects of the nasal cavity and the sinus paranasalis on the acoustic characteristics of nasal sounds. (In Japanese.) *Journal of the Acoustical Society of Japan* 43:133-145.

Terbeek, D. 1977. *A cross-language multidimensional scaling study of vowel perception* (Working Papers in Phonetics 37), 1-271. University of California at Los Angeles.

Terbeek, D., & R. Fox. 1975. An INDSCAL study of the perceptual space of American diphthongs. *Journal of the Acoustical Society of America* 58:S91.

Terbeek, D., & R. Harshman. 1971. *Cross-language differences in the perception of natural vowel sounds* (Working Papers in Phonetics 19), 26-38. University of California at Los Angeles.

Terbeek, D., & R. Harshman. 1972. *Is vowel perception non-Euclidean?* (Working Papers in Phonetics 22), 13-30. University of California at Los Angeles.

Ward, I. C. 1952. *An introduction to the Yoruba language.* Cambridge: W. Heffer.

Wilson, H. F., & Z. S. Bond. 1976. An INDSCAL analysis of vowels excerpted from four consonantal environments. *Journal of the Acoustical Society of America* 59:S25.

Wright, J. T. 1975. Effects of vowel nasalization on the perception of vowel height. In C. A. Ferguson, L. M. Hyman, & J. J. Ohala, eds., *Nasalfest. Papers from a symposium on nasals and nasalization*, 373-388. Language Universals Project, Stanford University.

Wright, J. T. 1976a. *Dynamic optical palatograph* (Report of the Phonology Laboratory 1), 117-118. University of California, Berkeley.

Wright, J. T. 1976b. *VOCALTS: Articulatory-based synthesis incorporating nasalization.* (Report of the Phonology Laboratory 1), 119-120. University of California, Berkeley.

4

On Describing Vowel Quality

SANDRA FERRARI DISNER

INTRODUCTION

Current theories about the forces which shape the distributions of vowels in the vowel space (e.g., Liljencrants & Lindblom 1972; Crothers 1978; Lindblom, this volume) require answers to questions such as: Are the vowels of language X evenly distributed in the vowel space, or are, say, the front vowels more widely spaced than those in the back? Are the vowels centralized or peripheral? Are the front rounded vowels lower than their unrounded counterparts? Is the [i] of language X higher than the [i] of language Y? To answer such questions, phonologists often have recourse to acoustic phonetic measures of vowels, primarily their formant frequencies. Although formant frequencies have long been recognized as a major determinant of phonetic vowel quality, the answers to the above questions would not be at all evident if the vowels of several speakers were plotted as clouds of individual data points on the traditional formant 1 versus formant 2 representation of the vowel space, as in Figure 4.1. The problem is that it is (probably) the relation between a vowel's formant values and the general range of the formant values for all vowels produced by a given speaker which determines vowel quality, whereas the absolute values of the formants are greatly influenced by individual differences in speakers' vocal anatomy—those between men and women, adults and children, bassos and tenors. Thus, plots such as that in Figure 4-1 incorporate too much between-speaker variation along with language-specific systematic variation.

69

EXPERIMENTAL PHONOLOGY

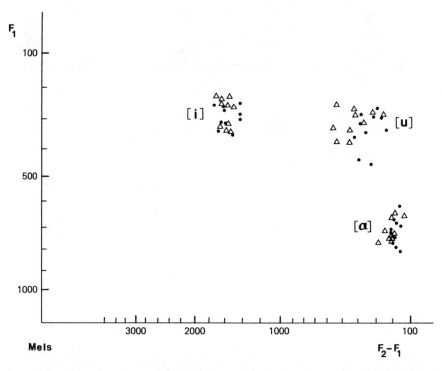

Figure 4.1 Plot of selected vowels of English (triangles) and Dutch (points), as pronounced by 10 native speakers of each language.

In order to compare vowel systems across languages, it must be possible to remove as much of the speaker variation as possible in order to restrict the cluster of data points for a given vowel to the smallest possible area.[1] Any of a number of vowel-normalization procedures can satisfactorily achieve this reduction by shifting, stretching, or shrinking the dimensions of each speaker's vowel system in proportion to where his formant values stand with respect to those of the population as a whole. Some of the better-known normalization procedures have been proposed by Gerstman (1968), Harshman (1970), Lobanov (1971), Sankoff, Shorrock, and McKay (1974), Harshman and Papçun (1976), Nearey (1977), and Bernstein (1977). Common to most of these procedures is the use of the overall means of each of the first few formant values as a correction factor for the frequencies of individual vowels.

But it has been found that many of the proposed normalization proce-

---

[1]The removal of personal variation must be done in a principled fashion and must not leave less than the characteristic amount of personal variation tolerated by the language. For this reason, a simple averaging technique is considered too powerful.

dures are simply inapplicable to cross-language studies of vowel quality (Disner 1980): When the vowel systems themselves differ, the correction factors may also differ significantly. For example, French has twice as many front vowels as Italian does, while the back vowels are comparable. As a result, the mean of the French vowels is considerably farther front than the mean of the Italian vowels. A normalization procedure based on the overall formant means would thus be likely to overnormalize the data by drawing the French front vowels back in the phonetic space. This backing is justified in within-language studies, where the difference in means reflects an anatomical (age-related or sex-related) difference between the speakers; however, when the difference in the means is purely linguistic, this backing is a procedural artifact which must be avoided. Similar procedural artifacts may arise when the vowels in a system are not symmetrically distributed around the mean.

Some normalization procedures do avoid making assumptions as to the comparability of different vowel systems. However, even a procedure that keeps the data relatively free of distortion—Harshman's (1970) PARAFAC procedure—has the drawback of leaving behind a great deal of the original variance. Clearly, then, there is a need for some alternative means of restricting the range of the phonetic data so that we may use it profitably in answering phonological questions.

ANOVA

One likely approach to the cross-linguistic analysis of vowel quality is the use of statistical procedures such as analysis of variance (ANOVA) or the T-test. In both of these procedures the magnitude of the difference between the languages is compared to the magnitude of the speaker-related differences within each language. If the between-language difference exceeds the within-language differences to a significant degree, the languages may be said to differ reliably from one another along the relevant parameters. Unlike other normalization procedures, ANOVA does not transform the data; it simply seeks out trends. This makes it an excellent tool for testing linguistic hypotheses.

Method

DATA

Formant-frequency data from numerous speakers of each language may be used as the input to ANOVA. Significant differences are more readily obtained from larger data sets than from small, and it is useful to enter as much data as is conveniently available. The data examined here are taken from studies by Peterson and Barney (1952) on English and by Pols, Tromp, and Plomp (1973) on Dutch. In each of these studies, 25 speakers were asked to pronounce the vowels of their respective languages, each one in the context of a preceding [h] and a following dental consonant; these utterances were then analyzed to determine their formant frequencies. The six vowels transcribed as [i, ɪ, ɛ, ɑ, ɔ, u] were selected for the present study, as these are the only vowels common to both languages.[2]

In order to minimize the amount of speaker-related variance from the outset, all of the speakers chosen for the present example were adult males.

ANALYSIS

Analysis of variance was used to test the hypothesis that the formant means of several different populations (i.e., speakers of different languages) are equal. The use of ANOVA allows each observation to be classified according to three linguistically relevant criteria of classification: the language spoken, the identity of the speaker, and the phonetic identity of the vowel. The total variation present in the data is thus broken down into separate, independent components that may be attributed to any of these three sources and is analyzed accordingly.

The ANOVA procedure determines whether there is a *language effect* in the data such that the vowels of one language are consistently higher or lower (in the F_1 domain) or fronter or backer (in the F_2 domain) than the vowels of another; whether there is a *vowel effect* such that, say, the vowel [i] for all speakers and languages in the sample differs reliably from the vowel [u]; and whether there is a *speaker effect* such that the vowels of speaker A are consistently different from those of speaker B. Not all of these effects are of equal linguistic importance, however. The presence of a speaker effect is entirely idiolectal and thus outside the scope of our linguistic investigation. A vowel effect, too, is of very little concern to us, since it is to be expected that different vowels have different acoustic specifications. But whether or not there is a language effect is of interest insofar as it can be associated with the well-known linguistic notion of 'base of articulation'— the characteristic articulatory set of a language. The language effect can be quantified in a way that the more impressionistic base of articulation cannot. Also of interest is whether there is a significant language-by-vowel inter-

---

[2]It may be argued that the steady-state portion of English diphthongs [eᶦ] and [oᵁ] should be added to this list, as comparable to the Dutch vowels [e] and [o]. Indeed, in some phonological accounts of English the vowels in *hayed* and *honed* are portrayed as monophthongs, and in certain dialects this is beyond doubt a phonetic fact. However, formant frequencies for these vowels were not included in the Peterson-Barney data.

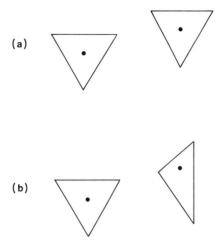

Figure 4.2   Schematic representation of language effect (a) and pattern effect (b).

action effect—that is, whether the vowels of one language align themselves in the same way as the vowels of another.[3] This interaction effect is different from either the language effect alone (which indicates that the mean of each formant differs from language to language) or the vowel effect alone (which indicates that individual vowels are different, regardless of the language). We may redefine this interaction as a *pattern effect* and note that it indicates a difference in the relative contribution of individual vowels toward the overall difference between languages; the absence of such an effect indicates that individual vowels participate equally in the determination of a language effect.

pattern effect (Figure 4.2). Yet we still lack a means of determining whether each individual vowel differs significantly from one language to another. For example, is Dutch [i] higher than English [i]? This more detailed indication of cross-language differences may be derived from *a posteriori* contrasts between pairs of group means. An *a posteriori* contrast test systematically compares all possible pairs of group means. Pairs which exceed a predetermined significance level (in the present case, $p < .05$; additional tests may be set at $p < .01$) may be said to differ significantly along a certain parameter, here, one or another of the formant axes.

In sum, then, these three criteria—language effect, pattern effect, and a posteriori contrasts—tell us a great deal about the way languages differ, in particular and in general.

---

[3]There is another possible interaction in the data, a speaker-by-vowel effect, which is not of linguistic interest. Since none of the speakers sampled was bilingual, the other possible interactions (speaker-by-language, speaker-by-language-by-vowel) do not occur here.

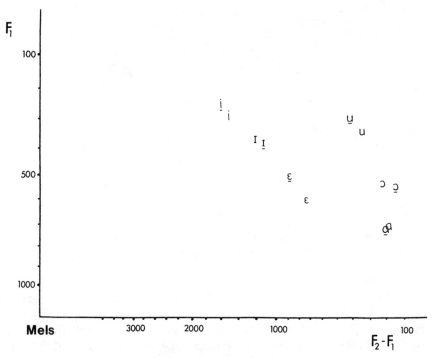

Figure 4.3 Mean values of 25 tokens each of 6 selected vowels of English (underscored) and Dutch.

For ease of interpretation, a first step in the analysis should be the graphing of the vowel tokens, or at least the mean value of the tokens of each vowel in each language, in a phonetic space. Figure 4.3 shows the means of the Dutch vowels and the English vowels (underscored) in two dimensions; these dimensions correspond to parameters which are widely recognized as the primary determinants of vowel quality—F_1 along the ordinate and the difference between F_2 and F_1 along the abcissa. The data points have been converted to mels, which better represent the perceived distances in phonetic space. Additional charts can be made to show $F_1 \times F_3$, $(F_2 - F_1) \times F_3$, and so on.

Results

Figure 4.4 is an elaboration of the basic vowel chart in Figure 4.3, adding the results of the ANOVA. Each of the vowel centroids in Figure 4.4 is projected onto a separate pair of axes parallel to, and identical in scale with,

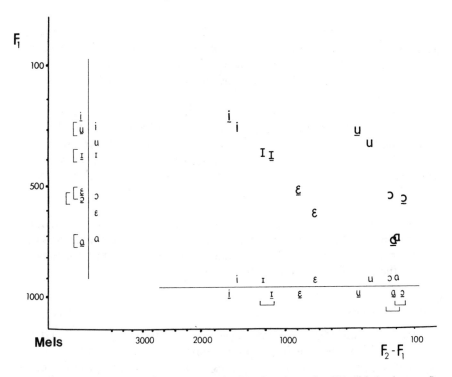

Figure 4.4 Mean values of 25 tokens each of 6 selected vowels of English (underscored) and Dutch. Means are plotted in a formant space and projected onto each of the axes, with brackets grouping the vowels which are not significantly different along a particular axis. Language effect: For F_1, $p < .10$; for F_2-F_1, $p < .10$. Pattern effect: for F_1 and F_2-F_1, $p < .001$.

the F_1 and F_2-F_1 axes. This provides us with two separate unidimensional representations of the relationships between vowels. The vowels along each interior axis can then be bracketed to mark the results of the *a posteriori* contrast tests. For example, the bracketing indicates that the English [ɔ] and the Dutch [ɔ] do not differ significantly along the F_1 (height) parameter, although they do differ significantly in terms of F_2-F_1 (backness).

From the plotted vowel means alone (Figure 4.3) we can see that certain vowels differ markedly from language to language, even when sampled across large numbers of speakers. An example is the vowel [ɛ], which in Dutch is recognized as being "more open than the English vowel in *bed*" (Koolhoven 1968). This fact is clearly evident in both Figure 4.3 and Figure 4.4. However, the differences between certain other vowels, while reliable and statistically significant, are not as dramatic as in the case of [ɛ]. Here the *a posteriori* test results help us in discovering these differences. The results show, for example, that the differences in degree of backness between English vowels and Dutch vowels are greatest in the intermediate range of the F_2-F_1 scale; vowels with extreme F_2-F_1 values tend not to be significantly different in English and Dutch.

There is not quite a significant language effect in either F_1 or F_2-F_1; that is to say, the differences in the overall height and backness of English and Dutch are not significant, compared to the large speaker-related differences within each language. This is not unexpected in two such genetically related languages with comparable numbers of vowel phonemes in their inventories. There are, however, highly significant ($p < .001$) pattern effects in both F_1 and F_2-F_1, indicating that the differences which do exist are not evenly distributed throughout the vowel system. The differences between individual vowels, such as Dutch [ɛ] and English [ɛ], thus cannot be explained solely in terms of a uniform shift from language to language—a shift corresponding to the notion of 'base of articulation'.

Other Languages

Data from other Germanic languages are presented in Figures 4.5 and 4.6. Figure 4.5 shows the four front vowels common to English and Danish. The symbols mark the mean formant values of these vowels, as pronounced by seven speakers of each language. The Danish data are from Fischer-Jørgensen (1972); the English data are from a study by Kahn (1978) and, unlike the Peterson-Barney data, do include formant values for the initial steady-state portion of [eᴵ] (as in *hayed*).

It is virtually a cliché that "Danish is spoken higher in the mouth" than other Germanic languages. This point is clearly illustrated in Figure 4.5: Along the F_1 dimension each Danish vowel is substantially higher than its English counterpart. This is reflected in the highly significant F_1 language effect. In the F_2-F_1 domain we find that, with the exception of [i], Danish vowels are also farther front than their English counterparts; this is reflected in the highly significant F_2-F_1 language effect. And, just as in the Dutch-English example, there is a highly significant pattern effect along each parameter as well. We cannot simply say that Danish has a higher base of articulation than English; the vowels of Danish are unevenly spaced, with [i, e, ɛ] high and close together, and [æ] a good deal lower.[4] Each Danish vowel is indeed higher than its English counterpart, but the difference does not suggest a uniform shift.

---

[4]The apparent unevenness of the English vowels is due to the fact that the vowel [ɪ] has been omitted from this illustration (since it lacks a Danish counterpart). If [ɪ] were inserted between [i] and [e], the intervals would be quite regular.

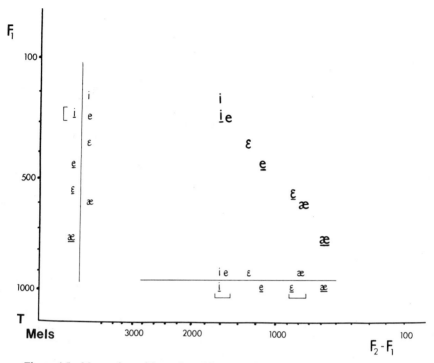

Figure 4.5 Mean values of four selected front vowels of English (underscored) and Danish. The means are plotted in a formant space and projected onto each of the axes, with brackets grouping the vowels which are not significantly different along a particular axis. Language effect: for F_1 and F_2-F_1, $p < .001$. Pattern effect: for F_1 and F_2-F_1, $p < .001$.

Figure 4.6 shows the vowels common to German and Dutch. The symbols mark the means of these vowels as pronounced by six speakers of each language. The Dutch data are a subset of the Pols *et al.* (1973) data used earlier; the German data are from Jørgensen (1969).

Only the vowel [a] is similar in height across the languages; the nonlow vowels are all significantly higher in German than they are in Dutch. As we would expect, there is a highly significant language effect in F_1. In contrast, we find no significant language effect in F_2-F_1; the overall backness of the two languages is similar. Even though the front vowels of German appear to be fronter than their Dutch counterparts, we can see from the *a posteriori* test results that most of these differences are not significant.

CONCLUSION

A method has been outlined for describing the quality of vowels in different languages. It provides a compact representation of a large amount of

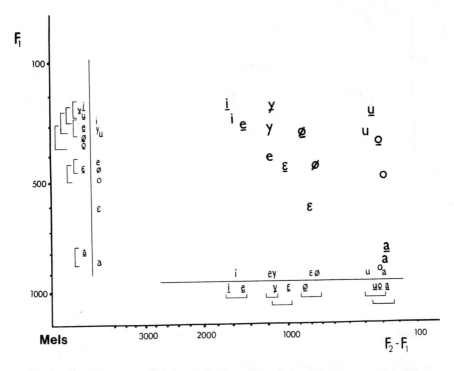

Figure 4.6 Mean values of eight selected vowels of German (underscored) and Dutch. The means are plotted in a formant space and projected onto each of the axes, with brackets grouping the vowels which are not significantly different along a particular axis. Language effect: for F_1, $p < .001$; for F_2-F_1, $p < .10$. Pattern effect: for F_1, $p < .001$; for F_2-F_1, $p < .01$.

acoustic data and also circumvents many of the problems encountered by normalization algorithms. Moreover, by using ANOVA one can find out whether the differences between languages are significant when compared with the accepted level of speaker-related differences within each language. A plot of the mean values alone cannot provide this information; without bracketing, the phonetic differences between vowels may appear to be greater than they actually are.

The overall differences in height and backness suggest differences in what is termed 'base of articulation' between languages. However, the unequal participation of individual vowels in these overall differences points to the inadequacy of a theory based on base of articulation alone. Beyond such general trends, an adequate description of a language must include more specific details about the phonetic quality of its vowels.

REFERENCES

Bernstein, J. C. 1977. Vocoid psychoacoustics, articulation, and vowel phonology. Ph.D. diss., University of Michigan.

Crothers, J. 1978. Typology and universals of vowel systems. In J.H. Greenberg, C. A. Ferguson, & E. A. Moravcsik, eds., *Universals of human language, Vol. 2, Phonology,* 93–152. Stanford: Stanford University Press.

Disner, S. F. 1980. Evaluation of vowel normalization procedures. *Journal of the Acoustical Society of America* 67:253–261.

Fischer-Jørgensen, E. 1972. Formant frequencies of long and short Danish vowels. In E. S. Firchow, K. Grimstad, N. Hasselmo, & W. O'Neil, eds., *Studies for Einar Haugen,* 189–213. The Hague: Mouton.

Gerstman, L. 1968. Classification of self-normalized vowels. *IEEE Transactions in Audio & Electroacoust.* AU-16:78–80.

Harshman, R. 1970. Foundations of the PARAFAC procedure: Models and conditions for an "explanatory" multi-modal factor analysis (Working Papers in Phonetics 16). University of California at Los Angeles.

Harshman, R., & G. Papçun. 1976. Vowel normalization by linear transformation. *Journal of the Acoustical Society of America* 59(S1):79.

Jørgensen, H. 1969. Die gespannten und ungespannten Vokale in der norddeutschen Hochsprache, mit einer spezifischen Untersuchung der Struktur ihrer Formantenfrequenzen. *Phonetica* 19:217–245.

Kahn, D. 1978. On the identifiability of isolated vowels (Working Papers in Phonetics 41), 26–31. University of California at Los Angeles.

Koolhoven, H. 1968. *Dutch.* London: The English Universities Press.

Liljencrants, J., & B. Lindblom. 1972. Numerical simulation of vowel quality systems: The role of perceptual contrast. *Language* 48:839–862.

Lobanov, B. 1971. Classification of Russian vowels spoken by different speakers. *Journal of the Acoustical Society of America* 49:606–608.

Nearey, T. 1977. Phonetic feature systems for vowels. Ph.D. diss., University of Connecticut, Storrs.

Peterson, G., & H. Barney. 1952. Control methods used in a study of the vowels. *Journal of the Acoustical Society of America* 24:175–184.

Pols, L. C. W., H. R. C. Tromp, & R. Plomp. 1973. Frequency analysis of Dutch vowels from 50 male speakers. *Journal of the Acoustical Society of America* 53:1093–1101.

Sankoff, D., R. Shorrock, & W. McKay. 1974. Normalization of formant space through the least squares affine transformation. Unpublished program and documentation. Philadelphia: University of Pennsylvania.

5

Phonetic Explanation for Phonological Universals: The Case of Distinctive Vowel Nasalization

HARUKO KAWASAKI

INTRODUCTION

Phonological universals can be of two types: diachronic universals which concern sound changes that have occurred repeatedly at different times and places, and synchronic universals which concern commonly observed patterns in phonemic inventories, allophonic variations, and morphophonemic alternations.[1] Greenberg (1966), however, pointed out that in spite of the dichotomy between diachrony and synchrony insisted on by Saussure and his followers, in the area of phonological universals there is an obvious link between the two. Every diachronic universal has its synchronic consequence, such as patterns in phonemic inventories or phonotactic constraints, which would then also be universal. Moreover, where a diachronic change has taken

[1]In this chapter, in accord with generally accepted practice, the term 'phonological universal' refers to any widespread cross-language sound pattern where there is prima facie reason to discount areal, genetic, or typological factors as responsible for it. It need not be universal in a strict sense. Nevertheless, it is my purpose to demonstrate that sound patterns said to be 'universal' in the loose sense are, when one looks carefully, universal in the strict sense, too, in that situations can be found or contrived—as in an experiment—where the pattern manifests itself in any language, or, more properly, in the behavior of the speakers of any language.

81

place, the old form may be preserved as a morphologically conditioned variant. In cross-language surveys such variation would naturally occur more frequently than variation due to other sources such as cultural, areal, or other language-specific factors. Conversely, widely attested synchronic allophonic variation may often lead to sound changes. Thus it is possible to find many parallels in diachronic processes and synchronic states.[2] It has been further argued that similar parallels exist in other linguistic domains such as child language acquisition, speech errors, and pathological speech (Jakobson 1968; Greenlee & Ohala 1980).

These arguments inevitably lead one to search for the cause of such parallels. If similar patterns are found in typologically, geographically, and geneologically unrelated languages, the causal factors must lie in what is common to all human beings, the physical system used for speech: the articulatory apparatus, the peripheral auditory system, or the central nervous system (Ohala 1974a, 1974b). From Greenberg's and Ohala's assumptions it follows directly that the seed of a given universal sound pattern must be present synchronically in any language which has the relevant segments; it will be manifested in the fine phonetic details of speech or in the behavior of the listeners to speech sounds. This is the assumption that lies behind the recent phonetic studies that attempt to account for phonological universals (J. Ohala 1974a, 1974b, 1975, 1978; Hombert 1975; Ohala & Lorentz 1977; Ohala, Riordan, & Kawasaki 1978; Javkin 1979; Wright, this volume) and it is the assumption underlying the present study, which examines a common pattern of interaction between nasalized vowels and adjacent nasal consonants.

PHONOLOGICAL UNIVERSALS
IN NASALS AND NASALIZATION

There have been several studies on the way nasals and nasal vowels behave in languages (Issatschenko 1937; Ferguson 1963, 1974; Lightner 1970; Schourup 1972; Bhat 1975; Crothers 1975; Ruhlen 1975, 1978). In this chapter I discuss the interaction between vowels and adjacent nasal consonants. The following are some of the major findings on this topic.

1. Vowels are often nondistinctively nasalized in the environment of nasal consonants (Ferguson 1963, 1974; Ruhlen 1978). Some languages which show this pattern are Akan, Alabaman, Armenian, Awadhi, Azerbaijani, Bengali,

---

[2]However, Hyman (1975) points out that it is also possible for a universal synchronic pattern to result not from a universal diachronic process but accidentally from the combination of some nonuniversal processes.

Capanahua, Cayapa, Chipewyan, Delaware, English, Ewe, Gã, Georgian, Greenlandic, Guarani, Hindi, Hupa, Kashmiri, Kpelle, Kunjen, Kurux, Land Dayak, Loma, Luo, Malagasy, Malay, Mazatec, Mixtec, Mundari, Nahuat, Nama, Navaho, Nez Perce, Nyangumata, Ojibwa, Paez, Panamanian Spanish, Picuris, Punjabi, Somali, Songhai, Sundanese, Swahili, Tagalog, Telugu, Tewa, Thai, Ticuna, Tolowa, Tunica, Wolof, Yao, Yerwa Kanuri, Yuchi, and Zulu.[3] Some examples are given in (1).

(1) English   /kænt/   [kʰǣnt]   'can't'
     Tagalog   /maŋanak/   [māŋānāk]   'to give birth'
     Tunica   /ʔimapan]   [ʔimapǟnʔ]   'I, too'
     Cayapa   /ʔɑpaiŋʔ/   [ʔɑpǟɪ̃ŋʔ]   'Hurry!'
     Kurux   /meed/   [mẽẽd]   'body'

In general, a syllable-final nasal nasalizes a vowel more than a syllable-initial nasal. Some languages with anticipatory nasalization are Azerbaijani, Cayapa, Chipewyan, Delaware, English, Hupa, Kashmiri, Malay, Nahuat, Nez Perce, Panamanian Spanish, Tagalog, Tewa, Tolowa, Tunica, and Wolof. Languages with perseveratory nasalization are Greenlandic, Kunjen, Kurux, Land Dayak, Loma, Mazatec, Nama, Paez, Sundanese, Ticuna, and Yuchi.

2. Synchronically, the sequence of a vowel and a nasal consonant, supposedly where the vowel is not noticeably nasalized, often has a free allophonic variant, a simple nasalized vowel or a nasalized vowel plus a very weak residual nasal consonant (Ferguson 1963; Greenberg 1966; Schourup 1972). Some languages showing this phenomenon are Azerbaijani, Bengali, Capanahua, Chontal, Dongolese Nubian, English, Georgian, Goajiro, Ila, Island Carib, Modern Greek, Mundari, Nahuat, Ojibwa, Panamanian Spanish, Sentani, Sinhalese, Somali, Spanish, Swahili, Telugu, Tillamook, and Western Ossetic. Some examples are given in (2).

(2) Bengali   /põcasi/   ~ /poncasi/   'eighty-five'
     Goajiro   /wĩpumə̃ĩ/   ~ /wimpuməĩ/   'northward'
     Panamanian   /kãpo/   ~ /kampo/   'field'
     Spanish
     Ila   /wá:ʒanina/   ~ /wá:ɲʒanina/ 'he danced to me'
     Chontal   /tɔ̃•ʃín/   ~ /tənʃín/   'in the middle'

3. Diachronically, distinctive nasal vowels often result from the stage mentioned in 2, followed by the complete loss of the conditioning nasal consonant

---

[3]References for the languages cited as examples are given in the appendix.

(Ferguson 1963, 1974; Greenberg 1966; Schourup 1972; Ruhlen 1978).[4] Such a development occurred in Breton, Burmese, Chinese (Changsha, Chaozhou, Jinan, Shanghai, Shuangfeng, Suzhou, Taiyuan, Xiamen, Xian, and Yangzhou dialects), Common Slavic, French, Gujarati, Hindi, Kashmiri, Kurux, Modern Irish, Nama, Old Church Slavonic, and Portuguese. Examples are given in (3).

(3) Middle Chinese   /laɲ/   > Suzhou   /lã/   'cold'
     Latin   centum   > French   /sã/   'hundred'
     Sanskrit   danta   > Hindi   /dãt/   'tooth'
     Old Portuguese   ganso   > Modern   /gõsu/   'goose'
                                  Portuguese
     Pre-Old Church   *klinti > Old Church   /klẽtī/   'to curse'
     Slavonic   Slavonic
                                  cf. Polish   /klinatʃ/

4. For distinctive nasal vowels, the position of maximum contrast (vis-a-vis oral vowels) is syllable-final after an oral consonant, whereas the position of minimum contrast is next to a nasal consonant (Ferguson 1963, 1974). Thus, the oral–nasal vowel opposition does not exist after a nasal consonant in Bengali, Ijo, Mazatec, Mixtec, Navaho, Nupe, and Quiotepec Chinantec. Examples are given in (4).

(4) Nupe   /ba/   'to cut'   /mã/   'to give birth'
                  /bã/   'to break'   */ma/
     Quiotepec   /toh/   'hole'   /mõh/   'bone'
     Chinantec   /tõh/   'thorns'   */moh/

Such an opposition does not exist before a nasal consonant in Beembe, Bengali, Brazilian Portuguese, Chinese, Goajiro, Hindi, Island Carib, Kashmiri, Mazatec, Mixtec, Punjabi, Takum Jukun, Tewa, and Yuchi.

This opposition is present but rare adjacent to a nasal consonant or it exists after a limited number of nasal consonants in Ọwọn Afa and Paez. In Ọwọn Afa, for example, /m/ and /n/ occur before either oral or nasal vowels, but /ŋ/ and /ŋ͡m/ only occur before oral vowels.

In a related pattern, only a limited number of nasal vowels may occur adjacent to a nasal consonant in Chaozhou Chinese, as exemplified in (5).

(5) /mia/   'life'   /mua/   'full'

[4]Far less frequently, distinctive nasal vowels result from the sequence of nasal plus vowel (Ferguson 1974; Ruhlen 1978); for example, Kwa, Portuguese, and Xiamen Chinese. The subsequent loss of the nasal consonant may or may not occur.

/mĩã/   'name'   */muã/

but

/pia$^\textapostrophe$/   'wall'   /pua/   'winnow'
/pĩã/   'soldier'   /puã/   'plate'

Historically in Kpelle, the oral–nasal opposition next to nasal consonants occurred after the development of this opposition next to oral consonants (Hyman 1975).

5. Partial or complete denasalization of nasal consonants adjacent to oral vowels often happens in languages in which the oral–nasal vowel opposition has been established in the environment of nasal as well as oral consonants (Hyman 1975)[5]. For example, nasal consonants are realized as partially denasalized near oral vowels in Amahuaca, Apinaye, Gbeya, Guarani, Otomi, Siriono, and Wukari Jukun. Examples are given in (6).

(6) Amahuaca   /tamó/   [tambɪ]   'cheek'
                 /hĩnĩ$^\textapostrophe$no/   [hĩndĩ$^\textapostrophe$no]   'lobo'
                 but
                 /nõnó/   [nõnó]   'duck'
     Apinaye   /ma/   [mba]   'liver'
                 /om/   [obm]~[om]   'mixture'
                 but
                 /mõ/   [mõ]   'to go'
                 /ũm/   [ũm]   'dirty (water)'
     Otomi   /nĩne/   [nĩnᵈe]   'your mouth'
     Siriono   /tena/   [teⁿda]   'sun'
                 but
                 /anã/   [anã]   'butterfly'

Nasal consonants are realized as voiced oral consonants before oral vowels in Chaozhou and Xiamen Chinese. The data in (7) (from Dong 1968, transcription simplified) show oral consonants in these dialects as reflexes of Middle Chinese nasals (these dialects also have distinctively nasal vowels).

[5]Hyman (1975) argues that such denasalization would occur only in languages with the oral-nasal vowel contrast. Languages exist, however, in which there are no phonemic nasal vowels but the denasalization of nasal consonants occurs, for example, Asmat, Cantonese, Cham, Diegueño, Korean, and Telefol. However, such denasalization occurs either preconsonantally (as epenthetic stops in English), before high vowels, or after long vowels. The intervocalic denasalization not specifically conditioned by the quality or length of the adjacent vowel, then, seems to be limited to the languages with distinctive nasal vowels, as Hyman predicted.

(7) Middle Chinese   Xiamen   Chaozhou
     /mu/   /bu/,/bo/   /bo/   'mother'
     /mjuaŋ/   /bɔŋ/   /buaŋ/   'die'
     /mjuo/   /bu/,/bɔ/   /bo/   'without'
     nuən/   /dzun/   /luŋ/   'tender'
     /nuɑi/   /lue/,/lai/   /lai/   'inside'
     /ŋa/   /ga/,/ge/   /ge/   'teeth'
     /ŋjæi/   /ge/   /goi/   'skill'

How can we account for these widespread patterns? It has been well documented that 1, nondistinctive nasalization, has a physiological cause: lowering of the velum adjacent to nasal consonants (Moll 1962; Lubker 1968; Ohala 1971a; Ushijima & Sawashima 1972; Ushijima & Hirose 1974; Clumeck 1976). This apparently automatic physical nasalization also underlies the patterns described in 2 and 3. The usual kind of explanation given claims that the feature [+nasal] is transferred from the nasal consonant to the preceding vowel and then the nasal consonant is dropped because of the tendency of languages both to weaken syllable-final segments and to eliminate redundant segments. Plausible as this may sound, it leaves many questions unanswered (Ohala 1971b).

The phonotactic constraints given in 4 may be explained in most cases by the fact that the nasal which brought about the distinctive nasal vowel through sound change was itself lost. Hindi, for example, does not exhibit the oral–nasal vowel opposition before a nasal consonant precisely because the existence of the distinctive nasal vowels presupposes the loss of a postvocalic nasal consonant.

Hyman (1975) suggests that the motivation for the denasalization in 5 is the reinforcement of the perceived contrast between oral and nasal vowels. That is, if a language has acquired the oral–nasal vowel opposition next to a nasal, it would be hard to determine the orality or nasality of a vowel which is intrinsically nasalized in this context. To avoid this perceptual ambiguity, the nasal consonant is denasalized to guarantee that there will be no spillover of nasalization onto adjacent vowels. This perceptually based hypothesis seems very promising, and it is probable that many of the ways in which a vowel and a nasal consonant interact with each other, whether these interactions manifest themselves as sound changes or phonotactic constraints, can be explained by referring to perceptual constraints.

The hypothesis offered here is that listeners' expectations in perceiving speech play a crucial role in giving rise to sound patterns in language, among them those discussed above (Ohala 1978, 1981, 1983; Ohala, Riordan, & Kawasaki 1978). Briefly, whatever a listener expects to hear, that is, some kind of automatic or commonly encountered perturbation of one segment by another, may be taken for granted and factored out of the phonetic percept constructed for a word, as long as the segment responsible for the perturbation is detected. This, I suggest, is what permits nondistinctive, that is, allophonic, nasalization on vowels next to nasal consonants. If the perturbing segment is not detected, for whatever reason, then the perturbation is not expected and is not factored out; it is then included as part of the phonetic percept of the word. In this latter case, the listener (who is also a speaker) draws on this perceptual image with the perturbation included as the model for his or her own pronunciation. It constitutes a sound change if what was previously just a phonetically caused perturbation in a word gets incorporated purposely. Thus, if a listener fails to detect a nasal consonant, the nasalization it caused on an adjacent vowel becomes perceptually evident. This is presumably why the nasal consonant is also missing in sound changes which involve the creation of a distinctive nasal vowel. The expectation of nasalized vowels around nasal consonants, however, may make it difficult for the listener to differentiate phonemic nasal vowels and oral vowels in this context. This may possibly lead some language to allow the nasal–oral vowel contrast only in non-nasal environments (i.e., impose a phonotactic constraint) or to develop a sound pattern where nasal consonants are partially "oralized" around oral vowels.

A testable consequence of this hypothesis is that the nasalization on a vowel should be perceptually more evident as adjacent nasal consonants become attenuated, for it is the presence of the nasal consonant that permits listeners to reconstruct the orality of a vowel and its absence or weakness which permits the nasalization to be heard.

EXPERIMENT 1

Design

In order to test the above hypothesis, the following perceptual experiment was conducted. Three syllables, /mɪm/, /mʊm/, and /mɑm/, were recorded by an adult male speaker of American English. These recorded syllables were digitized and processed as follows. The amplitude of the nasal consonants (which for this purpose included the transitions into the vowel) was attenuated in five steps: 0 dB, − 12 dB, − 24 dB, − 36 dB, and − ∞ dB. The first step represents the unchanged original syllables and the last step, the complete removal of the nasal consonants. A stimulus tape was constructed consisting of a randomization of five tokens of each of these five conditions

Table 5.1

Experiment 1: Number of Times Nasal Consonants Were Heard When
Nasals Were Attenuated.

Degree of Attenuation (dB)	/mɪm/	/mʊm/	/mɑm/	Total (%)
0	54	55	54	163 (99)
− 12	53	55	55	163 (99)
− 24	53	52	48	153 (93)
− 36	25	32	24	81 (49)
− ∞	7	7	3	17 (10)

for each of the three syllable types, for a total of 5 × 5 × 3 = 75 stimuli.
The tape was presented twice over headphones in a sound-treated room to
11 speakers of American English. In the first run Ss were asked to indicate
whether they heard nasal consonants in the stimuli. In the second run, Ss
judged the degree of nasality of the vowel on a five-point scale where 5 =
'heavily nasalized' and 1 = 'oral'. Examples of nasalized and oral vowels
were demonstrated before this second part. Subjects were also told that the
presence or absence of nasal consonants bore no relation to whether or not
a vowel was nasalized.

Results

The results of the first part of the experiment are given in Table 5.1. The
entry in a given cell in a column headed by a stimulus indicates how many
times, out of a possible 55, that stimulus was perceived as having nasal consonants, given the level of attenuation listed at the head of the row. The last
two columns give, respectively, the totals and the percentages of the responses
in the first three columns. Nasal consonants were perceived reliably until their
amplitude was reduced to − 24 dB of the original. At − 36 dB attenuation
Ss responded randomly. When the nasal consonants were removed completely, virtually all Ss indicated that they heard no nasals.

From this we were sure that if, in the second part of the experiment, Ss
perceived differences in the degree of nasalization of vowels in the stimuli
having 0, − 12, and − 24 dB attenuation, it would be due to the attenuation
itself, not to their failure to detect the nasal consonants. Reactions to the
− 36 dB attenuation might, however, be due to failure to detect the nasal
consonants.

The results of the second part of the experiment are given in graphic form
in Figure 5.1, where, for each of the subjects, the average response on the

five-point scale (ordinate) is plotted as a function of the degree of attenuation of the stimulus (abscissa).

In general, the stimuli containing the vowel /i/ were perceived as less nasal than those with the other two vowels. It is also evident that there were two groups of Ss: Ss 1 through 5 perceived less nasalization on vowels as the amplitude of the nasal consonants decreased, and Ss 6 through 11 showed the opposite (the predicted) tendency. I refer to the first group as 'fallers' and the latter as 'risers'. Figures 5.2 and 5.3 give the average responses for the fallers and risers, respectively. One-way analyses of variance showed that the effect of nasal attenuation on the nasality judgments was significant ($p < .001$) for both fallers ($F = 8.418$, $df = 4$) and risers ($F = 47.088$, $df = 4$). It was not expected that Ss would react in such a different way to the stimuli. As it happened, three of the five fallers were, at the time of the experiment, former or current students in linguistics; all of the risers, however, could more properly be described as 'linguistically naive' listeners. It could be that the judgments of the linguistics students were biased by their knowledge of phonetics, that is, that vowels are typically nasalized in the environment of nasals.

It is also possible that some amount of between-subject variation was due to the difficulty of the task, that is, in the requirement to rate the degree of nasalization in vowels without any reference level of nasality or orality being given in immediate proximity. Conceivably some subjects used one criterion and others used another. In order to have better control over the criteria Ss used in making their judgments of the degree of nasalization of vowels, a second experiment was conducted.

EXPERIMENT 2

Design

In the second experiment the degree of perceived nasalization of the vowels was obtained by the method of paired comparisons (House & Stevens 1956; Coleman 1963; Weinberg & Shanks 1971). Fourteen linguistically naive American English speakers, none of whom participated in Experiment 1, heard pairs of the same stimuli used in Experiment 1, excluding pairs of identical stimuli, stimuli with different vowel phonemes, and stimuli with attenuation of -36 dB. There was only one token of each of the resulting 18 pairs; that is, although the order (lesser vs. greater attenuation of stimuli) was randomly varied, only one order per pair was included. The Ss were asked to judge which member of each pair had the more nasalized vowel. As in the

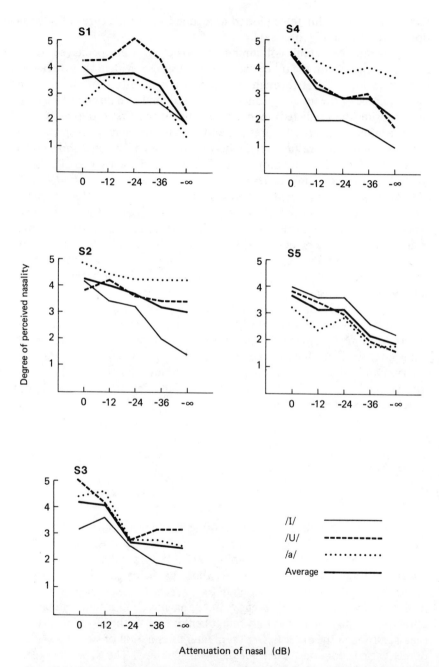

Figure 5.1 Experiment 1: nasality judgments by individual Ss on five point scale as a function of degree of attenuation of nasal consonants.

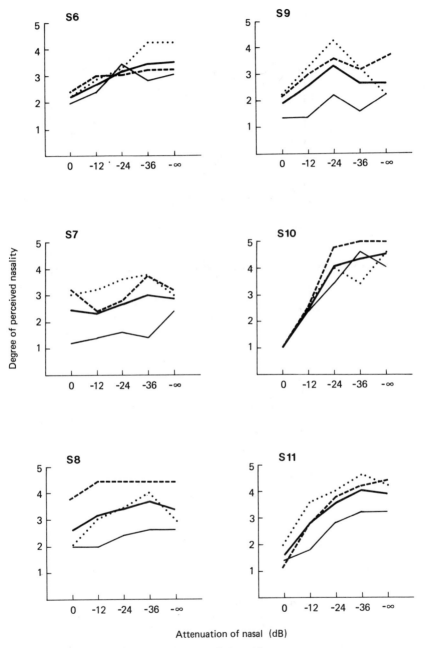

Figure 5.1 (*Continued*)

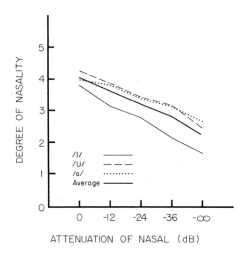

Figure 5.2   Experiment 1: average responses for 'fallers' (five Ss pooled).

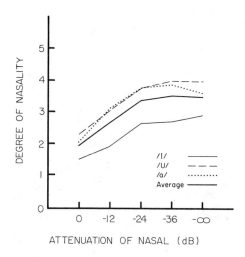

Figure 5.3   Experiment 1: average responses for 'risers' (six Ss pooled).

first experiment, the task was fully explained with a live (i.e., not taped) demonstration of nasalized and oral vowels. Also, before Ss' responses were obtained, the first several pairs of stimuli on the tape were presented to familiarize Ss with the range of stimuli they would be hearing.

Table 5.2

Experiment 2: Pairwise Judgments on Nasality for Stimuli with /ɪ/

Degree of nasal attenuation in stimuli perceived as less nasalized	Degree of nasal attenuation in stimuli perceived as more nasalized			
	−0 dB	−12 dB	−24 dB	−∞ dB
−0 dB		13	12	12
−12 dB	1		11	9
−24 dB	2	3		7
−∞ dB	2	5	7	

Results

The results of the second experiment are shown in Tables 5.2–5.5, which give the data for the stimuli with the vowels /ɪ/, /u/, /ɑ/, and all stimuli, respectively. In these tables the figure in a given cell indicates how many times, out of a possible total of 14, the stimulus listed in the column was judged to have a more nasalized vowel than the stimulus listed in the row. It should be recalled that, in fact, within any given table, all stimuli were identical, as far as their vowels were concerned. Thus, the cells above the diagonal line (from upper left to lower right) represent cases where the stimuli with the more attenuated nasals were judged to have more nasalized vowels than those with less attenuated nasals, and those cells below the diagonal represent cases where the opposite was true. It is clear from these results that, as predicted, the majority of the subjects perceived as more nasalized the vowels flanked by weaker (or no) nasal consonants. Out of 18 pairs, 2 showed no difference and 1 was in the direction opposite to that predicted. All of these involved comparisons of stimuli with − 24 and − ∞ dB attenuation.

Table 5.3

Experiment 3: Pairwise Judgments on Nasality for Stimuli with /u/

Degree of nasal attenuation in stimuli perceived as less nasalized	Degree of nasal attenuation in stimuli perceived as more nasalized			
	−0 dB	−12 dB	−24 dB	−∞ dB
−0 dB		13	13	12
−12 dB	1		11	8
−24 dB	1	3		7
−∞ dB	2	6	7	

Table 5.4

Experiment 2: Pairwise Judgments on Nasality for Stimuli with /a/

Degree of nasal attenuation in stimuli perceived as less nasalized	Degree of nasal attenuation in stimuli perceived as more nasalized			
	−0 dB	−12 dB	−24 dB	−∞ dB
−0 dB		9	12	12
−12 dB	5		11	9
−24 dB	2	3		4
−∞ dB	2	5	10	

Table 5.5

Experiment 2: Pairwise Judgments on Nasality for All Stimuli Pooled

Degree of nasal attenuation in stimuli perceived as less nasalized	Degree of nasal attenuation in stimuli perceived as more nasalized			
	−0 dB	−12 dB	−24 dB	−∞ dB
−0 dB		35	37	36
−12 dB	7		33	26
−24 dB	5	9		18
−∞ dB	6	16	24	

DISCUSSION

It is safe to conclude from the experiments using two different methods of psychological rating that, as predicted, the degree of perceived nasality of a vowel is enhanced by the attenuation of adjacent nasal consonants or, conversely, is reduced by the presence of adjacent nasal consonants. With this hypothesis we can explain many of the phenomena involving interactions of nasals and nasal vowels. The diachronic process which gives rise to distinctive nasal vowels from prior sequences of nondistinctively nasalized vowel and nasal consonant is seen to be the result of listeners either perceiving the final nasal consonant (and its predictable effect on the preceding vowel) or not.

With this hypothesis we are also in a position to explain certain detailed language-specific allophonic variations involving vowels and neighboring nasals. In Tunica, which has nondistinctive vowel nasalization before a nasal consonant, a nasal preceding a voiceless stop is devoiced, but when this happens, the vowel preceding it is reported to have even stronger nasalization than is normally found before nasal consonants (Haas 1941). Examples are given in (8).

(8) /ʔunnaʃiku/ [ʔũnnaʃiku] 'he leads them'
    /yunka/ [yũŋka] 'rope'

The phonotactic constraints and the denasalization of nasal consonants stated above are another consequence of the fact that nasal vowels do not sound nasal enough when nasal consonants stand next to them. In accord with this, in Guarani, the distinctive nasal vowels are reported to be only weakly nasalized after a nasal consonant (Gregores & Suárez 1967). What is more intriguing is the following description of the nasal vowels in Picuris (Trager 1971 p. 31–32).

Nasal vowels are most nasalized when they are not adjacent to a nasal consonant. After a nasal consonant, a nasal vowel is less nasalized at its beginning than it is at the end. Before a nasal consonant, a nasal vowel is more nasalized at the beginning than it is at the end. These two phenomena may be described together as the dissimilatory effect of a nasal consonant on a nasalized vowel. Between nasal consonants, the dissimilation of the nasality of a vowel is most apparent, i.e., there is only slight nasalization.

Trager suggests that such a phenomenon has an articulatory correlate, that is, that it involves different degrees of actual physiological nasalization. However, this seemingly dissimilatory process need not be explained in strictly articulatory terms. It is also possible that it is due to the perceptual effect proposed in this study. The described phenomenon may be just Trager's own auditory impression. This effect may also be the basis for the suggestion by Kelly (1934) that, since the perceived difference between oral and nasal vowels is much smaller in the context of nasals than when vowels are isolated, nasal consonants should be avoided in test items in therapeutic drills for excessive nasalization (e.g., for patients with repaired cleft palate).

The listener's expectation for perturbations of one segment upon another has been hinted at in previous phonetic studies. There is, for example, Sherman's (1954) finding that the abnormal nasality in cleft palate speakers can be evaluated more accurately when tape recordings of patients' speech are played backwards. I had personal experience of this when selecting stimuli for the experiments presented above. The natural speech token /san/ when played backwards sounded like [n:ãs]. The heavy nasalization that occurs before a syllable-final nasal is not expected after a syllable-initial nasal and therefore becomes more noticeable when played backwards. The advantage

of playing speech backwards, then, is that it allows the listener to hear phonetic details which would otherwise be discounted due to their predictability.
The results of this study have allowed us to resolve the paradox that
although for articulatory reasons nasalized vowels are most likely to be found
adjacent to nasal consonants, nevertheless, for perceptual reasons this is the
least favorable environment to perceive them.

ACKNOWLEDGMENTS

This is an expanded version of a paper entitled 'The Perceived Nasality of Vowels with Gradual
Attenuation of Adjacent Nasal Consonants' presented at the Joint Meeting of the Acoustical
Society of America and the Acoustical Society of Japan, Honolulu, Hawaii, November
27–December 1, 1978. The research was conducted while I was a member of the Phonology
Laboratory, Department of Linguistics, University of California, Berkeley.

I wish to thank the following people: Hideki Kasuya for giving me the original idea of the
experimental technique, Peter Ladefoged for allowing me to use the computer facilities in the
UCLA Phonetics Laboratory, Steve Greenberg and James Wright for their help in preparing
the stimuli, John Ohala for providing insightful guidance and some of the phonological data,
Mel Greenlee for her help in statistical analysis, and Gainor Tomokiyo and Wendy Weiner for
proofreading and typing initial versions of the manuscript. Most of the data were obtained from
the Phonology Archive Project, Stanford University, and I am especially grateful to John
Crothers, Donald Sherman, and James Lorentz for their assistance. This work was supported
in part by a grant from the National Science Foundation.

APPENDIX: REFERENCES TO THE
LANGUAGES CITED IN THE TEXT

Akan	Welmers (1946)	Capanahua	Loos (1969)
Alabaman	Rand (1968)	Cayapa	Lindskoog &
Amahuaca	Osborn (1948)		Brend (1962)
Apinaye	Burgess & Ham	Cham	Blood (1967)
	(1968)	Chinese	University of Bei-
Armenian	Allen (1950)		jing (1962),
Asmat	Voorhoeve (1965)		Dong (1968),
Awadhi	Saksena (1971)		Chen (1973),
Azerbaijani	Householder		Cheng (1973)
	(1965)	Cantonese	
Beembe	Jacquot (1962)	Changsha	
Bengali	Ferguson &	Chaozhou	
	Chowdhury	Jinan	
	(1960)	Shanghai	
Brazilian Por-		Shuangfeng	
tuguese	Brito (1975)	Suzhou	
Breton	Ternes (1970)	Taiyuan	
Burmese	Matisoff (1975)	Xiamen	

Xian		Nahuat	Wolgemuth (1969)	
Yangzhou		Nama	Beach (1938)	
Chipewyan	Li (1946)	Navaho	Sapir & Hoijer	
Chontal	Keller (1959)		(1967)	
Common Slavic	Shevelov (1965)	Nez Perce	Aoki (1970)	
Delaware	Voegelin (1946)	Nupe	Hyman (1975)	
Diegueño	Langdon (1970)	Nyangumata	O'Grady (1964)	
Dongolese Nubian	Armbruster (1960)	Ojibwa	Bloomfield (1956)	
English	Malécot (1960),	Old Church		
	Schourup	Slavonic	Lightner (1970)	
	(1972)	Otomi	Blight & Pike	
Ewe	Berry (1951)		(1976)	
French	Posner (1971)	Ọwọn Afa	Awobuluyi (1972)	
Gã	Berry (1930)	Paez	Gerdel (1973)	
Gbeya	Samarin (1966)	Panamanian		
Georgian	Robins & Water-	Spanish	Cedergren &	
	son (1952)		Sankoff	
Goajiro	Holmer (1949)		(1975)	
Greenlandic	Thalbitzer (1904)	Picuris	Trager (1971)	
Guarani	Gregores & Suárez	Portuguese	Foley (1975), Ruh-	
	(1967)		len (1978)	
Gujarati	Pandit (1961)	Punjabi	Gill & Gleason	
Hindi	M. Ohala (1975)		(1963)	
Hupa	Golla (1970)	Quiotepec		
Ijo	Williamson (1965)	Chinantec	Robbins (1961)	
Ila	Doke (1928)	Sentani	Cowan (1965)	
Island Carib	Taylor (1955)	Sinhalese	Coates & de Silva	
Kashmiri	Kelkar & Trisal		(1960)	
	(1964)	Siriono	Priest (1968)	
Korean	Chen & Clumeck	Somali	Armstrong (1964)	
	(1975)	Songhai	Prost (1956)	
Kpelle	Welmers (1962)	Spanish	Navarro Tomás	
Kunjen	Sommer (1969)		(1961)	
Kurux	Pfeiffer (1972)	Sundanese	Robins (1957),	
Kwa	Hyman (1972)		Anderson	
Land Dayak	Scott (1964)		(1972)	
Loma	Sadler (1951)	Swahili	Tucker & Ashton	
Luo	Gregersen (1961)		(1942)	
Malagasy	Dahl (1952)	Tagalog	Schachter &	
Malay	Verguin (1967)		Otanes (1972)	
Mazatec	Pike & Pike	Takum Jukun	Welmers (1968)	
	(1947)	Telefol	Healey (1964)	
Mixtec	Hunter & Pike	Telugu	Lisker (1963)	
	(1969)	Tewa	Hoijer & Dozier	
Modern Greek	Householder,		(1949)	
	Kazazis, &	Thai	Noss (1954), Kru-	
	Koutsoudas		atrachue	
	(1964)		(1960),	
Modern Irish	Mhac an Fhailigh		Abramson	
	(1968)		(1962)	
Mundari	Gumperz (1957)	Ticuna	Anderson (1959)	

98   HARUKO KAWASAKI

Tillamook	Thompson &	Wukari Jukun	Welmers (1968),
	Thompson		Hyman (1975)
	(1972)	Yao	Purnell (1965)
Tolowa	Bright (1964)	Yerwa Kanuri	Awobuluyi (1971)
Tunica	Haas (1941)	Yuchi	Crawford (1973)
Western Ossetic	Henderson (1949)	Zulu	Doke (1926)
Wolof	Sauvageot (1965)		

REFERENCES

Abramson, A. S. 1962. *The vowels and tones of Standard Thai: Acoustical measurements and experiments*. International Journal of American Linguistics Publication 20.
Allen, W. S. 1950. Notes on the phonetics of an Eastern Armenian speaker. *Transactions of the Philological Society (London)*, 180–206. Oxford: Basil Blackwell.
Anderson, L. 1959. *Ticuna vowels with special regard to the system of five tonemes*. Publicaos do Museu Nacional. Serie Linguistica Especial, 1:76–119. Rio de Janeiro.
Anderson, S. R. 1972. On nasalization in Sundanese. *Linguistic Inquiry* 3:253–268.
Aoki, H. 1970. *Nez Perce grammar*. University of California Publications in Linguistics 62.
Armbruster, C. H. 1960. *Dongolese Nubian. A grammar*. London: Cambridge University Press.
Armstrong, L. E. 1964. *The phonetic structure of Somali*. Ridgewood, NJ: Gregg Press.
Awobuluyi, O. 1971. *The phonology of Yerwa Kanuri*. Research Notes 4, 1–21. Department of Linguistics and Nigerian Languages, University of Ibadan, Nigeria.
Awobuluyi, O. 1972. *The morphophonemics of Qwǫn Afa*. Research Notes 5, 25–44. Department of Linguistics and Nigerian Languages, University of Ibadan, Nigeria.
Beach, D. M. 1938. *The phonetics of the Hottentot language*. Cambridge: Heffer.
Berry, J. 1930. *The pronunciation of Gã*. Cambridge: Heffer.
Berry, J. 1951. *The pronunciation of Ewe*. Cambridge: Heffer.
Bhat, D. N. S. 1975. Two studies of nasalization. In C. A. Ferguson, L. M. Hyman, & J. J. Ohala, eds., *Nasálfest. Papers from a Symposium on Nasals and Nasalization*, 27–48. Language Universals Project, Stanford University.
Blight, R. C., & E. V. Pike. 1976. The phonology of Tenango Otomi. *International Journal of American Linguistics* 42:51–57.
Blood, D. L. 1967. Phonological units in Cham. *Anthropological Linguistics* 9:15–32.
Bloomfield, L. 1956. *Eastern Ojibwa*. Ann Arbor: University of Michigan Press.
Bright, J. 1964. The phonology of Smith River Athabaskan (Tolowa). *International Journal of American Linguistics* 30:101–107.
Brito, G. 1975. The perception of nasal vowels in Brazilian Portuguese: A pilot study. In C. A. Ferguson, L. M. Hyman, & J. J. Ohala, eds., *Nasálfest. Papers from a Symposium on Nasals and Nasalization*, 49–66. Language Universals Project, Stanford University.
Burgess, E., & P. Ham. 1968. Multilevel conditioning of phoneme variants in Apinayé. *Linguistics* 41:5–18.
Cedergren, H., & D. Sankoff. 1975. Nasals: A sociolinguistic study of change in progress. In C. A. Ferguson, L. M. Hyman, & J. J. Ohala, eds., *Nasálfest. Papers from a Symposium on Nasals and Nasalization*, 67–80. Language Universals Project, Stanford University.
Chen, M. 1973. Nasals and nasalization in the history of Chinese. Ph.D. diss. University of California, Berkeley.
Chen, M., & H. Clumeck. 1975. Denasalization in Korean: A search for universals. In C. A. Ferguson, L. M. Hyman, & J. J. Ohala, eds., *Nasálfest. Papers from a Symposium on Nasals and Nasalization*, 125–131. Language Universals Project, Stanford University.

Cheng, T. M. 1973. The phonology of Taishan. *Journal of Chinese Linguistics* 1:256–322.

Clumeck, H. 1976. Patterns of soft palate movements in six languages. *Journal of Phonetics* 4:337–351.

Coates, W., & M. de Silva. 1960. The segmental phonemes of Sinhalese. *University of Ceylon Review* 18:163–175.

Coleman, R. O. 1963. The effect of changes in width of velopharyngeal aperture on acoustic and perceptual properties of nasalized vowels. Ph.D. diss., Northwestern University.

Cowan, H. K. J. 1965. *Grammar of the Sentani language.* Verhandelingen van het Koninklijk Instituut voor Taal-, Land- en Volkenkunde, No. 47. The Hague: Martinus Nijhoff.

Crawford, J. M. 1973. Yuchi phonology. *International Journal of American Linguistics* 39:173–179.

Crothers, J. 1975. Nasal consonant systems. In. C. A. Ferguson, L. M. Hyman, & J. J. Ohala, eds., *Nasálfest. Papers from a Symposium on Nasals and Nasalization*, 153–166. Language Universals Project, Stanford University.

Dahl, O. 1952. Etude de phonologie et de phonetique malagaches. *Norsk Tidsskrift for Sprogvidenskap* 16:148–200.

Doke, C. M. 1926. The phonetics of the Zulu language. *Bantu Studies* Vol. 2, special number.

Doke, C. M. 1928. An outline of Ila phonetics. *Bantu Studies* 3:127–153.

Dong, T.-H. 1968. *Hanyu Yinyunxue.* Taipei: Guangwen Shuju.

Ferguson, C. A. 1963. Assumptions about nasals: A sample study in phonological universals. In J. Greenberg, ed., *Universals of language*, 53–60. Cambridge, MA: MIT Press.

Ferguson, C. A. 1974. *Universals of nasality.* Working Papers in Language Universals 14, 1–16. Stanford University.

Ferguson, C. A., & M. Chowdhury. 1960. The phonemes of Bengali. *Language* 36:22–59.

Foley, J. 1975. Nasalization as universal phonological process. In C. A. Ferguson, L. M. Hyman, & J. J. Ohala, eds., *Nasálfest. Papers from a Symposium on Nasals and Nasalization*, 197–212. Language Universals Project, Stanford University.

Gerdel, F. 1973. Paez phonemics. *Linguistics* 104:28–48.

Gill, H. S., & H. A. Gleason, Jr. 1963. *A reference grammar of Panjabi.* Hartford Studies in Linguistics No. 3. Hartford: The Hartford Seminary Foundation.

Golla, V. 1970. Hupa grammar. Ph.d. diss., University of California, Berkeley.

Greenberg, J. H. 1966. Synchronic and diachronic universals in phonology. *Language* 42:508–517.

Greenlee, M., & J. J. Ohala. 1980. Phonetically motivated parallels between child phonology and historical sound change. *Language Sciences* 2:283–308.

Gregersen, E. A. 1961. Luo: A grammar. Ph.D. diss., Yale University.

Gregores, E., & J. A. Suárez. 1967. *A description of colloquial Guarani.* The Hague: Mouton.

Gumperz, J. J. 1957. Notes on the phonology of Mundari. *Indian Linguistics* 17:6–15.

Haas, M. 1941. Tunica. In F. Boas, ed., *Handbook of American Indian Languages* (Vol. 4), 1–143. New York: J. J. Augustin.

Healey, A. 1964. *Telefol phonology.* Pacific Linguistics, Series B, No. 3. Canberra: Australian National University.

Henderson, E. J. A. 1949. A phonetic study of Western Ossetic (Digoron). *Bulletin of the School of Oriental and African Studies* 13:36–79.

Hoijer, H., & E. Dozier. 1949. The phonemes of Tewa. Santa Clara dialect. *International Journal of American Linguistics* 15:139–144.

Holmer, N. 1949. Goajiro (Arawak) I: Phonology. International Journal of American Linguistics 15:45–56.

Hombert, J.-M. 1975. Towards a theory of tonogenesis: An empirical, physiologically and perceptually-based account of the development of tonal contrasts in language. Ph.d diss., University of California, Berkeley.

House, A. S., & K. N. Stevens. 1956. Analog studies of the nasalization of vowels. *Journal of Speech and Hearing Disorders* 21:218–232.

Householder, F. W., Jr. 1965. *Basic course in Azerbaijani.* Uralic and Altaic Series, Vol. 45 Bloomington: Indiana University Press.
Householder, F. W., Jr., K. Kazazis, & A. Koutsoudas. 1964. *Reference grammar of literary Dhimotiki.* International Journal of American Linguistics Publication 31.
Hunter, G., & E. Pike. 1969. The phonology and tone sandhi of Milinos Mixtec. *Linguistics* 47:24–40.
Hyman, L. M. 1972. Nasals and nasalization in Kwa. *Studies in African Linguistics* 3:167–205.
Hyman, L. M. 1975. Nasal states and nasal processes. In C. A. Ferguson, L. M. Hyman, & J. J. Ohala, eds., *Nasálfest. Papers from a Symposium on Nasals and Nasalization,* 249–264. Language Universals Project, Stanford University.
Issatschenko, A. 1937. A propos des voyelles nasales. *Bulletin de Société Linguistique de Paris* 38:267–279.
Jakobson, R. 1968. *Child language, aphasia, and phonological universals.* The Hague: Mouton.
Jacquot, A. 1962. Notes sur la phonologie du beembe (Congo). *Journal of African Languages* 1:232–242.
Javkin, H. R. 1979. *Phonetic universals and phonological change.* Report of the Phonology Laboratory 4, University of California, Berkeley.
Kelkar, A. R., & P. N. Trisal. 1964. Kashmiri word phonology: A first sketch. *Anthropological Linguistics* 6:13–22.
Keller, K. C. 1959. The phonemes of Chontal (Mayan). *International Journal of American Linguistics* 25:44–53.
Kelly, J. 1934. Studies in nasality. *Archives of Speech* 1:26–42.
Kruatrachue, F. 1960. Thai and English: A comparative study of phonology for pedagogical applications. Ph.D. diss., Indiana University.
Langdon, M. 1970. *A grammar of Diegueño: Mesa Grande dialect.* University of California Publications in Linguistics 66.
Li, F.-K. 1946. Chipewyan. In H. Hoijer, ed., *Linguistic structures of Native America,* 398–423. New York: Wenner-Gren Foundation.
Lightner, T. 1970. Why and how does vowel nasalization take place? *Papers in Linguistics* 2:179–226.
Lindskoog, J. N., & R. M. Brend. 1962. *Cayapa phonemics. Studies in equatorian Indian languages, I.* SIL Publication 7. Norman, OK: Summer Institute of Linguistics.
Lisker, L. 1963. *Introduction to spoken Telugu.* New York: American Council of Learned Societies.
Loos, E. E. 1969. *The phonology of Capanahua and its grammatical basis.* Norman, OK: Summer Institute of Linguistics.
Lubker, J. F. 1968. An electromyographic-cinefluorographic investigation of velar function during normal speech production. *Cleft Palate Journal* 5:1–18.
Malécot, A. 1960. Vowel nasality as a distinctive feature in American English. *Language* 36:222–229.
Matisoff, J. A. 1975. Rhinoglottophilia: The mysterious connection between nasality and glottality. In C. A. Ferguson, L. M. Hyman, & J. J. Ohala, eds., *Nasálfest. Papers from a Symposium on Nasals and Nasalization,* 265–287. Language Universals Project, Stanford University.
Mhac an Fhailigh, E. 1968. *The Irish of Erris, Co. Mayo.* Dublin: The Dublin Institute for Advanced Studies.
Moll, K. L. 1962. Velopharyngeal closure on vowels. *Journal of Speech and Hearing Research* 5:30-37.

Navarro Tomás, T. 1961. *Manual de pronunciación española*. Publicaciones de la Revista de Filología Española, No. 3. Madrid: Consejo Superior de Investigaciones Científicas, Instituto "Miguel de Cervantes".

Noss, R. B. 1954. An outline of Siamese grammar. Ph.D. diss., Yale University.

O'Grady, G. 1964. *Nyangumata grammar*. Oceania Linguistic Monographs, No. 9. Sidney: University of Sidney.

Ohala, J. J. 1971a. *Monitoring soft palate activity in speech*. Project on Linguistic Analysis Reports 13, J01-J015. University of California, Berkeley.

Ohala, J. J. 1971b. *The role of physiological and acoustic models in explaining the direction of sound change*. Project on Linguistic Analysis Reports 15, 25-40. University of California, Berkeley.

Ohala, J. J. 1974a. Experimental historical phonology. In J. M. Anderson & C. Jones, eds., *Historical linguistics II. Theory and description in phonology*, 353-389. Amsterdam: North Holland.

Ohala, J. J. 1974b. Phonetic explanation in phonology. In A. Bruck, R. A. Fox, & M. W. LaGaly, eds., *Papers from the Parasession on Natural Phonology*, 251-274. Chicago: Chicago Linguistic Society.

Ohala, J. J. 1975. Phonetic explanations for nasal sound patterns. In C. A. Ferguson, L. M. Hyman, & J. J. Ohala, eds., *Nasálfest. Papers from a Symposium on Nasals and Nasalization*, 289-316. Language Universals Project, Stanford University.

Ohala, J. J. 1978. Southern Bantu vs. the world: The case of palatalization of labials. *Proceedings of the Annual Meeting of the Berkeley Linguistics Society* 4:370-386.

Ohala, J. J. 1981. The listener as a source of sound change. In C. S. Masek, R. A. Hendrick, & M. F. Miller, eds., *Papers from the Parasession on Language and Behavior*, 178-203. Chicago: Chicago Linguistic Society.

Ohala, J. J. 1983. The direction of sound change. In A. Cohen & M. P. R. v. d. Broecke, eds., *Abstracts of the Tenth International Congress of Phonetic Sciences*, 253-258. Dordrecht: Foris

Ohala, J. J., & J. Lorentz. 1977. The story of [w]: An exercise in the phonetic explanation for sound patterns. *Proceedings of the Annual Meeting of the Berkeley Linguistics Society* 3:577-599.

Ohala, J. J., C. J. Riordan, & H. Kawasaki. 1978. The influence of consonant environment upon identification of transitionless vowels. Paper presented at the Joint Meeting of the Acoustical Society of America and the Acoustical Society of Japan, Honolulu, Hawaii, 27 November-1 December 1978.

Ohala, M. 1975. Nasals and nasalization in Hindi. In C. A. Ferguson, L. M. Hyman, & J. J. Ohala, eds., *Nasálfest. Papers from a Symposium on Nasals and Nasalization*, 317-332. Language Universals Project, Stanford University.

Osborn, H. 1948. Amahuaca phonemes. *International Journal of American Linguistics* 14:188-190.

Pandit, P. 1961. Historical phonology of Gujarati vowels. *Language* 37:54-66.

Pfeiffer, M. 1972. *Elements of Kurux historical phonology*. Leiden: E. J. Brill.

Pike, K. L., & E. V. Pike. 1947. Immediate constituents of Mazatec syllables. *International Journal of American Linguistics* 13:78-91.

Posner, R. 1971. On synchronic and diachronic rules: French nasalization. *Lingua* 27:184-197.

Priest, P. N. 1968. Phonemes of the Sirionó language. *Linguistics* 41:102-108.

Prost, R. P. A. 1956. *La langue songay et ses dialectes*. Memoires de l'Institut Français d'Afrique Noire, No. 47. Dakar: Institut Français d'Afrique Noire.

Purnell, H. C., Jr. 1965. *Phonology of a Yao dialect spoken in the province of Chiengrai, Thailand*. Hartford Studies in Linguistics No. 15. Hartford: Hartford Seminary Foundation.

Rand, E. 1968. The structural phonology of Alabaman, a Muskogean language. *International Journal of American Linguistics* 34:94–103.

Robbins, F. E. 1961. Quiotepec Chinantec syllable patterning. *International Journal of American Linguistics.* 27:237–250.

Robins, R. H. 1957. Vowel nasality in Sundanese: A phonological and grammatical study. In Philological Society (London), *Studies in Linguistic Analysis,* 87–103. Oxford: Basil Blackwell.

Robins, R. H., & N. Waterson. 1952. Note on the phonetics of the Georgian word. *Bulletin of the School of Oriental and African Studies, London* 15:55–72.

Ruhlen, M. 1975. The patterning of nasal vowels. In C. A. Ferguson, L. M. Hyman, & J. J. Ohala, eds., *Nasálfest. Papers from a Symposium on Nasals and Nasalization,* 333–371. Language Universals Project, Stanford University.

Ruhlen, M. 1978. Nasal vowels. In J. H. Greenberg, C.A. Ferguson, & E. A. Moravcsik, eds., *Universals of human language, Vol. 2. Phonology,* 203–241. Stanford: Stanford University Press.

Sadler, W. 1951. *Untangled Loma.* Monrovia, Liberia: The Board of Foreign Missions of the United Lutheran Church in America.

Saksena, B. R. 1971. *Evolution of Awadhi.* Delhi: Motilal Banarsidass.

Samarin, W. J. 1966. *The Gbeya language.* University of California Publications in Linguistics 44.

Sapir, E., & H. Hoijer. 1967. *The phonology and morphology of the Navaho language.* University of California Publications in Linguistics 50.

Sauvageot, S. 1965. *Description synchronique d'un dialecte Wolof: Le parler du Dyolof.* Memoires de l'Institut Français d'Afrique Noire, No. 73. Dakar: Institut Français d'Afrique Noire.

Schachter, P., & F. Otanes. 1972. *Tagalog reference grammar.* Berkeley: University of California Press.

Schourup, L. 1972. Characteristics of vowel nasalization. *Papers in Linguistics* 5:530–548.

Scott, N. 1964. Nasal consonants in Land Dayak (Bukar-Sadong). In D. Abercrombie, D. B. Fry, P. A. D. MacCarthy, N. C. Scott, & J. L. M. Trim, eds., *In honour of Daniel Jones,* 432–436. London: Longmans.

Sherman, D. 1954. The merits of backward playing of connected speech in the scaling of voice quality disorders. *Journal of Speech and Hearing Disorders* 19:312–321.

Shevelov, G. Y. 1965. *A prehistory of Slavic.* New York: Columbia University Press.

Sommer, B. A. 1969. *Kunjen phonology: Synchronic and diachronic.* Pacific Linguistics, Series B, No. 11. Canberra: Australian National University.

Taylor, D. M. 1955. Phonemes of the Hopkins dialect of Island Carib. *International Journal of American Linguistics* 21:233–241.

Ternes, E. 1970. Grammaire structurale du breton de l'île de Groix. Heidelberg: Carl Winter Universitätsverlag.

Thalbitzer, W. 1904. *A phonetical study of the Eskimo language.* Meddelelser om Grønland 31. Copenhagen: [s.n.].

Thompson, L. C., & M. T. Thompson. 1972. Language universals, nasals, and the Northwest Coast. In M. E. Smith, ed., *Studies in linguistics in honor of George L. Trager,* 441–456. The Hague: Mouton.

Trager, F. H. 1971. The phonology of Picuris. *International Journal of American Linguistics* 37:29–33.

Tucker, A. N., & E. O. Ashton. 1942. Swahili phonetics. *African Studies* 1:77–103; 161–182.

University of Beijing. 1962. *Hanyu Fangyin Zihui.* Beijing: Wenzi Gaige Chubanshe.

Ushijima, T., & H. Hirose. 1974. Electromyographic study of the velum during speech. *Journal of Phonetics* 2:315–326.

Ushijima, T., & M. Sawashima. 1972. Fiberscopic observation of velar movements during speech. *Annual Bulletin, Research Institute of Logopedics and Phoniatrics* (University of Tokyo) 6:25–38.

Verguin, J. 1967. *Le Malais. Essai d'analyse fonctionelle et structurale.* Paris: Mouton.

Voegelin, C. F. 1946. Delaware, an Eastern Algonquian language. In H. Hoijer, ed., *Linguistic structures of Native America*, 130–157. New York: Wenner-Gren Foundation.

Voorhoeve, C. L. 1965. *The Flamingo Bay dialect of the Asmat language.* The Hague: Smits.

Weinberg, B., & J. Shanks. 1971. The relationship between three oral breath pressure ratios and ratings of severity of nasality for talkers with cleft palate. *Cleft Palate Journal* 8:251–256.

Welmers, W. E. 1946. *A descriptive grammar of Fanti.* Language Dissertation No. 39. Philadelphia: Linguistic Society of America.

Welmers, W. E. 1962. The phonology of Kpelle. *Journal of African Languages* 1:69–93.

Welmers, W. E. 1968. *Jukun of Wukari and Jukun of Takum.* Occasional Publication No. 16, Institute of African Studies. Ibadan, Nigeria: University of Ibadan.

Williamson, K. 1965. *A grammar of the Kolokuma dialect of Ijo.* Cambridge: Cambridge University Press.

Wolgemuth, C. 1969. Isthmus Veracurz (Mecayapan) Nahuat laryngeals. In D. F. Robinson, ed., *Aztec Studies I. Phonological and grammatical studies in modern Nahuatl dialects*, 1–14. Norman, OK: Summer Institute of Linguistics.

6

The Size and Structure
of Phonological Inventories:
Analysis of UPSID *

IAN MADDIESON

INTRODUCTION

A database designed to give more reliable and more readily available answers to questions concerning the distribution of phonological segments in the world's languages has been created as part of the research program of the UCLA Phonetics Laboratory. The database is known formally as the UCLA Phonological Segment Inventory Database and for convenience is referred to by the acronym UPSID. UPSID has been used to investigate a number of hypothesized phonological universals and universal tendencies. Principal among these have been certain ideas concerning the overall size and structure of the phonological inventories. The design of the database is briefly described in this chapter. A full description is given in *Patterns of Sounds* (Maddieson 1984), and the appendices at the end of that book report on the data contained in UPSID files. The remainder of the present chapter discusses the overall structure and size of phonological inventories which have been examined through UPSID.

*This paper is essentially the same as Chapter 1 of *Patterns of Sounds* (Maddieson 1984) and is included here by permission of the Syndicate of Cambridge University Press. In the phonetic transcriptions in this chapter, "t", "d", "l", etc. stand for dental or alveolar place of articulation.

DESIGN OF THE DATABASE

The languages included in UPSID have been chosen to approximate a properly constructed quota sample, based on a genetic classification of the world's extant languages. The quota rule is that only one language may be included from each small family grouping; for example, among the Germanic languages, one is included from West Germanic and one from North Germanic (East Germanic, being extinct and insufficiently documented for a reliable phonological analysis to be made, is not included). Each such small family grouping should be represented by the inclusion of one language. Availability and quality of phonological descriptions are factors in determining which language to include from within a group, but such factors as the number of speakers and the phonological peculiarity of the language are not considered. The database includes the inventories of 317 languages. The analysis assumed for each language can be found in the data charts at the end of *Patterns of Sounds*. The language identification numbers after language names in this chapter are those used in that book.

In the database, each segment which is considered phonemic is represented by its most characteristic allophone, specified in terms of a set of 58 phonetic attributes. These are treated as variables which take the value 1 if the segment has the attribute and 0 if the segment lacks it. The list of attributes with the value 1 thus provides a phonetic description of the segment concerned.

For 192 of the 317 languages included, UPSID has profited from the work of the Stanford Phonology Archive (SPA). Our decisions on phonemic status and phonetic description do not always coincide with the decisions reached by the compilers of the SPA, and we have sometimes examined additional or alternative sources, but a great deal of effort was saved by the availability of this source of standardized analyses. It should be noted that UPSID, unlike the SPA, makes no attempt to include information on allophonic variation, syllable structure, or phonological rules.

In determining the segment inventories, there are two especially problematical areas. The first involves choosing between a unit or sequence interpretation of, for example, affricates, prenasalized stops, long (geminate) consonants and vowels, diphthongs, or labialized consonants. The available evidence which bears on the choice in each language individually has been examined but with some prejudice in favor of treating complex phonetic events as sequences (i.e., as combinations of more elementary units). The second problem area involves the choice between a segmental and a suprasegmental analysis of certain properties. Stress and tone have always been treated as suprasegmental; that is, tonal and stress contrasts do not by themselves

:dd to the number of distinct segments in the inventory of a language, but if differences in segments are found which accompany stress or tone differences, these may be regarded as segmental contrasts when the association does not seem a particularly natural one. For example, if there is an unstressed vowel which is a little shorter or more centralized than what can be seen as its stressed counterpart, these vowels are treated as variants of the same segment. However, larger qualitative differences between the set of stressed and unstressed vowels lead us to enter such sets of vowels as separate segments. In all cases, sets of vowels which are divided into vowel-harmony series are all entered separately; the factor which distinguishes the vowel-harmony series is not extracted as·a suprasegmental.

VARIATIONS IN INVENTORY SIZE

The number of segments in a language may vary widely. The smallest inventories included in the survey have only 11 segments (Rotokas, 625; Mura, 802) and the largest has 141 (!Xū, 918). However, it is clear that the typical size of an inventory lies between 20 and 37 segments; 70% of the languages in the survey fall within these limits. The mean number of segments per language is a little over 31; the median falls between 28 and 29. These values are very close to the number 27 ± 7 which Hockett (1955) estimated as the most likely number of segments in a language.

The variability in segment totals can be reflected in a number of statistical measures. These show that the curve formed by plotting the number of languages against the segment totals is not normally distributed. It is both positively skewed and platykurtic, that is, there is a longer tail to the distribution at the high end of the scale, and the shape of the curve is one with a low peak and heavy tails. This implies that the mean number of segments is not a good way to sum up the distribution. For this reason, more attention should be paid to the range of 20–37 than the mean of 31.

Whether the tendency to have from 20 to 37 segments means that this is an optimum range is an open question. It seems likely that there is an upper limit on the number of segments that can be efficiently distinguished in speech and a lower limit set by the minimum number of segments required to build an adequate vocabulary of distinct morphemes. But these limits would appear to lie above and below the numbers 37 and 20, respectively.

Consider the following: The Khoisan language !Xū (918) with 141 segments is related to languages which also have unusually large inventories. Comparative study of these languages (Baucom 1974; Traill 1978) indicates that large inventories are a stable feature which has persisted for a long time in the Khoisan family. If the number of efficiently distinguished segments were substantially smaller, there would be constant pressure to reduce the number of segments. There does not seem to be any evidence of such pressure.[1]

Similarly, the facts do not seem to show that languages with small inventories (under 20 segments) suffer from problems due to lack of contrastive possibilities at the morphemic level. The symptoms of such difficulties would include unacceptably high incidence of homophony or unmanageably long morphemes. Dictionaries and vocabularies of several languages with small phoneme inventories, such as Rotokas (625, Firchow, Firchow, & Akoitai 1973), Hawaiian (424, Pukui & Elbert 1965) and Asmat (601, Voorhoeve 1965), do not provide evidence of symptoms of stress. Hawaiian, for example, with 13 segments, has been calculated to have an average of just 3.5 phonemes per morpheme (Pukui & Elbert 1965), clearly not unacceptably long. And again, comparative evidence indicates that small inventory size may be a phenomenon which persists over time, as, for example, in the Polynesian language family, which includes Hawaiian (Grace 1959).

The restrictions on inventory size may therefore not be theoretical ones relating to message density and channel capacity in language processing. Although such considerations have been the most widely discussed, they are far from the only ones likely to influence the typical language inventory. Linguistic messages do have to be sufficiently varied to be able to deal with myriad situations, and they do need to be successfully conveyed via a noisy channel, but the design of language is also subject to many pressures of a nonfunctional kind. Most languages exist in a multilingual social context. Limits may be placed on the size of a typical inventory through language contact, especially in situations where a language is gaining speakers who are learning the language after early childhood. The mechanism may be one which approximates the following: Speakers acquiring a new language make substitutions for any segment that is not matched by a closely similar segment in their own language or is not capable of being generated by a simple process of adding familiar features (e.g., acquiring /g/ is easy if you already have /p, b, t, d, k/ in the first language). The resulting inventory in the acquired language contains only the segments common to both input languages plus a few segments generated by the process outlined above. The smaller the inventory of the first language, the greater the probability that some segments will be generated in the fashion outlined. The greater the inventory, the smaller the probability that similar segments will coincide in the two languages and thus the greater the probability of inventory simplification.

This proposal predicts not only that upper and lower limits on inventory size tend to be rather flexible, as is the case, but also that areal-genetic devi-

[1]If languages with large phoneme inventories were approaching some kind of limit on the ability to discriminate contrasts, it would be expected that speakers of these languages would show higher error rates in tasks involving phoneme recognition than speakers of languages with small inventories. I know of no experimental data which bear on this point.

ations from the central tendency should be expected. Thus, greater than average size inventories in Khoisan or Caucasian languages and smaller than average in Polynesian are understandable results: Local deviations are perpetuated because primary contact is with other languages tending in the same direction. This proposal also avoids a difficulty: If human processing limitations are postulated as the cause of limitations on the size of inventories, then they ought invariably to exert pressure to conform on the deviant cases. The evidence for this is lacking.

RELATIONSHIP BETWEEN SIZE AND STRUCTURE

The data in UPSID have been used to address the question of the relationship between the size of an inventory and its membership. The total number of consonants in an inventory varies between 6 and 95 with a mean of 22.8 (and a mode of 21). The total number of vowels varies between 3 and 46 with a mean of 8.7. The balance between consonants and vowels within an inventory was calculated by dividing the number of vowels by the number of consonants. The resulting ratio varies between 0.065 and 1.308 with a mean of 0.402. The median value of this vowel ratio is about 0.36; in other words, the typical language has less than half as many vowels as it has consonants. There are two important trends to observe: Larger inventories tend to be more consonant dominated, but there is a tendency for the absolute number of vowels to be larger in the languages with larger inventories. The first is shown by the fact that the vowel ratio is inversely correlated with the number of consonants in an inventory ($r = -.40, p = .0001$) and the second by the fact that the total of vowels is positively correlated with the consonant total ($r = .38, p = .0001$). However, a large consonant inventory with a small vowel inventory is certainly possible, as, for example, in Haida (700: 46C, 3V), Jaqaru (820: 38C, 3V), or Burushaski (915: 38C, 5V). Small consonant inventories with a large number of vowels seem the least likely to occur (Hockett, 1955), although there is something of an areal or genetic tendency in this direction in New Guinea languages such as Pawaian (612: 10C, 12V), Daribi (616: 13C, 10V), and Fasu (617: 11C, 10V). In these cases a small number of consonants is combined with a contrast of vowel nasality. Despite some aberrant cases, however, there is a general though weak association between overall inventory size and consonant–vowel balance: Larger inventories tend to have a greater proportion of consonants.

Such an association suggests that inventory size and structure may be related in other ways as well. A simple form of such a hypothesis would propose that segment inventories are structured so that the smallest inventories contain the most frequent segments, and, as the size of the inventory increases, segments are added in descending order of their overall frequency of occurrence. If this were so, all segments could be arranged in a single hierarchy. Such an extreme formulation is not correct, since no single segment is found in all languages. But if we add a corollary, that larger inventories tend to exclude some of the most common segments, then there is an interesting set of predictions to investigate. We may formulate these more cautiously in the following way: A smaller inventory has a greater probability of including a given common segment than a larger one, and a larger inventory has a greater probability of including an unusual segment type than a smaller one.

The extent to which languages conform to the predictions can be tested in two straightforward ways. One is to examine inventories of some given size and see what segments they contain; the other is to examine given segment types and see how they are distributed across inventories by size. Using the second approach, the distribution of 13 of the most frequent consonants was investigated in a set of UPSID languages with relatively small inventories and in a set of languages with relatively large inventories. For the small-inventory set, languages with 20–24 segments were chosen. A language with fewer than 20 segments usually has fewer than 13 consonants, so that exclusions would occur simply because of the small numbers involved. For the large-inventory set, all UPSID languages with over 40 segments were selected. These choices resulted in subsamples containing 57 and 54 languages, respectively.

The set of consonants investigated and their distribution is shown in Table 6.1, together with three percentages. The first is the percentage of the 57 small-inventory languages with the given segment, the second is the percentage of all UPSID languages which have the segment, and the third is the percentage of the large-inventory languages which have the segment. Note that consonants in the dental–alveolar region have not been considered here because of the frequent uncertainty as to whether they are dental or alveolar.

The consonants investigated fall into three groups. Using the overall frequency of the segment as the expected value, the first and third groups of these consonants show significant deviations ($p < .005$), while the central group shows no significant difference from the expected value (using a χ^2 test). There is a set (especially plain voiceless plosives) which is more common in the smaller inventories; for example, /p/ and /k/ occur in 90% or more of these languages but in less than 80% of the languages with larger inventories. There is also a set of these frequent consonants that are much more likely to occur in languages with larger inventories, these being notably the voiced stops /b/ and /g/ and the fricatives /f/ and /ʃ/. There is a tendency for smaller inventories to have no voicing contrast in stops and to lack fricatives apart from some kind of /s/. Note that the common nasals in the table are divided one to each group; /ŋ/ is more common in smaller

Table 6.1

Inventory Size and Frequency of Selected Segments

Segment	Small inventory languages (%)	All languages (%)	Large inventory languages (%)
More likely in small inventories			
/p/	89.5	82.6	77.8
/k/	93.0	89.3	79.3
/ŋ/	59.6	52.7	51.9
Equally likely in large or small inventories			
/m/	94.7	94.3	92.6
/w/	75.4	75.1	77.8
More likely in large inventories			
/b/	45.6	62.8	77.8
/g/	42.1	55.2	75.9
/ʔ/	33.3	30.3	55.6
/tʃ/	22.8	44.5	64.8
/f/	15.8	42.6	51.8
/ʃ/	17.5	46.1	70.4
/j/	78.9	85.5	94.4
/ɲ/	22.8	33.8	37.0

inventories, /m/ is equally common in small and large, and ɲ is more common in the larger inventories.

From this examination, we must conclude that the relationship between the size and the content of an inventory is a matter that concerns individual types of segments, rather than being amenable to broad generalizations.

A second test of aspects of the relationship of inventory size and structure was conducted by considering what kind of consonant inventory would be formed if only the most frequent segments were included. In this case, only the number of consonants in an inventory was considered. Recall that the modal number of consonants in an inventory is 21. The most frequently occurring individual consonant segment types in the UPSID data file would form a "modal" inventory containing the 20 consonants below plus one other:

p, b	*t, *d	tʃ	k, g	ʔ	
f	*s	ʃ			
m	*n	ŋ	ŋ		
m	*n	ɲ	ŋ		
w	*l,*r	j		h	

A certain amount of pooling of similar segments is assumed to be valid for this exercise; for example, dental or alveolar segments have been pooled and are represented by /*t, *d, *n/. The twenty-first consonant in the inventory might be one of several with rather similar frequencies, especially /z/ or /ts/, which are both about as frequent. A little less probable would be /x/, /v/ or /dʒ/, as these are a little less common. The aspirated stops /pʰ/, /tʰ/ and /kʰ/ are about as frequent as this last group, but they almost always occur as part of a series of aspirated stops, and so one of them alone as the twenty-first consonant is not plausible. Because of the several possible candidates, distribution of only 20 consonants was examined.

Languages are most likely to have between 5 and 11 stops (including affricates but excluding clicks in this class for these purposes); 63% of the languages fall within the range given but the scatter is quite wide (minimum 3, maximum 36, mean 10.5). For fricatives, one to four is the most likely (58% of languages), and from two to four is most likely for nasals (91% of languages). Languages are most likely to have two liquids and two vocoid approximants (41% and 72%, respectively). About 63% of the languages have the consonant /h/, which is not included in any of the categories already named.

The inventory made up from the most frequent consonant segments does conform to the predominant patterns concerning the numbers of stops, fricatives, and so on reported above. For example, there are eight (or, with /dʒ/, nine) stops, and three (or, with /z/, /x/ or /v/, four) fricatives. By simply considering frequency, we obtain an inventory which is typologically most plausible in its structure. This is encouraging. However, none of the 29 languages with 21 consonants contains all 20 of the segments outlined above. Bambara (105) is very close with 19 of them, having /z/ and /dʒ/ but lacking ʔ . Fur (203) only deviates by having ɣ instead of ʔ and having /dʒ/ rather than /tʃ/ and is thus also very close to the idealization generated. But at the other extreme, Wichita (755) has only 7 of the 20 segments (although two other segments are phonemically long counterparts of /s/ and /n/). Other languages with relatively few of the most common consonants include the Australian languages Kariera–Ngarluma (363) with 10 and Arabana–Wanganura (366) with 11, as well as Mongolian (066) with 11. The majority of the languages examined have between 14 and 16 of the most frequent segments.

Leaving aside the consonants in the dental–alveolar region because of difficulties in arriving at exact counts, a calculation was done comparing the expected frequency of these consonants in any random subsample of 29 languages, and the observed frequency in the 29 languages with 21 consonants. The expected frequency is simply derived from the overall frequency in the UPSID languages. For the 14 segments compared, there is only one case in which the expected and observed frequencies differ by more than 3. The difference between these frequencies is not significant ($\chi^2 = 1.505$ for 13 df). In general, the conclusion suggested is that at the modal inventory size for consonants there is no greater tendency for more frequent segments to occur than in the UPSID data file as a whole.

PHONETIC SALIENCE AND
THE STRUCTURE OF INVENTORIES

Although the idea of a single hierarchy cannot be sustained, there are many strong implicational hierarchies between particular types of segments (although very few are exceptionless). Some examples of these, validated by the data in UPSID and discussed in more detail in *Patterns of Sounds*, are given below:

1. /k/ does not occur without /*t/. (One exception in UPSID: Hawaiian, 424.)
2. /p/ does not occur without /k/ . (Four exceptions in UPSID: Kirghiz, 062, with /p, "t", q/ ; Beembe, 123; Tzeltal, 712; and Zuni, 748. These last two languages have an aspirated velar plosive /kʰ/ beside unaspirated /p/ and /t/. There are 24 languages with /k/ but no /p/; 18 of these have /b, d, g/.) Nasal consonants do not occur unless stops (including affricates) occur at (broadly speaking) the same place of articulation. (Five exceptions in UPSID: Ewe, 114, Efik, 119, and Auca, 818, have ɲ but no palatal or palato-alveolar stops. Hupa, 705, has /m/ but no bilabial stops. Igbo, 116, has /mŋ/ but no labial–velar stops; it does have labialized velars. There are numerous examples of languages with stops at particular places of articulation with no corresponding nasal consonant.)
4. Voiceless nasals and approximants do not occur unless the language has the voiced counterparts. (No exceptions in UPSID.)
5. Mid vowels do not occur unless high and low vowels occur. (Two exceptions in UPSID: All languages have at least one high vowel but Cheremis, 051, and Tagalog, 414, are reported to lack low vowels.)
6. Rounded front vowels do not occur unless unrounded front vowels of the same basic height occur. (Two exceptions in UPSID: Bashkir, 063, and Khalaj, 064.)
7. /ø/ and /œ/ do not occur (separately or together) unless /y/ also occurs. (Hopi, 738, is a clear exception. Wolof, 107, has one front rounded vowel, /ø/, but this has allophones as high as /y/. Akan, 115, has marginal phonemes /ø:/ and /œ:/ but no /y/.)

Yet, as briefly illustrated above, such observations cannot be compiled into a single composite hierarchy. At the very least, alternate choices must be built in at certain points. This is because equally valid general prohibitions on the co-occurrence of segments within an inventory can also be found; for example,

1. A language does not contain both (voiced) implosives and laryngeal-ized plosives at the same place of articulation. (No counterexamples in UPSID.)
2. A language does not contain a voiceless lateral fricative and a voiceless lateral approximant. (No counterexamples in UPSID.)
3. A language does not contain both /ɸ/ and /f/ or both /β/ and /v/. (Two counterexamples in UPSID, Ewe 114, and Tarascan, 747).
4. A language does not usually include a dental stop, fricative, nasal, or lateral and an alveolar stop, fricative, nasal, or lateral of the same type. (There are 22 exceptions to this observation, but this number is significantly fewer than would be anticipated if the co-occurrence were unrestricted; 43 co-occurrences of /t̪/ and /t/ alone would be expected otherwise on the basis of a calculation which partitions those stops which are unspecified as being dental or alveolar into dental and alveolar plosives according to the frequency with which the plosives with known place occur.)

These statements could be subsumed under a general observation that segments do not (usually) function contrastively unless they are sufficiently phonetically distinct. The mutual exclusions cited here are all between phonetically similar segments; without defining what "phonetically similar" means with any greater precision, note that the segments referred to could be collapsed under more inclusive labels; for example, /β/ and /v/ are both voiced labial fricatives. The distinctions between these pairs of segments verge on being noncontrastive phonetic differences of the type that have been discussed by Ladefoged (1978; 1980).

The hypothesis referred to here is that there are measurable phonetic differences between segments which are generally similar but which occur in different languages. These differences are assumed to be found along parameters that do not serve as the basis for phonemic contrast in any language or are of smaller magnitude than the differences which form phonemic contrasts. In this light, the difference between, say, dental and alveolar stops approaches membership in this class of distinctions which are generally unavailable for meaningful contrast in a language. (A more typical member of this class would be, say, a difference in relative timing of the release of the oral and glottal closures in the production of ejectives [Lindau 1982]).

This interpretation of prohibitions on co-occurrence introduces a concept of phonetic distance or phonetic salience as an explanatory factor in the design of phonological inventories. If we can explain why certain kinds of segments never (or rarely) occur together in an inventory on the grounds that the distinctions between them are not salient enough, perhaps the favoring of certain segments can be explained on the grounds that they are the most salient and that an appropriate selection of such sounds maintains generous phonetic distance between the segments of the language involved. While such ideas have principally been discussed in relation to vowel inventories (e.g., Liljencrants & Lindblom 1972; Crothers 1978; Disner 1982), they can be extended to the whole inventory. From this perspective, implicational hierarchies can be interpreted as involving steps down in phonetic salience, with the most salient segments at the top of any hierarchical arrangement and segments which are less distinct (distant) from each other lower down. Note that this leaves open the possibility that the mean phonetic distance between the members of an inventory is approximately constant, as an expanded inventory includes additional members whose distance from their closest neighbor is less, even though the total phonetic space used by the language is being expanded.

It is far from a straightforward matter to determine appropriate measures of salience and phonetic distance. Nevertheless, there are probably some questions which can be answered with only an informal characterization of these notions. For example, to the question "Is maximization of distinctiveness the principle on which inventories are constructed?" the answer is obviously no. Clicks are highly salient, yet few languages (about 1%) use them. Moreover, those that do, have multiple series of clicks rather than exploiting this feature to make a highly salient contrast between, say, a dental click and a velar plosive in a limited series of stops. The most frequent vowel inventory is /i, e, a, o, u/, not /i, ẽ, a̰, o̤, uˤ/, where each vowel not only differs in quality but is distinctively plain, nasalized, breathy, laryngealized, and pharyngealized. Yet this second set of vowels surely provides for more salient distinctions among them and approaches maximization of contrast more than the first set whose differences are limited to only the primary dimensions conventionally recognized for vowel quality.

A more adequate theory of inventory structure must recognize that certain dimensions of contrast are preferentially used before others in ways that do not seem related to salience. For example, a language, generally speaking, only adds the additional parameters of contrast to vowels if it includes a fairly wide sample of simple contrasts on the primary vowel-quality dimensions. In a sense, then, these additional ways of contrasting vowels are themselves involved in an implicational hierarchy whose arrangement is not predicted by a principle of selecting maximally salient contrasts.

Independent of the above discussion, it must be recognized that phonetic distance cannot explain some of the prohibitions on co-occurrence of segments. There is a class of these prohibitions that differs from those cited above in that the distinctiveness of the segments concerned is not really in doubt. An example of this is the co-occurrence restriction which applies to subinventories of laterals. A language with several lateral segments contrasts them either by manner (voiced approximant, voiceless fricative, ejective affricate, etc.) or by place (all the laterals being voiced approximants). Only one language in UPSID (Diegueño 743) clearly violates this rule, although Irish (001) is an arguable exception too. Even two exceptions are significantly fewer than expected. Thus, while multiple-lateral subsystems almost invariably contain an apical or laminal lateral approximant, which is therefore at the top of an implicational hierarchy, at the lower end of this hierarchy there are two branches, one permitting elaboration by place and the other permitting elaboration of laterals sharing the same place of articulation by variation in the manner of production.

COMPENSATION IN INVENTORY STRUCTURE

The fact that certain types of mutual exclusions occur which do not seem to be based on principles of phonetic distance suggests that there is a principle of "compensation" controlling the structure of inventories. Martinet (1955), for example, suggests that a historical change which simplifies an inventory in one area is counterbalanced by a compensating elaboration elsewhere. Similar ideas are discussed at length by Hagège and Haudricourt (1978).

If diachronic changes do generally follow this pattern, then the consequence should be measurable relationships between various facets of inventories which follow a pattern of negative correlation. We have already seen, though, one aspect of inventory structure in which compensation does not occur. The tendency mentioned above for vowel inventories to increase in step with increases in consonant inventories is the opposite of the prediction made by a compensation theory. Several other inventory sectors were investigated for general signs of the operation of a compensation process.

The stop inventories of the languages in UPSID were examined to see if there was a tendency for the elaboration of the number of place contrasts and vice versa. Such a compensation is suggested by the inventories of Australian languages. These typically have a rich range of places of articulation for stops (and nasals) but no contrasts of manner (such as voicing differences) within the stops (Wurm 1972; Dixon 1980). Is this a local aberration or just a particularly striking example of a basic pattern in human language? Has the atypical language Mabuiag (365) compensated for its reduction to three places of articulation by adding a voicing contrast, creating the stop inventory /p, "t", k; b, "d", g/?

There are a number of ways in which this comparison of places and manners could be done. In this instance, it was decided to treat doubly articulated stops (in practice, this means labial-velars) as having a place of articulation distinct from that of either of their components, that is, labial-velar is treated as a place of articulation. Secondary articulations, on the other hand, since they are more likely to appear with a range of primary places of articulation, seem more akin to the series-generating nature of the differences in initiation and phonation type and hence were treated as differences in manner. So, of the two inventories given below, (1) is treated as having four places of articulation and two manners, whereas (2) is treated as having three places of articulation and three manners.

(1)   p   t   k   kp
       b   d   g   gb
(2)   p   t   k
       p^w k^w
       b   d   g

The correlation was obtained between the number of places out of a list of 10 and the number of manners out of a list of 14 series-generating manner components for each language.[2] (Glottal was not included in the calculation of places because glottal stops do not ordinarily have contrasting manners.) The numbers of languages involved are shown in Table 6.2. Those rows with very sparse representation, that is, less than three and more than five places, or more than four manners, have been eliminated, removing 29 languages from the calculation. There is essentially no correlation between the numbers of places and the numbers of manners for stops, whereas the hypothesis of compensation would predict a strong negative correlation.

A similar computation was performed for fricatives, relating place to manner with cases with over five places or over four manners dropped (resulting in 16 languages being excluded over and above the 21 languages which have no fricatives). The results are given in Table 6.3. The observed data are significantly different from those expected under the hypothesis that place and manner are unrelated ($p = .0001$), and in this case a fairly substantial positive correlation ($r = .46$) between the two variables is found. Again this is counter to the predictions of a compensation hypothesis, and more strongly so than is the case with stops.[3]

The example given by Martinet (1955) of a compensatory adjustment in

[2]The manner components are plain voiceless, plain voiced, voiceless aspirated, breathy, preaspirated, laryngealized, implosive, ejective, prenasalized, nasally released, labialized, palatalized, velarized, and pharyngealized.

[3]Of course, other compensations may exist between aspects of the segmental inventories not examined here; the failure to find evidence for gross compensatory tendencies does not affect the validity of any posited historical evolution in a particular case.

Table 6.2

Cross-tabulation of the Number of Places of Articulation
and Manners of Articulation of Stop Consonants

		Manners			
Places	1	2	3	4	Total
1	19	83	35	20	157
2	14	28	32	21	95
3	3	16	11	6	36
	36	127	78	47	

Table 6.3

Cross-tabulation of the Number of Places of Articulation
and Manners of Articulation of Fricative Consonants

		Manners		
Places	1	2	3	Total
1	37	8	1	46
2	46	35	1	82
3	21	45	8	74
4	6	32	8	46
5	4	22	6	32
	114	142	24	

segment inventories concerns elaboration of the fricative inventory by reduction of the stop inventory. Therefore, a similar comparison of fricative and stop numbers was made. In this computation, languages with fewer than 5 or more than 13 stops were dropped and languages with more than 8 fricatives were dropped, resulting in 92 languages being eliminated from the total. No tabulation of these numbers is provided because the table requires an inconveniently large number of cells. Statistical tests showed a weak positive correlation between the number of fricatives and the number of stops ($r = .35$), but this correlation is probably not reliable since its significance level is under .05. However, the absence of an inverse correlation is still notable.

SEGMENTS AND SUPRASEGMENTALS

Despite the failure to find any confirmation of a compensation hypothesis in several tests involving segmental subinventories, it is possible that the compensation exists at another level. One possibility was evidently in the minds of Firchow and Firchow (1969:271). In their paper on Rotokas (625),

Table 6.4

Relation of Segment Inventory Size to Complexity of Suprasegmentals

	Languages with small segment inventory (⊕ 20)	Languages with large segment inventory (◊ 45)
Stress		
Contrastive	6	8
Predictable	7	9
Pitch accent	2	2
None	5	4
Inadequate data	8	5
Tone		
Complex system	2	6
Simple system	2	4
None	22	15
Inadequate data	2	5

which has an inventory of only 11 segments, they remark that "as the Rotokas segmental phonemes are simple, the supresegmental are complicated."[4] A similar view of a compensatory relationship between segmental and suprasegmental complexity seems implicit in much of the literature on the historical development of tone. For example, Hombert, Ohala, and Evan (1979:38) refer to "the development of contrastive tones on vowels because of the loss of a voicing distinction on obstruents." If this phenomenon is part of a pervasive relationship of compensation we would expect that, in general, languages with larger segmental inventories would tend to have more complex suprasegmental characteristics.

In order to test this prediction, the languages in UPSID which have less than 20 or more than 45 segments were examined to determine if the first group had obviously more complex patterns of stress and tone than the second. Both groups contain 28 languages. The findings on the suprasegmental properties of these languages, as far as they can be ascertained, are summarized in Table 6.4.

Despite some considerable uncertainty of interpretation and the incompleteness of the data, the indications are quite clear that these suprasegmental properties are not more elaborate in the languages with simpler segmental inventories. If anything, they tend to be more elaborate in the languages with larger inventories.

There are more "large" languages with contrastive stress and complex tone

---

[4]Rotokas is not really very complex in its suprasegmentals. It has a partially predictable stress and a contrast of vowel length that seems only partly independent of stress (Firchow, Firchow, & Akoitai 1973). Long vowels are not treated as separate segments in UPSID for this language.

systems (more than two tones) than "small" languages. There are more "small" languages lacking stress and tone. The overall tendency appears once again to be more that complexity of different kinds goes hand in hand, rather than for complexity of one sort to be balanced by simplicity elsewhere.

SEGMENT INVENTORIES
AND SYLLABLE INVENTORIES

Another hypothesis is that the size of the segment inventory is related to the phonotactics of the language in such a way as to limit the total number of possible syllables that can be constructed from the segments and suprasegmental properties that it has. Languages might then have approximately equal numbers of syllables even though they differ substantially in the number of segments. Rough maintenance of syllable-inventory size is envisaged as the function of cyclic historical processes by, for example, Matisoff (1973:82–83). He outlines an imaginary language in which, at some arbitrary starting point, "the number of possible syllables is very large since there is a rich system of syllable-initial and -final consonants." At a later stage of the language these initial and final consonant systems are found to have simplified but "the number of vowels has increased and lexically contrastive tones have arisen," maintaining contrasting syllabic possibilities. If tone or vowel contrasts are lost, consonant clustering increases again at the syllable margins. Matisoff also suggests that the morphological complexity of the language would evolve along with the phonological shifts.

A brief investigation of the relationship between segmental-inventory size and syllable-inventory size was carried out by calculating the number of possible syllables in nine languages. The languages are Tsou (418), Quechua (819), Thai (400), Rotokas (625), Gã (117), Hawaiian (424), Vietnamese (303), Cantonese, Higi, and Yoruba (the last three are not in UPSID but detailed data on the phonotactics are available in convenient form for these languages). The nine languages range from those with small segment inventories (Rotokas, Hawaiian) to those with relatively large inventories (Vietnamese, Higi, Quechua) and from those with relatively simple suprasegmental properties (Tsou, Hawaiian, Quechua) to those with complex suprasegmental phenomena (Yoruba, Thai, Cantonese, Vietnamese). In calculating the number of possible syllables, general co-occurrence restrictions were taken into account, but the failure of a particular combination of elements to be attested if parallel combinations were permitted is taken only as evidence of an accidental gap, and such a combination is counted as a possible syllable. The calculations reveal very different numbers of possible syllables in these languages. The totals are given in Table 6.5. Even with the uncertainties involved in this kind of counting, the numbers differ markedly enough for the con-

Table 6.5

Syllable-Inventory Size
of Nine Selected Languages

Language	Total possible syllables
Hawaiian	162
Rotokas	350
Yoruba	582
Tsou	968
Gã	2,331
Cantonese	3,456
Quechua	4,068
Vietnamese	14,430
Thai	23,638

clusion to be drawn that languages are not strikingly similar in terms of the size of their syllable inventories.

In following up this study, several tests were done to see which of a number of possible predictors correlated best with syllable-inventory size. The predictors used were the number of segments, the number of vowels, the number of consonants, the number of permitted syllable structures (CV, CVC, CCVC, etc.), the number of suprasegmental contrasts (e.g., number of stress levels times number of tones), and a number representing a maximal count of segmental differences in which the number of vowels was multiplied by the number of suprasegmentals. Of these, the best predictor is the number of permitted syllable types ($r = .69$), an indication that the phonotactic possibilities of the language are the most important factor contributing to the number of syllables. The next best predictor is the number of suprasegmentals ($r = .59$), with the correlation with the various segmental counts all being somewhat lower. Although all the predictors tested show a positive simple correlation with the number of syllables, in a multiple regression analysis only the number of vowels contributes a worthwhile improvement to the analysis (r^2 change $= .19$) beyond the number of syllable types. Thus we can say that syllable-inventory size does not depend heavily on segment-inventory size. Nonetheless, because the predictors do have positive correlations with syllable-inventory size, the picture is once again of a tendency for complexity of different types to go together.

CONCLUSIONS

Work with UPSID has confirmed that segment inventories have a well-defined central tendency as far as size is concerned. Nonetheless, considerable variation in their size and structure occurs. Their structure is subject to

122   IAN MADDIESON

a hierarchical organization in many particulars but cannot be substantially explained in terms of a single unified hierarchy of segment types. This is partly because segments of certain types are subject to rules of mutual exclusion. The mutual exclusions cannot all be explained as due to the avoidance of inadequate phonetic contrasts, as some involve strongly salient distinctions. Evidence that languages maintain a balance by compensating for complexity in one phonological respect with simplicity elsewhere could not be found by looking at balances between classes of segments, between segments and suprasegmental contrasts, or between segments and phonotactic conditions. These investigations suggest that complexity of various kinds occurs together in languages, and that languages really do differ in their phonological complexity.

REFERENCES

Baucom, K. L. 1974. Proto-Central Khoisan. In E. Voeltz, ed., *Third Annual Conference on African Linguistics* (Indiana University Publications, African Series, 7), 3–38. Bloomington: Indiana University.
Crothers, J. 1978. Typology and universals of vowel systems. In J. H. Greenberg, C. A. Ferguson, & E. A. Moravcsik, eds., *Universals of human language. Vol. 2, Phonology*, 93–152. Stanford: Stanford University Press.
Disner, S. F. 1982. Vowel quality: the relationship between universal and language specific factors (Working Papers in Phonetics 58). University of California at Los Angeles.
Dixon, R. M. W. 1980. *The languages of Australia*. Cambridge: Cambridge University Press.
Firchow, I., & J. Firchow. 1969. An abbreviated phoneme inventory. *Anthropological Linguistics* 11:271–276.
Firchow, I., J. Firchow, & D. Akoitai. 1973. Vocabulary of Rotokas–Pidgin–English. Ukarumpa: Summer Institute of Linguistics, Papua New Guinea Branch.
Grace, G. W. 1959. The position of the Polynesian languages within the Austronesian (Malayo-Polynesian) language family. *International Journal of American Linguistics*, Memoir 16.
Hagège, C., & Haudricourt, A. 1978. *La phonologie panchronique*. Paris: Presses Universitaires de France.
Hockett, C. F. 1955. A manual of phonology. *International Journal of American Linguistics*, Memoir 11.
Hombert, J. -M., J. J. Ohala, & W. G. Ewan. 1979. Phonetic explanations for the development of tones. *Language* 55:37–58.
Ladefoged, P. 1978. *Phonetic differences within and between languages*. (Working Papers in Phonetics 41), 32–40. University of California at Los Angeles.
Ladefoged, P. 1980. What are linguistic sounds made of? *Language* 56:485–502.
Liljencrants, J. & Lindblom, B. 1972. Numerical simulation of vowel quality contrasts: The role of perceptual contrast. *Language* 48:839–862.
Lindau, M. 1982. Phonetic differences in glottalic consonants (Working Papers in Phonetics 54), 66–77. University of California at Los Angeles.
Maddieson, I. 1984. *Patterns of sounds*. Cambridge: Cambridge University Press.
Martinet, A. 1955. *Economie des changements phonétiques*. (2nd ed.). Berne: Francke.

Matisoff, J. M. 1973. Tonogenesis in Southeast Asia. In L. M. Hyman, ed., *Consonant types and tone*. Southern California Occasional Papers in Linguistics 1.

Pukui, M. K., & S. H. Elbert. 1965. Hawaiian–English dictionary (3rd ed.). Honolulu: University of Hawaii Press.

Sheldon, S. N. 1974. Some morphophonemic and tone perturbation rules in Mura-Pirahã. *International Journal of American Linguistics* 40, 279–282.

Snyman, J. W. 1975. *Žu|'hõasi fonologie en woordeboek*. Cape Town: Balkema.

Traill, A. 1978. Research on the Non-Bantu African languages. In L. W. Lanham & K. P. Prinsloo, eds., *Language and communication studies in South Africa*. Cape Town: Oxford University Press.

Voorhoeve, C. L. 1965. *The Flamingo Bay dialect of the Asmat language* (Verhandelingen van het Koninklijk Instituut voor Taal-, Land- en Volkenkunde 46). The Hague: Nijhoff.

Wurm, S. A. 1972. *Languages of Australia and Tasmania*. The Hague: Mouton.

7

Quichean (Mayan) Glottalized and Nonglottalized Stops: A Phonetic Study with Implications for Phonological Universals*

SANDRA PINKERTON†

INTRODUCTION

A considerable amount of work in phonological universals has focused on co-occurrence restrictions between different types of stops and place of articulation. For example, Chao (1936), Haudricourt (1950), Wang (1968), Greenberg (1970), Hamp (1970), Gamkrelidze (1973, 1975), and Sherman (1975), looking at both pulmonic and glottalic stops, notice asymmetries in stop inventories of the sort exemplified in (1).

(1)   Hausa   Efik
   t   k   kʷ   kʲ   t   k   kʷ   kp
 b   d   g   gʷ   gʲ   b   d
     k'   kʷ'   kʲ'
 ɓ   ɗ

---

*I use the terms 'glottalized' and 'nonglottalized' only when referring to the phonological classes of stops in the Quichean languages. There is no phonological contrast between ejectives and implosives in these languages.

†Present address: Speech Recognition Group, Hewlett-Packard Laboratories, Palo Alto, California 94304.

	Tacana			Mazahua		
p	t	k	p	t	k	kʷ
			pʰ	tʰ	kʰ	kʷʰ
b	d				g	gʷ
			t′	k′	kʷ′	
			ɓ	ɗ		

	Vietnamese	
t	c	k
tʰ		
ɓ	ɗ	

Greenberg, focusing on glottalic consonants concludes, following Haudricourt and Wang, that front articulations favor implosives and back articulations, ejectives. Greenberg, although acknowledging some exceptions, hypothesizes the following universal co-occurrence constraint on the incidence of implosives at different places of articulation: "if a language has one injective [implosive] obstruent it is ʔb; if it has two they are ʔb and ʔd . . . ; if there are three they are ʔb, ʔd, ʔj . . . ; and if four they are ʔb, ʔd, ʔj, and ʔg" (p. 128).[1] Gamkrelidze and Sherman, however, conclude that it is the voicing of the stops which favors front articulations and voicelessness which favors back articulations.

As they apply to glottalic stop systems, either generalization—the one that attributes their asymmetries to the ingressive versus egressive nature of the stop or the one that attributes asymmetries to their voicing characteristics—would seem to be appropriate, since voicing typically co-occurs with implosiveness and voicelessness must, of physical necessity, co-occur with ejectiveness. What would help to differentiate between these two explanations would be evidence on the behavior of voiceless implosives—which are considered to be quite rare.[2] Such evidence is provided by Campbell (1973), who cites counterexamples to Greenberg's hypothesis in the Quichean languages. He notes that these languages have a set of glottalized stops which he symbolizes ʔb, t', k', ʔq, this last stop being a voiceless uvular implosive. If Greenberg's hypothesis holds for these languages, the presence of the uvular implosive would imply that all the stops in the glottalized set which are articulated farther forward of that place of articulation would also be implosive. However, only the bilabial and the uvular stops are implosive, the apical and velar being ejectives. Apparently, then, the explanation that the asymmetries are tied to the voicing character of the stops has more generality.

[1]Greenberg and Campbell use ʔC for implosives. I use the following phonetic symbols: C′ = ejective, Cˤ = voiceless implosive, [ɓ] and [ɗ] = voiced implosives.

[2]See also Javkin (1977) for phonetic arguments against the claim that the ingressive versus egressive character of glottalic stops favors oral cavities of different dimensions.

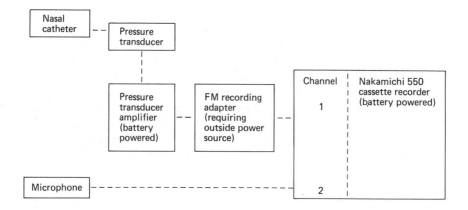

Figure 7.1   Principal pieces of equipment used in the study.

Both Greenberg and Campbell, however, allude to the problem that many of the phonetic descriptions given by writers who provide the data that these generalizations are based on are ambiguous, and that further phonetic research is necessary both to find out exactly what kinds of sounds exist in the languages discussed and to identify the causal factors behind their behavior.

It was with the goal of trying to obtain some reliable data about the phonetic character of the glottalized stops, particularly uvulars, in the Quichean languages, that I undertook the following study.

METHOD

Although acoustic recordings might give some useful information about the character of the glottalized stops in the Quichean languages, only physiological recordings of a parameter like oral air pressure would provide (largely) unambiguous evidence about their ingressive versus egressive nature as well as verify their glottalic character (Ladefoged 1962). Since there were few Quichean speakers in the vicinity of the Phonology Laboratory at Berkeley (where I was located at the time of this study), it was necessary to take air pressure recording instrumentation to Guatemala. This was relatively easily done, thanks to the miniaturization of several of the needed components.

Figure 7.1 shows the principal pieces of equipment used in this study. The heart of the apparatus was a portable battery-powered stereo cassette tape recorder (Nakamichi 550).[3] Audio recordings were made on one channel of

---

[3]This model is no longer available. However, many other portable stereo cassette tape recorders of sufficient quality for fieldwork are now readily and cheaply obtainable.

the tape recorder (using a conventional microphone) and the air pressure recordings on the other. Air pressure was recorded by means of a pressure transducer (Statham PC-151), which was driven by and whose output was (DC) amplified by a custom-made battery-powered unit.[4] This DC signal was then input to an FM transducer (modulator/demodulator) (manufactured by A. R. Vetter Co., Rebersburg, PA); this FM signal was then recorded on the second channel. Only the FM transducer required external power (110 V AC); a separate transformer was necessary to convert 220 V (occasionally found in Guatemala) to the required 110 V. All of the equipment, including a U-tube water manometer (for calibrating the air pressure signal), plastic catheters, extra cassette tapes, and a battery charger (to power up the rechargeable batteries), was packed in one small suitcase, thus making it relatively easy to get around in the Guatemalan countryside using local transportation.

Graphic recordings of the data recorded on tape and subsequent analyses were made in phonetics laboratories in the United States. For this purpose the demodulator function of the FM transducer was utilized.

Since air pressure had to be measured for the full range of places of articulation, including uvular, a nasal catheter was used so that air pressure variations in the pharyngeal region could be sampled. I demonstrated the use of the nasal catheter on myself first if any subject required it.

There are seven Quichean languages. Figure 7.2 is a map of Guatemala; the area where the Quichean languages are spoken is delimited by the heavy line. The regions where the five languages which I investigated are spoken are indicated by numbers.

Twenty-seven male speakers, 17 to 32 years of age, were recorded. Of these, 15 were native speakers of K'ekchi, and the remaining 12 consisted of 3 each from the other 4 languages. The K'ekchi data include different dialects characteristic of the three urban centers in the department of Alta Verapaz (San Pedro Charcha, San Juan Chamelco, and Coban). I also report on some Pocomchi dialect variation for two speakers from the towns of San Cristobal and Tactic. Figure 7.3 locates these towns on a map of Alta Verapaz.

Each of the Quichean languages has a set of four voiceless, unaspirated stops which contrast phonologically with a set of four glottalized stops, at the bilabial, alveolar, velar, and uvular places of articulation. During the recording sessions, subjects read a prepared list of real words, embedded within a carrier phrase. This list contained eight minimal pairs illustrating the glottalized–nonglottalized contrast in word-initial position and an additional eight minimal pairs showing the same contrast in intervocalic word-

[4]I thank Steve Pearson for designing and constructing this unit as well as testing, "portablizing," and organizing all the other components taken into the field.

Figure 7.2 Map of Guatemala showing areas where languages studied are spoken: (1) K'ekchi, (2) Pocomchi, (3) Cakchiquel, (4) Quiche, (5) Tzutujil.

Figure 7.3 Alta Verapaz. K'ekchi-speaking towns: (1) Coban, (2) Chamelco, (3) Carcha; Pocomchi-speaking towns: (4) San Cristobal, (5) Tactic.

medial position. Each token appeared ten times in the corpus. Examples of two minimal pairs in K'ekchi are given in (2).

(2) *t'oqok*   'to throw'   *ʃaːt'oq*   'you threw it'
     toqok   'to break'   *ʃaːtoq*   'you broke it'

RESULTS AND ANALYSIS

Samples of the audio and intraoral air pressure for typical stops in the five Quichean languages, graphically transduced by an Oscillomink (an ink-jet oscillograph, manufactured by Siemens), are shown in Figures 7.4 through 7.10.

The figures give sample tokens of the productions of one speaker of each language or dialect. The averages reported are based on 10 tokens of peak (or in cases of implosives, minimum) pressure of the particular stop under discussion. Class averages are based on averages made from the individual tokens. Likewise, voice onset time measures are based on 10 tokens of a given stop type. Detailed analysis, especially quantitative analysis, of the entire set is being prepared and will be presented in subsequent papers. Only details that are relevant to the issues of universal constraints on stop inventories are discussed here.

Figures 7.4c, 7.5c, 7.6c, 7.7c, and 7.8c give representative traces for ejectives, in all cases [k']. The pressure signal, which in all cases is positive with respect to atmospheric pressure, is typically much greater than that of surrounding nonglottalized obstruents (see, e.g., the [t] following the [k'] in Figure 7.4c). There is an average difference of 5 cm of water between the air pressure of [k'] and the surrounding nonglottalized obstruents. Similar differences hold for the other ejectives in each of the languages investigated. (See also the traces for [t'] in Quiche, Figure 7.4b; Cakchiquel, Figure 7.5b; Chamelco K'ekchi, Figure 7.6b; and San Cristobal Pocomchi, Figure 7.9b. As is true for all egressive stops, the pressure in the production of [k'] starts to build up upon closure of the stop and falls abruptly at the moment of stop release. All of these ejectives are, of course, voiceless. The onset of voicing of the following vowel in the production of ejectives in these speakers begins an average of 45 msec after stop release.

Figures 7.4–7.9 Audio and intraoral pressure data: (A) /ɓ/, (B) /t/, (C) /k'/, (D) /q'/.

Figure 7.4 Quiche   Figure 7.7 Tzutujil
Figure 7.5 Cackchiquel   Figure 7.8 Tactic Pocomchi
Figure 7.6 Chamelco K'ekchi   Figure 7.9 San Cristobal Pocomchi

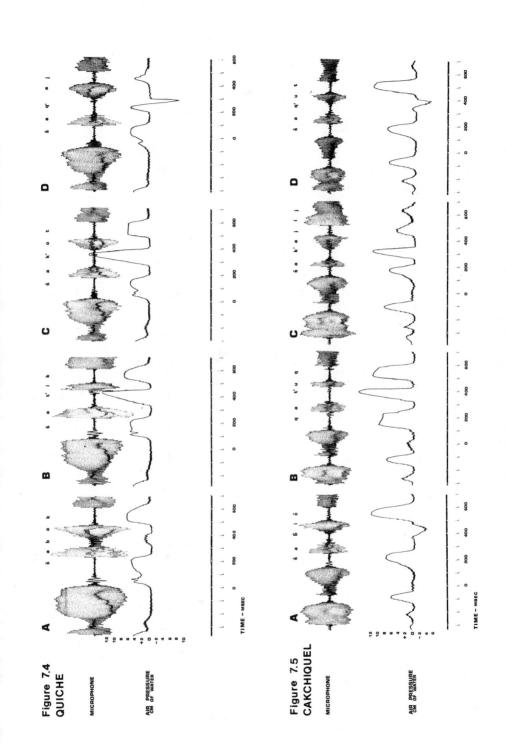

Figure 7.4
QUICHE

Figure 7.5
CAKCHIQUEL

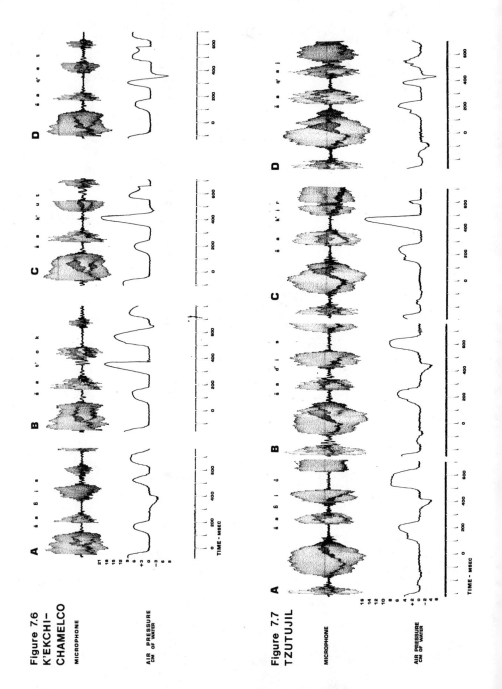

Figure 7.6
K'EKCHI-
CHAMELCO

Figure 7.7
TZUTUJIL

132

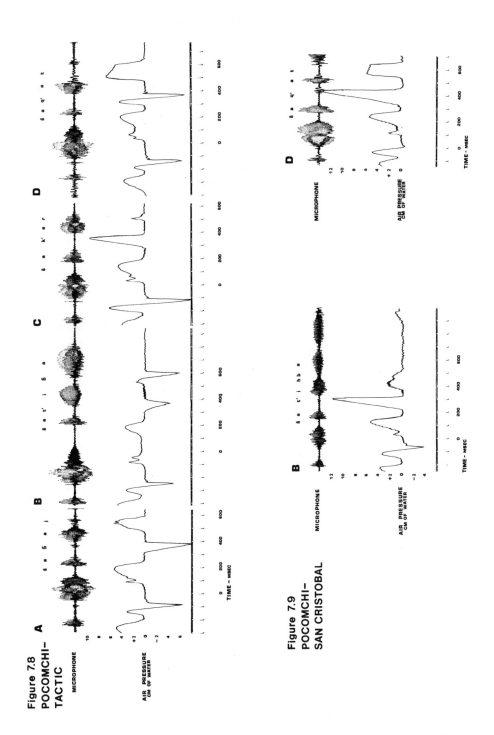

Figure 7.8
POCOMCHI–
TACTIC

Figure 7.9
POCOMCHI–
SAN CRISTOBAL

133

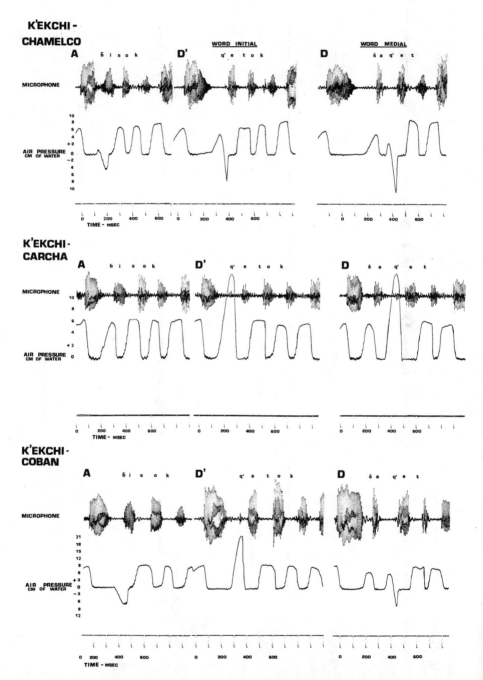

Figure 7.10 Dialect variation for speakers of Chamelco, Carcha, and Coban K'ekchi: (A) /ɓ/, (D') word-initial /q'/, and (D) word-medial /q'/.

Bilabial implosives are evident in Figures 7.5a, 7.6a, 7.7a, and 7.8a. In the first three, representing the languages Cakchiquel, Chamelco K'ekchi, and Tzutujil, these implosives are produced with a negative pressure impulse averaging − 4 cm of water, and they have an average duration of prevoicing of 30 msec. Voiced alveolar implosives are found in Figures 7.7b (Tzutujil) and 7.8b (Tactic Pocomchi). The sounds which are cognate to these voiced bilabial implosives in other languages show some variation. Figure 7.4a indicates that in Quiche the glottalized bilabial stop is produced with an average positive pressure impulse of 1 cm of water and that there is voicing throughout the 80 msec closure. Although not strictly speaking ingressive (since there is no negative pressure impulse), this is a well-recognized variant of a voiced implosive. As Ladefoged (1971: 26–27) remarks:

> In many of the languages I have observed . . . the pressure of the air in the mouth during an ingressive glottalic stop is approximately the same as that outside the mouth since the rarefying action of the downward movement of the glottis is almost exactly counterbalanced by the leakage of lung air up through the vocal cords . . . .
> . . . The difference between [glottalic voiced] implosives and [pulmonic voiced] plosives is one of degree rather than kind.

Also, in Pocomchi (Figure 7.,8a) the glottalized bilabial stop is produced with an extreme negative pressure impulse of − 8 cm of water and there is an average voicing lag of about 30 msec.

Glottalized uvular stops are shown in Figures 7.4d, 7.5d, 7.6d, 7.7d, and 7.8d, representing Quiche, Cakchiquel, Chamelco K'ekchi, Tzutujil, and Tactic Pocomchi, respectively.[5] In all but Figures 7.5d there is an initially high positive pressure impulse—averaging about 9 cm of water, which is about the same as surrounding nonglottalized stops—followed immediately by a negative impulse averaging about − 6 cm of water. These stops are voiceless and have a voice-onset time of about 20 msec. The cognate uvular stop in 7.5d, for Cakchiquel, has a smaller positive pressure impulse (averaging 2 cm of water for this subject) followed by a negative impulse similar to those in the other languages.

There is, however, considerable regional (and possibly individual) dialect variation. Figures 7.8 and 7.9 show such variation in Pocomchi. The subject from Tactic (Figure 7.8) produces the bilabial, alveolar, and uvular glottalized stops as implosives with an average voicing lag of 25 msec. His velar stop, though, is ejective. Although the subject from San Cristobal (Figure 7.9) also produces the bilabial and velar glottalized stops as an implosive and ejective, respectively, the same as the Tactic speaker, his alveolar and uvular glottalized stops are both ejectives with a very high positive pressure

---

[5]Although no examples of nonglottalized uvular stops are shown, these stops have pressure curves similar to those of other nonglottalized stops. It is safe to conclude that nonglottalized uvular stops do not have any unusual pressure impulse vis-a-vis those of stops at other places of articulation.

impulse (about 12 cm of water). One note of caution about the interpretation of this variation: While these two speakers are from different regions, they also have significantly different ages, making it difficult to attribute this variation to regional or social factors.

Figure 7.10 illustrates dialect variation in K'ekchi. All of these speakers produce the alveolar and velar glottalized stops as ejectives. However, whereas speakers from Chamelco and Coban produce the bilabial glottalized stop as implosives with voicing lead, speakers from Carcha produce the cognate stop as nonglottalized, that is, a voiced pulmonic stop. The realization of the uvular glottalized stop varies from town to town and with position in utterance. Speakers from Chamelco produce uvular implosives in both word-initial and word-medial positions, but those from Carcha produce uvular ejectives in the same environments. Speakers from Coban produce the cognate sound as ejective in word-initial position and as an uvular implosive in word-medial position.

DISCUSSION

In summarizing the types of glottalized stops found in this study of Quichean languages, it is important to note the extent of the phonetic variation in the production of the glottalized stops across languages and within Pocomchi and K'ekchi. Thus, the identification of a set of stops as phonologically "glottalized" by no means indicates their phonetic nature. Across the Quichean languages and among their dialects one sees, as shown in Table 7.1, considerable variety in the phonetic realizations of the members of this glottalized set. There are three variants at the bilabial place of articulation: [ɓ] with a voicing lead in Cakchiquel, Tzutujil, and Chamelco and Coban K'ekchi; [p<] with a voicing lag in Pocomchi; and [b] in Quiche and Carcha K'ekchi, although Quiche does not have a pressure impulse typical of pulmonic egressive stops. There are three variants at the alveolar place: [t'], an ejective, in Quiche, Cakchiquel, K'ekchi, and San Cristobal Pocomchi; [ɗ], an implosive with voicing lead in Tzutujil; and [t<], a voiceless implosive with voicing lag in Tactic Pocomchi. There is one type of velar: [k'], an ejective, in all languages. Finally, there are two variants at the uvular place: [q'], an ejective, in Coban and Carcha K'ekchi and in San Cristobal Pocomchi; and [q<], a voiceless implosive with a voicing lag and a biphasic pressure impulse, initially positive and then negative, in Quiche, Cakchiquel, Tzutujil, Tactic Pocomchi, and Chamelco and Coban K'ekchi.

The data reveal, in accord with Campbell, that the stop inventories of the Quichean languages present a clear counterexample to Greenberg's prediction. Quiche, Cakchiquel, Chamelco and Coban K'ekchi, Pocomchi, and

Table 7.1

Quichean Stop Inventories

	Unaspirated, egressive					Glottalized		
Cakchiquel								
voiceless	p	t	k	q		t'	k'	q<
voiced					ɓ			
Chamelco K'ekchi								
voiceless	p	t	k	q		t'	'k	q<
voiced					ɓ			
Quiche								
voiceless	p	t	k	q		t'	k'	q<
voiced	(b)				(ɓ)			
Tzutujil								
voiceless	p	t	k	q			k'	q<
voiced					ɓ	ɗ		
Carcha K'ekchi								
voiceless	p	t	k	q		t'	k'	q'
voiced	b							
San Cristobal Pocomchi								
voiceless	p	t	k	q	p<	t'	k'	q'
voiced								
Coban K'ekchi								
voiceless	p	t	k	q		t'	k'	q'/q<
voice					ɓ			
Tactic Pocomichi								
voiceless	p	t	k	q	p<	t<	k'	q<
voiced								

ª p	t	k	q	voiceless unaspirated egressive stops
b				voiced unaspirated egressive stop
ɓ	ɗ			voiced implosives
p<	t<	q<		voiceless implosives
	t'	k'	q'	ejectives

Tzutujil all realize their uvular glottalized stop as an implosive and yet do not have implosives at all points of articulation which are further forward; instead they have ejectives at the alveolar or velar places or at both. It should be noted, however, that this uvular implosive is voiceless whereas the implosives made further forward (bilabial and alveolar) are (with one exception) voiced. These data, therefore, do adhere to the implicational constraints stated by Gamkrelidze and Sherman: It is true for both pulmonic and glottalic stops series that front articulations favor voicing and back articulations favor voicelessness. Implicationally, a voiced stop at a given place of articulation (within a given series) would indicate the existence of voiced stops articulated further forward. Voicelessness at a given place of articulation would imply the existence of voiceless stops articulated farther back. The two dialects of

Pocomchi therefore represent crucial cases because their bilabial glottalized stop is voiceless. By the generalization just made, it would be predicted that all the other places of articulation in the glottalized series should also be voiceless. This prediction is borne out.

Greenberg's predictions may have statistical validity since most implosives tend to be voiced and all ejectives must be voiceless; however, it is apparently not the implosive or ejective character per se which determines any pattern of the places of articulation at which these two types of glottalic segments are found. If the implosive or ejective character of a stop can be predicted on the basis of other co-occuring phonetic features, including place of articulation, these generalizations have yet to be discovered.

The grouping of ejectives and voiceless implosives as a class in these languages has interesting implications for another set of facts about Mayan. Campbell notes that implosives in the Mayan languages do not seem to have originated from any of the kinds of sources identified in the development of implosives in other languages (e.g., voiced stops, in the case of Sindhi). He provides examples which suggest that many of the implosives in Mayan languages come from original ejectives. Also, in one case, an ejective, a labial one, has come from an implosive. It is interesting, then, that the dialect data for Pocomchi and K'ekchi also suggest a close relation between ejectives and implosives. In Pocomchi, the alveolar and uvular glottalized stops are ejectives in the San Cristobal dialect but implosives in Tactic. In K'ekchi, the uvular glottalized stop is an ejective in Carcha but an implosive in Chamelco. Finally, in Coban K'ekchi, the uvular glottalized stop is an ejective in word-initial position and an implosive in word-medial position. If it is accepted that in order to explain how sound A can develop into sound B, it would be helpful to identify a situation in which both appear as natural, presumably phonetically caused variants, then it is interesting to speculate that the development of implosives from ejectives in these languages may come about due to (1) variation in the timing of the articulatory gestures (laryngeal, pharyngeal, etc.) which, in the voiceless implosives discovered here, result in a biphasic pressure impulse which is positive and then negative, or (2) phonetic differences created by position within the word.

Finally, it is important to note that given the trends in miniaturization as well as the reliability of electronic equipment, it is possible to take "laboratory" equipment into the field and gather data—acoustic and physiological—which are crucial to the evaluation of phonological claims.

ACKNOWLEDGMENTS

    Support for this research was received from a National Institute of Health Post-Doctoral Grant taken at the Phonology Laboratory, Department of Linguistics, University of California, Berkeley, and from a University of Minnesota Faculty Research Grant.

Winifred Strange (Human Learning Center, University of Minnesota) and Peter MacNeilage (Department of Linguistics, University of Texas) very generously lent me the use of the facilities in their respective laboratories, for which I am very grateful. I want to thank Robert Harms, Carol Riordan, Peter Ladefoged, Lyle Campbell, and Jim Fox for their helpful comments at different stages in the writing of this paper; I especially want to thank John Ohala for extensive comments which helped me to integrate my findings with the literature on phonological universals. Of course, they are not responsible for any errors in fact or analysis. Finally, I want to thank the members of the Summer Institute of Linguistics in Guatemala, the Instituto Lingüístico Francisco Marroquin, and the Centro San Benito, as well as all the Guatemalen language consultants who helped me during the collection of the data.

REFERENCES

Campbell, L. 1973. On glottalic consonants. *International Journal of American Linguistics* 39:44–46.

Chao, Y.-R. 1936. Types of plosives in Chinese. *Proceedings of the 2nd International Congress of Phonetic Sciences*, 106–110. Cambridge: Cambridge University Press.

Gamkrelidze, T. V. 1973. Ueber die Wechselbeziehung zwischen Verschluss-und Reiblauten im Phonemsystem. *Phonetica* 27:213–218.

Gamkrelidze, T. V. 1975. On the correlation of stops and fricatives in a phonological system. *Lingua* 35:231–261.

Greenberg, J. H. 1970. Some generalization concerning glottalic consonants, especially implosives. *International Journal of American Linguistics* 36:123–145.

Hamp, E. 1970. Maya-Chipaya and typology of labials. *Proceedings of the 6th Annual Meeting of the Chicago Linguistics Society*, 20–22.

Haudricourt, A. 1950. Les consonnes préglottalisées en Indochine. *Bulletin de la Société Linguistique de Paris* 46:172–182.

Javkin, H. 1977. Towards a phonetic explanation for universal preferences in implosives and ejectives. *Proceedings of the 3rd Annual Meeting of the Berkeley Linguistics Society*, 559–565.

Ladefoged, P. 1962. *A phonetic study of West African languages*. London: Cambridge University Press.

Ladefoged, P. 1971. *Preliminaries to linguistic phonetics*. Chicago: University of Chicago Press.

Sherman, D. 1975. Stop and fricative systems: a discussion of paradigmatic gaps and the question of language sampling (Working Papers in Language Universals 17), 1–31. Stanford University.

Wang, W. S.-Y. 1968. *The basis of speech* (Project on Linguistic Analysis Reports 4), University of California, Berkeley.

8

Phonological Contrast in Experimental Phonetics: Relating Distributions of Production Data to Perceptual Categorization Curves

TERRANCE M. NEAREY
JOHN T. HOGAN

PHONOLOGICAL UNITS OF PERCEPTION

The nature of phonetic features has been of concern to linguists since the time of the Sanskrit grammarians. Modern linguistic theory has generally considered the basic phonetic framework to be universal in that the same set of phonetic features is available to speakers of all languages, even though there are language-specific choices to be made concerning the combinations and specific values of these features. Phonological theories, whether classical structuralist or generative, are fundamentally concerned with the mapping between language-specific phonological entities and the universal phonetic ground. It is our view that experimental phonetics is also fundamentally concerned with this mapping and hence is inextricably linked with phonology. In this chapter, we outline a quantitative framework for the study of what might be viewed as a language-specific warping (related to phonological units) of a universal phonetic space.

Sapir (1933) makes the distinction between 'phonetic' and 'phonemic' hearing. He argues that the difficulty encountered in having untrained listeners

141

EXPERIMENTAL PHONOLOGY

respond to phonologically irrelevant variation is due to the fact that the phonological structure of a listener's language imposes itself more or less immediately on the input signal. Considerable effort is required to direct listeners' attention to finer phonetic detail, however salient to a speaker of another language. Modern experimental phonetics has provided powerful evidence of the influence of phonology even on elementary discrimination tasks.

A particularly well-documented case of the influence of phonology on perception is the series of experiments by Lisker and Abramson (1970) involving a voice onset time (VOT) continuum for stop consonants. When English speakers are presented with a series of synthetic speech stimuli varying from a strongly prevoiced [d] (-150 msec VOT) to a strongly aspirated [t^h], they break the continuum into two broad areas, one of which they label d and the other t. There is only a short transition region in between, centered at about 30 msec VOT. When Thai speakers are presented with the same continuum, they break it into three regions, corresponding to the three apical stop phonemes of Thai /d, t, t^h/. There are then two transition regions, one corresponding to the /d-t/ boundary, the other to the /t-t^h/ boundary.

The fact that different labeling behavior is demonstrated by the two sets of subjects is perhaps not surprising in that English orthography provides only two characters in the region of concern, while Thai orthography has three. However, there is good evidence that more basic perceptual forces are involved, forces strongly suggestive of Sapir's 'phonemic hearing'. This evidence comes from discrimination tasks performed by the same Thai and English speakers (Abramson & Lisker 1970). The basic experimental technique is to present subjects with a series of triads of stimuli chosen from the continuum. The first two elements of the triad are different and the third is the same as either the first or the second. Listeners are asked to judge whether the third is the same as either the first or second. Previous experiments have revealed that listeners almost invariably show greater sensitivity to small differences (an increase in discrimination) when stimuli are near a category boundary (as determined from previous categorization experiments with the same listeners) than when the stimuli are in a stable categorization region, that is, well inside phoneme boundaries. Abramson and Lisker's experiments clearly demonstrate that listeners from different language backgrounds show enhanced discrimination at the category boundaries of their own languages. While there are a number of interesting questions concerning the degree of enhancement around boundaries that takes place for different types of phonetic categories (e.g., consonants versus vowels), virtually all experiments have indicated some such enhancement.

These results are by no means new. However, it is doubtful that their implications for both phonetics and phonology have been fully appreciated. As far as phonology is concerned, the presence of well-defined 'tuning curves' on physical continua, such as VOT, provides strong evidence for language-dependent (and hence phonological rather than phonetic) units of perception that are largely autonomous from the point of view of higher grammatico-semantic considerations. Superficially, these units would appear to behave much like taxonomic phonemes in that they are less abstract than morphophonemes and are more closely related to phonetic dimensions. In addition, they are clearly related to lexically important contrasts.

On the other hand, phonetic experiments are typically conducted on fixed phonological contexts, for example, initial stops. The important question of membership of allophones into surface phonemes is not addressed. The marked difference in the physical properties of such contextual variants as initial versus final stops does not seem amenable to the intuitive 'tuning curve' notion that seems so natural in the case of VOT for initial /t–d/. It thus seems reasonable to suggest that the most familiar paradigm of perceptual experimentation involves the study of contrasting sets of allophones in specific syntagmatic environments. In the next section, we develop a model of such elementary phonological units that can account in a simple way for the warping of the phonetic space in different ways by different languages. This model allows for a more detailed study of the relationship between measurements of naturally produced phonetic events and listeners' judgments of synthetic stimuli.

RELATING DISTRIBUTIONS OF NATURAL SPEECH PRODUCTION TO PERCEPTUAL CATEGORIZATIONS

Prior Efforts

In experimental phonetic research, acoustic analysis of sets of contrasting allophones and the synthesis of perceptually relevant continua are closely linked. Ordinarily, when an analytically salient difference is discovered to cooccur with a set of phonological oppositions, experiments utilizing synthetic speech corroborate the perceptual relevance of the acoustic parameter in question. Clearly, there is a strong expectation for a close relationship between consistent acoustic differences and phonological categories.

An early attempt to explore the relationship between the distribution of speech-production data and listeners' perception is presented by Lisker and Abramson (1970). These authors give perceptual data from experiments involving a VOT continuum for stop consonant series categorized by speakers of a number of different languages. They used a graphic technique to compare the results of these perceptual experiments to measurements of VOT

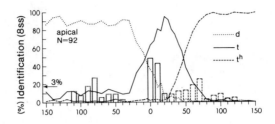

Figure 8.1 Histograms of production data and categorization functions for Thai apical stops (from Lisker & Abramson 1970).

in the various languages gathered in an earlier study. Figure 8.1 is a reproduction of one such graph, that for the /d, t, tʰ/ distinction of Thai. The identification curves are shown by lines. The speech-production data are indicated by the vertical bars of the histogram which give the frequency of occurrence of VOT values for the separate phonemic categories. It is evident that there is a reasonably good correspondence between the two sets of data. Lisker and Abramson point out, in particular, that the categorization curves tend to have crossover points (i.e., where the identification curves cross the 50% level) near the gaps that occur between the adjacent clusters in the histogram of the production data. Other studies show that this close correlation is generally found in other languages, too. They point out, however, that there appear to be cases where there is deviation between the production measurements and the categorization data. Thus, the crossover point between Thai [t] and [tʰ] occurs at a larger value than would be expected from the production distributions. They suggest that the reason for this might lie in the fact that "other acoustic variables play a role in fixing the category boundaries studied" (1970). This graphic technique is highly informative, but it obviously has its limitations. For one thing, it is practically limited to studying the relationships on only one-dimensional continua. It also relies heavily on very limited portions of the data set, namely the gaps in the production distributions and crossover points in the categorization curves. In what follows, we sketch a quantitative technique that can readily be generalized to multidimensional continua and that furthermore utilizes information from every part of the production distribution and every part of the categorization function. We point out that we are considering acoustic phenomena only, not articulatory. In principle, however, it would also be possible to apply this approach to a set of underlying articulatory parameters, provided (a nontrivial proviso) those articulatory parameters are recoverable from the acoustic signal.

A Model of Optimal Categorization

PRELIMINARY CONSIDERATIONS

Our method of relating production distributions to perceptual categorization may be developed by considering an elementary statistical pattern-recognition device (Fukunaga, 1972) that behaves as an optimal categorizer (in the sense of making the fewest misidentifications) of a collection of acoustic signals that represent a set of phonologically distinct classes. Let us consider the Thai /d/-/t/-/tʰ/ distinction. For convenience we assume that (1) the only relevant acoustic parameter for this distinction is VOT; (2) /d, t, tʰ/ are equally likely to occur in this language, that is, in the long run they are equally frequent; and (3) our recognizer has a knowledge of how each of the categories is distributed along the VOT continuum. This situation would be approximated if we provided the recognizer with a large training set of stimuli whose phonetic value was known. For the moment, we can think of this knowledge as represented by a set of bar graphs or histograms like those given by Lisker and Abramson. Under these conditions, the optimal categorization rule may be stated simply as "assign a new (unknown) stimulus to the group it is most likely to have come from." More formally (and less ambiguously), the rule is to assign a stimulus with a VOT value of x to the category for which it has the highest *a posteriori* probability for group membership (henceforth APP), which may be estimated as follows (for distributional knowledge represented as the frequency of occurrence of each category at a number of different x values, as in the bar graph example):

$$P(G_i|x) = \frac{N_i}{\sum\limits_{j} N_j} \tag{1}$$

where $P(G_i|x)$ is the probability of membership in the ith group, G_i; N_i is the number of tokens for the ith group at x msec VOT; and N_j is the number for the jth. This formula may be readily understood by considering an example. Suppose in the training set at $+30$ msec VOT we found that out of 100 measurements taken at that point, 90 were /tʰ/, 9 were /t/, and 1 was /d/. Then the APP for /tʰ/ is $90/(90 + 9 + 1) = .9$. The APP for /t/ is $9/(90 + 9 + 1) = .09$ and that for /d/ is $1/(90 + 9 + 1) = .01$. In this case the decision is obvious: Since 90% of all cases in our measurements were /tʰ/, we will assign any new cases with $+30$ msec VOT to /tʰ/.

The bar-graph model for the distribution of measurements illustrates nicely the concept of probability of group membership at a given value of measurement. However, there are some difficulties associated with such a model of the distribution. For example, if our training set were a small sample we might have values of VOT for which no tokens were observed, and it would be impossible to assign an APP value for any group since they would all have the indeterminate form $0/(0 + 0 + 0)$. This problem (and others, such as allowing for finer measurements of VOT than 5 msec intervals) can be avoided by adopting a continuous, parametric model of the probability distributions of our measured stimuli. Since the data in question display roughly a mound-like distribution, it seems reasonable to adopt a Gaussian (or normal) distribution.[1] But any other parametric model for continuous distributions could be used as well, if a compelling reason were found for doing so. The APP for continuous distributions is analogous to that above for discrete distributions:

$$P(G_i|x) = \frac{f_i(x)}{\sum_j f_j(x)} \tag{2}$$

where $f_i(x)$ is the probability density function for the ith group evaluated at x.[2] Thus in the case of a Gaussian distribution,

$$f_i(x) = \frac{1}{s\sqrt{2\pi}} \exp \frac{-\frac{1}{2}(x - m_i)^2}{s^2} \tag{3}$$

where m_i is the mean of the ith group and s is its standard deviation.

A hypothetical example with accompanying graphs serves to illustrate these functions. Assume we have measured data from a language with the following means (x) and standard deviations (SD); /d/, $x = -70$, SD $= 30$; /t/, $x = 0$, SD $= 30$; /t^h/, $x = 40$, SD $= 30$. The probability densities, calculated by Equation 3 above, are given in Figure 8.2. Substituting these densities in Equation 2 yields the 'APP' curves of Figure 8.2b.

Under these conditions, the optimal decision rule may be stated as follows:

R1   Assign stimulus x to the group for which its APP is the highest.

[1]However, compare Lisker and Abramson's remarks concerning the nonmodal distribution of some of their measurements. Note that their samples were relatively small, involving only a few speakers for each language.

[2]If the overall probability of occurrence in the language is not assumed to be equal, then a full Bayesian APP function requires the inclusion of prior probabilities such that

$$P(G_i|x) = \frac{f_i(x)P_i}{\sum_j f_j(x)P_j}$$

where Pi is the relative probability for group i and P_j is that for group j for the language as a whole.

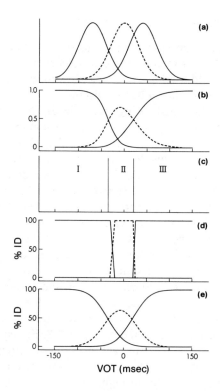

Figure 8.2 Illustration of categorization data generated by a statistical model: (a) probability density functions; (b) *a posteriori* probabilities; (c) regions of dominance for each category; (d) optimal categorization functions; (e) threshold Thurstonian categorization.

For the present discussion, we consider only the case for which the standard deviations of each of the groups are the same. Under these circumstances, the procedure just described is equivalent to that of linear discriminant function analysis (henceforth DFA). With the assumption of equal standard deviations in the groups, the result of the maximum APP decision rule is to divide the continuum into three regions, separated by two boundaries. The boundaries will ordinarily coincide with crossover points in the APP curves. We refer to these as the 'equi-APP' points. The areas within which the APP for each category is greater than those of others are indicated as regions I, II, and III in Figure 8.2C. Under the optimal decision rule, all observations in Region I are assigned to /d/, all those in II to /t/, and all those in III to /tʰ/. If our listeners were optimal categorizers of the type described above, categorization curves would be nearly rectangular, as in Figure 8.2d.

THE THRESHOLD THURSTONIAN MODEL

Obviously, it would be unreasonable for us to expect listeners to behave in exactly this way. We know that categorization curves are never as steep as indicated in Figure 8.2d. Perhaps the most obvious way to get our optimal categorizer to behave more like a human listener is to introduce noise into the stimulus effects of the signals being categorized. The stimulus effect for a given stimulus can be viewed as the psychophysical mapping of the stimulus variable plus a random error that varies from trial to trial on repeated presentation of the same stimulus. We assume that the mean of the stimulus-effects distribution for a fixed stimulus is a linear function of the VOT value of that stimulus. If these stimulus effects are assumed to be normally distributed, with equal variances and zero correlation, then the categorization model we are left with is essentially a variety of Thurstone's case V of categorical judgment (Thurstone 1927; Green & Swets 1966). This is also the categorization model of signal detection theory (hereafter SDT; Green & Swets 1966). For a more thorough discussion of the application of SDT to speech perception, the reader is referred to Elman (1979) and Stevenson (1979). Following Bock (1975), we refer to this model as the 'threshold Thurstonian' or simply the 'Thurstonian' model. The hypothetical stimulus-effects distributions for three stimuli are illustrated in Figure 8.3. For each stimulus, the predicted proportion of responses in each group is the area of the normal curve for the stimulus in question that lies within the region for the category in question. Thus for the stimulus in Figure 8.3a, the mean of the distribution is on the /d–t/ boundary. Half of the area of the normal curve lies below this point and hence we would predict 50% identification as /d/. We would predict slightly less than 50% categorization as /t/, because most of the area of the curve above the /d–t/ boundary lies between it and the /t–d/ boundary. However, a slight portion of the upper tail of the distribution also lies in the /t^h/ region, so we would predict a small but nonzero percentage of identification as /t^h/. Figure 8.3b depicts the hypothetical stimulus effects for a stimulus near the middle of the /t/ region. Clearly, most of the area under the normal curve lies within the /t/ region, although there are tails in both of the other regions. Formally, the predicted categorization for stimulus x for category j can be represented as

$$P(j,x) = \frac{1}{s\sqrt{2\Pi}} \int_{l_j}^{h_j} \exp\left[\frac{-\frac{1}{2}(y-x)^2}{s^2} \right] dy \qquad (4)$$

where l_j and h_j are the appropriate lower and upper limits of the areas in question (i.e., $-\infty$ to the /d–t/ boundary for /d/, the /d–t/ boundary to the /t–t^h boundary for /t/, and the /t–t^h/, boundary to $+\infty$ for /t^h/; s

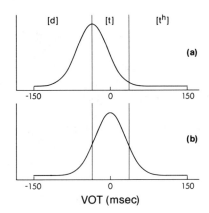

Figure 8.3 Distributions of stimulus effects for (a) stimulus centered on /d–t/ boundary and (b) stimulus at central /t/ value.

is the standard deviation of the stimulus effects. Since no analytic solution exists for the above integrals, a numerical approximation is required. Practically this may be done by standardizing the distributions about the mean stimulus value and changing the limits of integration appropriately. Certain procedures such as probit analysis or other techniques to fit normal ogives to categorization curves are closely related to models of this kind, although these are usually seen in connection with two-category cases only.

In applications of the Thurstonian model to speech perception, the precise relationship between listeners' categorization and measurements of production data does not seem to have been explicitly discussed. However, it would generally be consistent with SDT to expect the boundaries to occur at the points of equal *a posteriori* probability.[3] These are the boundaries at the equi-APP points in Figure 8.2b. In the case of the hypothetical natural distributions just described, these points will occur halfway between the means of the categories, that is, at -35 and $+25$ msec.[4] If this approach is taken, then their hypothetical boundary points could be predicted in advance on the basis of the production data. However, the question of the standard deviation of the stimulus effects appears to have no obvious relationship to

[3]This is clearly implied by Green and Swets (1966) in their consideration of automatic speech recognition experiments in which DFA of vowel data is discussed.

[4]When the means of the three categories are relatively well separated, the equi-APP values between the adjacent distributions are a function of only two groups, since the third, more remote, category contributes only a small value to the denominator.

production distributions, since the former is generally taken to represent internal noise or some combination of internal and external noise. Since the stimuli in a typical synthetic speech experiment are precisely controlled and presented in high signal-to-noise ratio conditions, there seems to be no reason for any correlation between observed natural SDs and those of the stimulus effects.[5] Nonetheless, in the following discussion, we take the production SDs as default values for estimating the stimulus effects. When this is done for our hypothetical data, the predicted categorization curves of Figure 8.2d result.

Under a Thurstonian categorization model, we may make comparisons between speech-production data and the perceptual categorization data in the following two ways:

1. Predict categorization curves in advance from the production data. This is done by estimating the probabilities of identification of each group from equation (4), using the midway points between production means as the finite boundaries and the average SD from the production data for the stimulus effects SDs.

2. Estimate parameter values of the boundaries and stimulus effects SDs so as to optimize some goodness-of-fit criterion to the categorization data. When we have optimal values, these can be compared to the production-data parameters.

THE NORMAL *A POSTERIORI* PROBABILITY (NAPP) MODEL

While the Thurstonian model of categorical judgment seems to have much to recommend it, there are other ways of generating both ogival and mound-like shapes for categorization curves that have interesting properties. In fact, APP values for each group as generated by equations 3 and 4 and illustrated in Figure 8.2b have roughly the right kinds of shapes. As noted above, at any given stimulus value, the APP value may be considered as a relative strength of group membership. A classification rule to produce APP-type curves might be formulated as follows:

R2   Assign a stimulus to a category proportionally to its relative strength of group membership.

When 'relative strength of membership' is defined as the APP based on normal distributions, we refer to the model as a whole as the normal *a posteriori* probability model of categorization, or NAPP. Note the difference between NAPP and the optimal classification rule (R1), above, which involved assign-

---

[5]Note that we are dealing here with the categorizations of a group of subjects. The SDs would likely be smaller for single-subject data.

ing an element to the group for which APP was maximum. If at some value the APP for /d/ is .9 and that for /t/ is .1, R2 will assign 90% of all x at that value to /d/ and 10% to /t/. The maximum APP rule will assign 100% to /d/.

The basic form of R2 is also not without precedent in psychophysics. When strength of membership is not strictly limited to normal APPs, it may be seen as a variety of the Bradley–Terry–Luce (B-T-L) model of choice (Baird & Noma 1978). To the best of our knowledge, the only application of an equivalent of our NAPP model to a perceptual situation of any kind is the micro-matching model of Lee (1963). Lee's experiments involved visual stimuli. He compared his results with what was in essence a Thurstonian (or SDT) model. He interpreted his results as falling somewhere between the two, some subjects behaving more like Thurstonian classifiers and others like APP classifiers. A different model also involving the B-T-L approach has been adopted for speech categorization behavior by Oden and Massaro (1978) and Massaro and Oden (1980). Their model also involves the concept of APP. However, it should be pointed out that they suggest no explicit relationship to APP functions based on speech production distributions. Oden and Massaro's APP functions are essentially ad hoc in nature.

The key difference of the present NAPP model then, compared to that Oden and Massaro, is in the nature of the underlying functions used to generate the APP values. The NAPP model provides us with a specific link between production data and categorizations. An analogous pair of comparisons to those discussed in connection with the threshold Thurstonian model above are applicable for the NAPP model.

1.' Predict categorization curves directly from the production data. This is done by substituting the measured means and SDs of the production data in the probability distributions of Equation 3 and applying Equation 4. Note in this case there is a direct relationship between all the parameters of the data and all those of the categorization curve.

2.' Estimate the means and SD for Equations 2 and 3 so as to optimize a criterion of goodness of fit to the categorization data. These values can then be compared directly to the corresponding production data.

It should be pointed out in passing that the general form of the NAPP function is in fact a 'multivariate logistic' (Lachenbruch 1975). Because of this, the NAPP model has close links to the log-linear and related logistic models that have been the object of considerable interest in applied statistics (Bishop, Fienberg, & Holland 1975; Fienberg 1980: Ch. 6). In some cases, the NAPP equations can be reduced to logistic models with fewer parameters.

In these instances, the production data parameters cannot be uniquely estimated from the categorization data. In general, this situation arises only when there are a small number of categories per dimension.[6] There are two potential benefits of the NAPP model over the threshold Thurstonian. The first is the ready generalization of the NAPP model to multivariate, multicategory cases. This may be accomplished by substituting multivariate normal probability distributions for the univariate distributions of Equation 3. Then, Equation 2 may be used without change as an implementation of categorization R2. Second, the NAPP model posits direct links between the means and SDs of production data and categorization. This last benefit is not without cost in the case of parameter optimization. For three categories, for example, the threshold Thurstonian requires only two boundary parameters, while the NAPP model requires three means. Both require a standard deviation parameter.

We should also make explicit a possible psychological interpretation of the NAPP model. Suppose listeners are equipped with 'allophone detectors', or better, with 'segment likelihood estimators' that are tuned so that their outputs for any combination of input parameters are proportional to the probability density of the corresponding segments in the relevant population of signals in the language. If a B-T-L choice procedure were then applied to this array of outputs, listeners' categorizations would look just like APP curves calculated from measurements of production data. In the following section, application of both the Thurstonian and NAPP models to empirical data is presented as an illustration of their utility in dealing with the problem at hand.

APPLICATION OF THE THURSTONIAN AND NAPP MODELS

The production data we use are the measurements of VOT for Thai labial and apical stop consonants of Lisker and Abramson (1964). Since they do not give SDs, it was necessary to reconstruct a table of values from their graphs.

Since this is the case, some doubt must remain as to the exactness of the present results. The categorization data of Lisker and Abramson (1970) of labial and apical synthetic VOT continua were selected as the corresponding perceptual data. Table 8.1 shows the means and SDs measured from this data. The identification rates were also reconstructed from the original graphs.

Direct estimates of the categorization functions from the production data

---

[6]Other possible generalizations of the NAPP model to allow for response bias parameters (which would serve as multipliers for each group's probability density) would also raise problems for unique estimation of assumed underlying production data distributions. However, it would still be possible to evaluate weaker hypotheses of compatibility between production measurements and categorization.

Table 8.1

Means and Standard Deviations (in msec) for Production Data VOT

	Labials			Apicals		
	/b/	/p/	/pʰ/	/d/	/t/	/tʰ/
Mean	− 105.8	6.4	59.4	− 84.4	6.1	60.6
SD	28.1	6.0	19.2	23.2	6.6	18.1
	Pooled SD = 17.7			Pooled SD = 17.0		

are instructive, if not too impressive. For the Thurstonian model, the estimates are obtained by substituting the estimated boundary points (midway between adjacent means) and SD into Equation 4. For the NAPP model, the three category means and the SD are substituted in Equations 2 and 3. Figure 8.4 shows the fit of the two models to the categorization data of the labials. Figure 8.5 shows the fit to the apicals. Some aspects of the apparent lack of fit are in accord with Lisker and Abramson's observations about the position of the gaps in the distributions vis-a-vis the categorization boundaries. In addition, in the case of the NAPP model, the steepness of the curves in the region of the boundaries is too great.

MEASURES OF ERROR AND OPTIMIZED MODELS

Quantitative measures of error (or lack of fit) are necessary for optimized parameter estimates. Such measures are easily defined for both Thurstonian and NAPP approaches. Perhaps the simplest is rms (root mean squared) deviation of observed and predicted values (in units of percent identification). However, the measure we have actually minimized in all optimizations is the likelihood ratio chi-squared, or G^2 (Fienberg 1980), which is widely used in goodness-of-fit tests for categorical data.[7] Values of both G^2 and rms deviations for the data of Figures 8.4 and 8.5 are given in the first two rows of Table 8.2. The *a priori* NAPP model fits are worse than the Thurstonian for both labials and apicals according to both error measures.

Figure 8.6 shows optimized (minimum G^2 fits to the labial data for the Thurstonian and NAPP models. Figure 8.7 shows analogous fits to the apical data. Slightly modified versions of the models were actually used in the fitting procedure. In preliminary fits using the unmodified models, the left tail of the /t/ response distribution (into negative VOT values in Figure 8.7)

---

[7]No standard statistical tests appear to be available either for goodness of fit or for comparing models for categorical data of this type pooled over listeners. For a discussion of some of the problems and some partial solutions, see Assmann, Nearey, and Hogan (1982). See also Bock (1975: 551–552) for a discussion of related statistical issues.

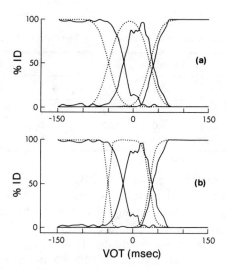

Figure 8.4 Observed categorizations (solid lines) and *a priori* predictions (dotted lines) for
Thai labials obtained by (a) the threshold Thurstonian model and (b) the NAPP model.

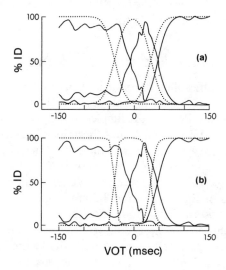

Figure 8.5 Observed categorizations (solid lines) and *a priori* predictions (dotted lines) for
Thai apicals obtained by (a) the threshold Thurstonian model and (b) the NAPP model.

appeared to have a large influence on the fit at the expense of the /d/–/t/
boundary. This effect was reduced by adding a term similar to the 'natural
responsiveness' factor of probit analysis (Finney 1971). It was assumed,
arbitrarily, that exactly 1% of the responses were random guesses, with each

Table 8.2
Summary of Goodness-of-Fit Statistics

Model	Labials			Apicals		
	G^2	df	rms (%)	G^2	df	rms (%)
A priori Thurstonian	1815.0	74	19.6	1971.9	74	19.6
A prior NAPP	3542.8	74	19.8	3538.8	74	23.1
Optimal Thurstonian	186.4	71	2.7	549.1	71	5.8
Optimal NAPP	149.4	70	2.7	311.2	70	6.2

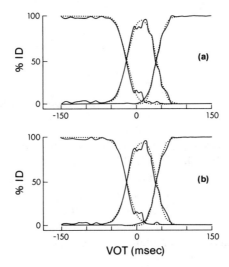

Figure 8.6 Observed categorizations (solid lines) and optimally fitted values (dotted lines) for Thai labials obtained by (a) the threshold Thurstonian model and (b) the NAPP model.

of the three phoneme responses equally likely. This natural responsiveness factor serves as a floor on the prediction of the probability of any cell and reduces the influence of cells with very low predicted values on G^2. Even so, the influence of the left tail of the /t/ curve is still noticeable for the NAPP model in Figure 8.7b. This figure also shows that the NAPP model is capable of generating asymmetrical shapes for the middle VOT categories. The Thurstonian model must produce a symmetrical shape for the /t/ responses. In Figure 8.7, the Thurstonian model appears to fit better in the /d/-/t/ boundary region, while the NAPP model fits better in the long /t/ tail. The tail of the observed curve does not appear to be typical of most categorization responses, and it is not clear what the correct modeling behavior should be.

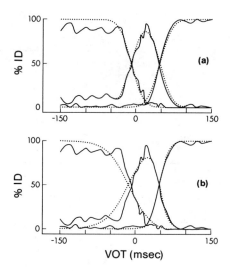

Figure 8.7 Observed categorizations (solid lines) and optimally fitted values (dotted lines) for Thai apicals obtained by (a) the threshold Thurstonian model and (b) the NAPP model.

The last two rows of Table 8.2 give the rms and G^2 values for the optimized model. For the labials, both models show essentially the same degree of fit on both measures. For the apicals, the Thurstonian model shows a smaller rms deviation, while the NAPP model shows a smaller G^2. The latter probably reflects the fact that errors for the low predicted values in the long /t/ tail have a greater influence on G^2 than on rms.

Table 8.3 presents optimal parameter estimates corresponding to the prediction curves in Figures 8.6 and 8.7. The corresponding statistics from the production data are included for comparison. The boundaries in both the production data and in the NAPP model are taken to be halfway between the means of adjacent categories. (Mean estimates cannot be calculated for the Thurstonian model.) The estimated boundary values for both the NAPP and Thurstonian models are generally quite similar and show systematic divergences from the production data. For both the labial and apical data, the voiced–voiceless boundary shows a value closer to zero than the corresponding production midpoints. Both also show values farther from zero than the production values in the case of the plain–aspirated boundary. The SDs are 5 to 13 msec higher for the NAPP model. For the Thurstonian model, the value is slightly lower for the labial data but higher for the apicals. The estimates of the mean in the case of the NAPP model are generally farther out of alignment from the production data than are the boundaries. It is encouraging to note, however, that the optimal values are at least within the range of the measured values.

Table 8.3

Comparison of Production Data Values and Optimal Estimates

	Mean voiced	Boundary voiced-voiceless	Mean voiceless	Boundary plain-apirated	Mean	SD
Labials						
observed natural	−105.8	(−49.7)	6.4	(32.9)	59.4	17.7
optimal Thurstonian	—	−17.9	—	41.2	—	15.8
optimal NAPP	−43.1	(−18.9)	5.2	(40.5)	75.8	22.8
Apicals						
observed natural	−84.4	(−39.2)	6.1	(33.3)	60.6	17.0
optimal Thurstonian	—	−14.9	—	50.8	—	27.8
optimal NAPP	−32.9	(−16.6)	−0.3	(47.6)	95.5	29.9

In some ways, it might be argued that we have learned no more than we already knew from the informal discussion of the graphic results by Lisker and Abramson. We would agree with the objection on the substantive issue of the production and perception of Thai stops. However, what we have done is to provide some specific models for relating production data to perception. The particular advantage of this approach becomes more evident when we consider briefly how the present models, especially the NAPP model, might be used as tools in broader research tasks.

FURTHER APPLICATION OF THE NAPP MODEL

Imagine that we wanted to explore the relevance of other phonetic variables to the perception of the phonological voicing distinctions in Thai. Suppose that we suspect that burst amplitude is relevant. In this case, the production of Thai stops in the VOT dimension and the burst amplitude dimension might be measured. If statistical analysis, say DFA, indicates that there is potentially useful information in the data to separate the groups, we might proceed to construct a stimulus continuum to present to listeners in order to ascertain the relevance of this pair of variables. It might also be possible to get some guidance in the construction of these stimuli by having listeners categorize the natural speech production tokens that were originally measured and comparing their categorizations to the statistical analysis along the lines sketched in this section. (It is also possible to pursue a mixed strategy in which one or more of the variables is manipulated artificially while the others are controlled for statistically; see Hogan and Rozsypal, 1980.)

Some preliminary efforts to apply NAPP principles to multivariate, multicategory data have led to encouraging results. As noted above, the NAPP model of identification has strong ties with DFA. In fact, the development of the NAPP model stems from our efforts to relate perceptual data to multivariate statistical analysis of natural data in connection with two M. Sc. theses completed in our department.

The first of these involves You's (1979) study of the spectra of English fricatives. DFA was performed on a filter-bank analysis of fricative segments gated from natural speech produced by three native speakers of Canadian English. Two repetitions by each subject for the fricatives /f, θ, s, ʃ, v, ð, z, ʒ/ were analyzed, each of the fricatives being followed by each of the four vowels /i, æ, ʌ, u/. Hence a total of 192 tokens were studied. The filter bank consisted of 32 adjacent (nonoverlapping) 250 Hz bins, covering the range 0–8000 Hz. (Amplitude values were normalized within each fricative segment by subtracting the maximum amplitude value over all the bins from each bin.) As a result of this analysis, the spectrum of each fricative was summarized by 32 numbers which were used as the independent variables in the DFA. The dependent variable was the group membership (phonemic class) of each of the spectra. This analysis resulted in 81% correct partition of the data using the four most significant eigenvectors. When two additional variables corresponding to overall amplitude and duration were included, about 87% correct partition resulted. Further analysis by You indicated that place-of-articulation differences could be even more accurately predicted if an overall adjustment for voicing were made. Inspection of the discriminant functions and some further statistical analyses gave indications of the spectrally important regions for the separation of various subsets of the fricatives. For the most part, these results were consistent with hypotheses from the literature. However, it was also found that the θ-f pair was also reasonably well distinguished statistically, though previous studies had shown their spectra to be highly similar.

Although this procedure indicated that there was adequate information in the spectra for the consonants to be distinguished statistically, the question remained whether the statistical analysis bore any resemblance to the processing of speech by human listeners. Therefore, You compared the statistical categorization of /θ-f/ to listeners' categorization of the same stimuli. The results revealed that frication segments totally isolated from vocalic context were also well identified by the listeners. (In fact, they were slightly better identified than were the identical fricative segments in their original vowel context!) To see if there was a more detailed correspondence between the listeners and the statistical analysis, You examined the behavior of the 19 tokens identified by listeners with less than 90% accuracy. (There were a total of 48 tokens in the set used in this perceptual study.) Five of six tokens misidentified by the statistical procedure were among those 19 which gave listeners some difficulty. Furthermore, 10 other of the worst perceptual tokens were correctly identified by the DFA but had relatively low APP values for the correct group. Only four of the items in this worst-token list had high (near 1.0) APP values for the intended category. Thus it appeared that the statistical identification procedure had at least some parallels to perception in its treatment of individual tokens.

A more direct comparison of the results of DFA and listeners' categorizations of the same set of natural speech data is presented by Assmann (1979). Assmann studied listeners' categorization of 100 msec segments gated from 10 vowels spoken by 5 male and 5 female Canadian English speakers. Measurements of the fundamental frequencies and the first four formants of these same stimuli were obtained. Assmann compared a number of DFAs involving different combinations of these measurements. He found significant correlations (though generally small, r ranging from about .3 to .5) between APP scores for the intended group and identification rates for listeners. Inspection of scatterplots (not reported by Assmann) of the cases of highest correlation indicated that nearly all of the tokens poorly identified by listeners showed low correct APP scores and most of the items with high APP scores were well identified by listeners. However, listeners also showed high identification rates on some of the tokens that showed relatively low APP scores. This might mean that listeners were, at least in these cases, attending to aspects of the signal that had not been measured. Further study of such tokens might reveal the relevance of other signal parameters. A more detailed analysis of this data using NAPP models is presented in Assmann, Nearey, and Hogan (1982).

In general, we find these tentative results, which can be related to the NAPP classification model, to be quite encouraging. Further experimentation involving some of the relatively better-understood phonetic phenomona are in order to better test the suitability of the model.

CONCLUSION

We have presented two models that appear to account for the warping of listeners' perceptual space given different language-specific production data. One of these, the NAPP model, is readily generalizable to multivariate, multicategory data. It provides a convenient theoretical framework for the comparision of measurements of production data with listeners' categorizations of speech-signal continua.

REFERENCES

Abramson, A. & L. Lisker. 1970. Discriminability along the voicing continuum: Cross-language tests. In B. Hala, M. Romportl, and P. Janota, eds., *Proceedings of the 6th International Congress of Phonetic Sciences*, 569–573. Prague: Academia Publishing House of the Czechoslovak Academy of Sciences.

Assmann, P. F. 1979. The role of context in vowel perception. M.Sc. thesis, University of Alberta.

Assmann, P. F., T. Nearey, & J. Hogan. 1982. Vowel identification: Orthographic, perceptual and acoustic aspects. *Journal of the Acoustical Society of America* 71:975–989.

Baird, J., & E. Noma. 1978. *Fundamentals of scaling and psychophysics*. New York: Wiley.

Bishop, Y., S. Fienberg, & P. Holland. 1975. *Discrete multivariate analysis: Theory and practice*. Cambridge, MA: MIT Press.

Bock, R. D. 1975. *Multivariate statistical methods in behavioral research*. New York: McGraw-Hill.

Elman, J. 1979. Perceptual origins of the phoneme boundary effect and selective adaptation of speech: A signal detection approach. *Journal of the Acoustical Society of America* 65: 190-207.

Fienberg, S. 1980. *The analysis of cross-classified data*. (2nd ed.). Cambridge, MA: MIT Press.

Finney, D. J. 1971. *Probit analysis* (3rd ed.). Cambridge: Cambridge University Press.

Fukunaga, K. 1972. *Introduction to statistical pattern recognition*. New York: Academic Press.

Green, D. M., & J. A. Swets. 1966. *Signal detection theory and psychophysics*. New York: Wiley.

Hogan, J., & A. Rozsypal. 1980. Evaluation of vowel duration as a cue for the voicing distinction in the following word final consonant. *Journal of the Acoustical Society of America* 67:1764-1771.

Lachenbruch, P. A. 1975. *Discriminant analysis*. New York: Haffner.

Lee, W. 1963. Choosing among confusably distributed stimuli with specified likelihood ratios. *Perceptual and Motor Skills* 16:445-467.

Lisker, L. & A. Abramson. 1964. A cross-language study of voicing in initial stops: Acoustical measurements. *Word* 20:384-422.

Lisker, L., & A. Abramson. 1970. The voicing dimension: Some experiments in comparative phonetics. In B. Hala, M. Romportl, & P. Janota, eds., *Proceedings of the 6th International Congress of Phonetic Sciences*, 563-567. Prague: Academia Publishing House of the Czechoslovak Academy of Sciences.

Massaro, D. & G. Oden. 1980. Evaluation and integration of acoustic features in speech. *Journal of the Acoustical Society of America* 67:996-1013.

Oden, G. & D. Massaro. 1978. Integration of featural information in speech perception. *Psychological Review* 85:172-191.

Sapir, E. 1933. La réalité psychologique des phonèmes. *Journal de Psychologie Normale et Pathologique* 30:247-265.

Stevenson, D. 1979. Categorical perception in speech. Ph.D. diss., University of Alberta.

Thurstone, L. 1927. A law of comparative judgment. *Psychological Review* 34:273-286.

You, H-Y. 1979. An acoustic and perceptual study of English fricatives. M.Sc. thesis, University of Alberta.

9

Testing Phonology in the Field

LYLE CAMPBELL

INTRODUCTION

In this chapter I consider some ways of testing phonology—both as an aspect of individual grammars and with regard to theoretical claims—with empirical evidence that can be obtained in linguistic field work. Specifically, I discuss strategies for testing psychological reality. At the outset, the research program established in the mid-1950s by generative phonology (henceforth GP) and followed by most practitioners of phonology since then is briefly reviewed. This is followed by cases illustrating how psychological reality can be tested. Finally, recommendations for future research are presented, and certain general questions concerning the research program suggested here are anticipated.

THE GP PROGRAM

In GP, explanation has been bound closely to the notion 'linguistically significant generalization' (i.e., the kind of generalization children make in learning language). The notation used by GP for the representation of linguistic constructs and processes was designed to permit the degree of generality of the representation to be inversely related to the length of the notation. Notational length is the formal measure of simplicity, and simplicity along with psychological reality are the two criteria used to evaluate linguistic

163

descriptions. A proposed generalization (or rule), notational device, or even an evaluation metric can be shown to be false by confronting it with empirical evidence relating to the actual grammar underlying speakers' competence. In principle there is nothing wrong with this program. In practice, however, little attention has been paid to psychological reality; rather, it is assumed that the child language learner is somehow constrained to acquire the simplest possible grammar. Then, by inference, the simplest grammar the linguist can write is assumed to be psychologically real. That is, arguments based on formal simplicity alone are considered sufficient (since the formal notational devices are supposedly designed to allow only true generalizations about language, the kind the child language learner would make). It is clear, however, that children at times fail to make the simplest generalizations as predicted by the notation of GP (see, e.g., Kiparsky 1971; Hale 1973; Campbell 1974). Thus is is clear that considerations of formal simplicity alone are not enough.

Questions about psychological reality (and learnability), then, cannot be answered solely through considerations of surface patterns, distribution of allomorphs, and combinatory properties of phonological elements within a linguistic system. The real question is: How can linguists be certain that the rules they write to account for the phonological patterns they perceive in their data correspond to the rules that the speakers of the language establish? There are at present no successful formal criteria which determine for a given set of linguistic data what the speakers' rules may be. Rather, we must seriously seek answers to such questions as (1) How different from the surface may underlying forms be and still be learned by speakers? (2) In how many forms must a rule be manifested before speakers learn the rule rather than the variant forms in an item-by-item way? (3) How do such factors as exceptions, nonproductivity, non-phonetic conditioning, and opacity affect the learnability of rules and underlying forms? (4) Just how good are language learners at linguistic analysis (especially at internal reconstruction, which is essentially the basis of much of GP's method of analysis)? To answer questions such as these we need tests for the psychological reality of our linguistic descriptions.

We need sources of "external evidence", that is, evidence not confined to surface-pattern regularities, but evidence showing speakers behaving linguistically in ways where they must call upon their knowledge of the rules and underlying forms of their language in overt and revealing ways. Some sources of external evidence that have been employed with some success are metrics and verse, word games (secret languages, disguised speech), experiments, borrowing, speech errors, orthography construction, and language change. My main goal in this paper is to describe some promising cases of external evidence that I have encountered in doing fieldwork. I consider first some cases that show the reality of aspects of individual language descriptions and then cases which have implications for larger theoretical claims.

EXTERNAL EVIDENCE

Evidence for Language-Specific Claims

K'EKCHI *JERIGONZA*

The first case is from a K'ekchi word game called *Jerigonza* (for details see Campbell 1974). Evidence from this secret language shows several rules of K'ekchi (a Mayan language of Guatemala) to be psychologically real. In *Jerigonza* a /p/ is placed after each vowel and then followed by a copy of that vowel. For example, /q'eqtʃiʔ/ 'K'ekchi' (the name of the language) in *Jerigonza* is /q'epeqtʃipiʔ/.

The rule of vowel epenthesis, to take just one example, is shown to be real by *Jerigonza*. The rule, which is obligatory in normal speech but optional in *Jerigonza*, is given in (1) with examples of its application in (2).

(1) $\emptyset \phi \rightarrow V_2 / V_1 C\_\_\_\{m, \beta\}; V_2 = V_1$

(2) /kwiq'-ɓa:nk/   [kwiq'iɓa:ŋk]   'to bend'
     /pets-ɓa:nk/   [petseɓa:ŋk]   'to sit on the ground'

Some examples of this rule in *Jerigonza* are given in (3) (where " > " henceforth is to be read as "is transformed by the word game into").

(3) /kwiq'iɓa:nk/   'to bend'   >   /kwipiq'ɓapa:nk/ or
                                     /kwipiq'ipiɓapa:nk/
     /k'uluɓa:nk/   'to accept'   >   /k'upulɓapa:nk/ or
                                     /k'upulupuɓapa:nk/
     /pereɓa:nk/   'to set'   >   /peperɓapa:nk/ or
                                     /peperepeɓapa:nk/

The rule of vowel epenthesis is psychologically real, since speakers leave out (optionally) only those vowels which are from epenthesis, never those which are lexically specified.

FINNISH WORD GAMES

Finnish has several secret languages. *Kontin kieli* (or *kontti kieli*) 'knapsack language' is one which shows the reality of several Finnish rules (for details, see Campbell 1977, 1980, 1981). The essential aspects of *kontin kieli* are that the first consonant(s) and vowel of a word are replaced by *ko* (of *kontti*), and the material for which *ko* is substituted is placed before *ntti* (of *kontti*). Examples are given in (4).

(4) *veitsi* 'knife' > *koitsi ventti*
     susi   'wolf'   > *kosi suntti*

Finnish vowel harmony is shown to be psychologically real in this language game, since vowel harmony adjusts the remaining vowels of the word to agree with the newly substituted *ko*. The harmonic series are back *a, o, u*; front *ä* ([æ]), *ö* ([ø]), *y*; and neutral *i, e*. Some examples of how vowels are modified by vowel harmony when words are transformed in *kontin kieli* are given in (5).

(5) *pysähtyköön* 'let him stop'   > *kosahtukoon pyntti*
     kylpylöissä 'in the baths'   > *kopuloissa kyntti*
     täynnä   'full'   > *kounna täntti*

Vowel harmony is a psychologically real rule of Finnish, then, since speakers adjust vowel harmony correctly when they produce words with *kontin kieli*.

It cannot be argued, incidentally, that vowel harmony is merely some kind of phonetic constraint and not a real rule that speakers know, since words that violate vowel harmony otherwise also violate vowel harmony in *kontin kieli*, as shown by the examples in (6).

(6) *jonglööri*   'juggler'   > *konglööri jontti*
     hydrosfääri 'hydrosphere'   > *kodrosfääri hyntti*
     manööveri   'maneuver'   > *konööveri mantti*

Kontin kieli also shows several other rules of Finnish to be real, for example, the rules involving diphthongs. In *kontin kieli* when *ko* is substituted for the first consonant(s) and a long vowel, the indication of length is retained on *ko*, as exemplified in (7).

(7) *maahan* 'land' (illative sg.) > *koohan mantti*

Finnish has three kinds of diphthongs: underlying diphthongs, diphthongs derived from long mid vowels, and diphthongs derived from loss of an intervocalic consonant. These are exemplified in (8).

(8) underlying diphthongs: *aika*   'time'
                                             keula   'bow (prow)'
                                             täynnä 'full'
                                             veitsi 'knife'
     diphthongs from long mid vowels: *lyödä* 'to hit'
                                             suo   'swamp'
                                             viedä   'to bring'

derived diphthongs: *hien* 'sweat' (gen. sg.; cf. *hiki* nom. sg.)

ien 'gums' (cf. *ikenen*, gen. sg.)

ies 'yoke' (cf. *ike(h)en*, gen. sg.)

ruon 'haycock' (gen. sg.; cf. *ruko*, nom. sg.)

The treatment of these different kinds of diphthongs in *kontin kieli* provides evidence for the reality of certain other Finnish rules.

First, the underlying diphthongs are treated as expected by the regular rules of *kontin kieli*, where /ko/ is substituted for the first consonant(s) and vowel, leaving the second vowel (or vocoid) in place, as shown in (9).

(9) *keula* > *koula kentti* 'bow (prow)'
    nousta > *kousta nontti* 'to rise'
    auttoi > *kouttoi antti* '(he) helped'
    aika > *koika antti* 'time'
    täynnä > *kounna täntti* 'full'
    löytää > *koutaa löntti* 'to find'

However, diphthongs derived from long mid vowels are treated like long vowels, with length retained on the substituted /ko/, as shown in (10).

(10) *kieli* > *kooli kientti* 'tongue'
    tiellä > *koolla tientti* 'on the road'
    tyossa > *koossa tuontti* 'in that'
    vyötää > *koottaa vyöntti* 'to gird (belt)'

Since short vowels and underlying diphthongs never take /koo/, showing vowel length, this suggests that the rule relating these diphthongs to long mid vowels in Finnish is real for speakers.

The interpretation of these diphthongs as underlying long mid vowels is supported further by *kontin kieli's* treatment of the derived diphthongs (from loss of medial consonants). Some derived diphthongs are not phonetically distinct from the diphthongs which come from underlying long vowels (just discussed), but are treated distinctly in *kontin kieli*, not as long vowels but as sequences of short vowels, as shown in (11).

(11) *hiessä* > *koessa hintti* 'sweaty' (from /hike-/), not **koossa hientti*
    ien > *koen intti* 'gums' (from /ikene-/), not **koos ientti*
    ies > *koes intti* 'yoke' (from /ikese-/), not **koos ientti*
    piellä > *koella pintti* 'on the beach' (from /pike-/), not **koolla pientti*

Were these treated like the phonetically identical diphthongs from long vowels we would expect, for example, *koossa hientti 'sweaty,' which does not occur. This evidence helps to confirm the rule deriving diphthongs from underlying long mid vowels; moreover, it suggests the reality of the rule which produces these derived diphthongs by deletion of certain intervocalic consonants. That is, to produce the correct kontin kieli forms, one must know whether a diphthong such as ie on the surface comes from ee (treated as long vowel) or from ike (where k is lost in the weak grade of consonant gradation and the form is treated as a sequence of two vowels).

Kontin kieli is not the only Finnish word game which confirms these and other phonological rules. In another Finnish secret language, the first consonant(s) and vowel of each succeeding pair of words are interchanged; in this game vowel harmony is also adjusted to accomodate the new first vowel, as shown in (12).

(12) Saksalaisia hätyytettiin   >   häksäläisiä satuutettiin 'the Germans were attacked'
      Ruotsalaisia hätyytettiin   >   hätsäläisiä ruotuutettiin 'the Swedes were attacked'
      kenkänsä polki   >   ponkansa kelki 'his shoe kicked'

The word game also distinguishes the different kinds of diphthongs, as shown in (13).

(13) kieli päässä   >   pääli kiessä 'tongue in head' (underlying long mid vowel)
      otsansa hiessä   >   hitsansa oessa 'in the sweat of his brow' (from /hike-/, derived diphthong; not *hietsansa ossa)
      ruon takana   >   taon rukana 'behind the haycock' (from /ruko-/)

Thus this game also supports the reality of the vowel-harmony rule and the rules involving diphthongs.

External Evidence and Linguistic Theory

In these examples we have seen how external evidence shows the reality of aspects of individual grammars. However, external evidence may often have implications for testing larger theoretical claims as well. I present just one example here, also involving K'ekchi.

In Coban, Guatemala, most speakers are bilingual in K'ekchi and Spanish. Consultants were presented a list of loan words, some from Spanish into K'ekchi and some from K'ekchi into local Spanish. They were asked to judge whether they thought the forms were borrowed and, if so, which they thought was the original language. Judgments were based on several parameters (cultural expectations, semantics, and phonology). The parameters were determined by asking the consultants why they thought particular loans originated from one or the other of the two languages. Reasons volunteered by these consultants involved, among other things, native views of morpheme structure in the two languages. For example, consultants said /pio:tʃ/ 'pickax' (from Spanish *piocha*), /tʃilte:p/ 'small chile' (from Spanish *chiltepe*), and similar forms were from Spanish because, they reported, K'ekchi does not have those kinds of sounds together (referring to the vowel-vowel and consonant-consonant clusters). In fact, K'ekchi does have such clusters, but only across morpheme boundaries, for example, /ke-ok/ 'get cold' (/ke/ 'cold' plus a verbal suffix), but never within a morpheme. These judgments are a very good verbalization of K'ekchi morpheme structure conditions. This shows, then, that these morpheme structure conditions of K'ekchi are psychologically real, since speakers actively call upon them in making judgments about the origin of lexical items (see Campbell 1974, 1976 for further details).

To be sure, this evidence helps validate aspects of K'ekchi grammar, namely its morpheme structure conditions. Perhaps more importantly, however, this external evidence has implications for theoretical claims. It shows that morpheme structure rules can be psychologically real, and this fact cannot be accounted for by syllable structure rules alone, as proposed in Natural Generative Phonology (Hooper 1975). The evidence does not indicate that speakers have no knowledge of syllables, but that with only knowledge of syllable structure and no knowledge of morpheme structure conditions they would be unable to distinguish these borrowed forms which have no morpheme boundaries breaking up such clusters from native forms which do. Thus any theory which claims that morpheme structure conditions are not needed is unable to account for these facts directly.

RECOMMENDATIONS

External evidence found in fieldwork is often largely a matter of chance. It is like a naturally occurring experiment (e.g., solar eclipses in astronomy); if it is found, the linguist takes full advantage of it, but too frequently no such external evidence occurs. A proper procedure in such cases might be just to describe the language as best one can using internal evidence, perhaps hoping that the future may produce some additional (external) evidence to support such a description. Another procedure, however, might be more rewarding and satisfactory. One might help nature along by contriving some experiments which give added external evidence. For example, one may teach language consultants word games that are not currently known to them (as Hombert, this volume, has done). These introduced games may produce evidence just as valid as that derived from the language games the investigator may have had the good fortune to find already existing in the culture. This introduction of games by the investigator should not raise any objections, since word games are often borrowed from other languages anyway. K'ekchi *Jerigonza*, as described above, is no doubt taken originally from a similar Spanish game which uses either *p* or *f*. The Finnish word game which interchanges the first consonant(s) and vowel of succeeding pairs of words is very similar to a Danish word game which interchanges the consonants before the first vowel of succeeding pairs of words. Some of the word games used by the Cuna Indians of Panama are also taken from Spanish (Sherzer 1970). Thus, there is nothing particularly unnatural about the linguistic investigator becoming the agent for introducing new word games. The important thing is not where the games come from but what they show about the speakers' knowledge of their language.

Another way the investigator may intervene to induce means of obtaining more external evidence is to train consultants in the basic principles and methods of linguistic analysis (but not in details of analysis for their own language or closely related languages) and then to examine the kinds of analyses they produce. These native analyses do not always coincide with the linguist's expectations. For example, for K'ekchi the traditional generative phonologist would postulate as a rule of final-consonant-cluster simplification.

(14) $C \rightarrow \emptyset$ / C___#

Such a rule would account for examples such as those in (15).

(15)   *kaɓl-ak*   'to make a house'   *kaɓ*   'house'
        naxt-i:nk   'to go far'   *nax*   'far'
        ts'axn-ok   'to get dirty'   *ts'ax*   'dirty'
        molɓ-ek   'to lay eggs'   *mol*   'egg'
        r-ism-al   'his pubic hair'   *is*   'pubic hair'

However, K'ekchi speakers appear not to have acquired this rule but rather to have learned the related forms piecemeal. Consultants trained in morphological analysis were asked to segment these K'ekchi forms into component morphemes. Given, for example, /molɓek/ (the linguist's /molɓ + ek/) and /ts'axnok/ (/ts'axn + ok/), they segmented these as /mol + ɓek/ and /ts'ax + nok/. When reminded that (according to their training) morphemes are recurrent partials that recur with the same meaning in other cases, they replied that /-ɓek/ and /-nok/, were morphemes that occur only once (i.e., they characterized these as "cranberry" morphs). When prompted with the recurrence of /-ek/ and /-ok/ as morphemes in other cases, some responded that the morpheme divisions must then be /mol + 6 + ek/ and /ts'ax + n + ok/ and had no idea what the posited morphemes /-6-/ and /-n-/ might mean. Finally, when asked directly if /6/ and /n/ could be part of the root morphemes, they responded with certainty that they could not be. This suggests that for K'ekchi speakers the rule of consonant-cluster simplification is probably not psychologically real. Other investigators have had similar experiences in working with linguistically trained consultants in other Mayan languages.

A procedure for obtaining additional external evidence in some cases, then, might be to train consultants in linguistic analysis with clear cases, and then to consider the analyses they produce with less clear cases which have implications for important phonological rules. This is, in fact, the strategy behind the 'concept formation' technique used in the psycholinguistic studies described by Jaeger (this volume). In all such methods, including word games, speakers' performance is based on their knowledge of the structure of their language.

Another kind of intervention involves instruction in use of or construction of orthography (for a classic case, see Sapir 1949). Interesting results sometimes emerge when previously illiterate speakers are taught to write. Often their rendering of less clear forms (for which they have had no direct instruction) has strong implications for the psychological reality of aspects of their language.

If new evidence may be obtained through the instruction of native speakers in words games, linguistic analysis, orthography, and the like, then perhaps with some brainstorming and a little imagination many other ways can be found to enlarge the store of evidence from fieldwork.

QUESTIONS

Some questions about external evidence in phonology should be anticipated. First, is there really a distinction between internal and external evidence? I believe that in most cases the distinction is entirely clear, though naturally the distinction depends on one's definitions. Opinions vary widely. I hold external evidence to be that obtained from situations where speakers must call upon their knowledge of their language(s) in overt and revealing ways, cases where the productive or active employment of this knowledge yields information not normally considered in the corpus of material upon which linguistic descriptions are typically based. The important thing is not to achieve some exact definition but to find evidence with direct implications for the psychological reality of linguistic descriptions.

Perhaps ultimately there should be no firm distinction between external and internal evidence. Given our current state of knowledge, however, there are no formal principles that guarantee descriptions which correlate with the way language is represented in the mind of the speaker. As we obtain more and more cases of such evidence, it should become possible to begin to formulate more reliable principles which will approach psychological reality without necessarily requiring testing in each case. At that stage perhaps a distinction between external and internal evidence will not be so crucial. The distinction, however, is necessary when we are dealing—as at the present time—with uncertain proposals.

Another question is, what is to be done when the interpretation of some external evidence is not clear? Some have complained that a few scholars, in their zeal to obtain external evidence, have interpreted their data incorrectly. The interpretation problem is not limited, of course, to the quest for external evidence but is rather a problem of all scientific investigation. Bad practice does not mean that the entire enterprise is misguided. One poorly made cabinet should not lead us to conclude that all cabinetmaking is of no value. Moreover, if some data are hard to interpret, that should not make us think less of the clear and revealing cases. It is to be expected in any scholarly endeavor that some things lend themselves more readily to unambiguous interpretation than others. The important thing here is that the clearly helpful cases far outweigh those that may be more controversial.

Related to this is another question: what about cases of conflicting external evidence, where different kinds of such evidence suggest different and conflicting analyses? Again, this is a problem that all scientific investigations face. Ultimately we believe that all valid evidence must not conflict. The resolution may involve the discovery that some of the data are unreliable, that they have been misinterpreted, or that we are asking the wrong question (witness the wave vs. particle conflict in the conceptualization of the nature of electromagnetic energy). Thus there should ultimately be no cases of conflicting external evidence, rather only cases of bad data, bad practice, and bad theory. Fortunately, these are problems science has shown itself able to solve, given enough time.

CONCLUSION

I urge that more serious attention be given to the criteria used to declare phonological constructs and processes psychologically real. I have emphasized the use of external evidence and have presented cases to illustrate its value for validating both aspects of individual language descriptions and for testing larger theoretical claims. Finally, I have suggested several ways in which more abundant external evidence might be obtained in the field.

REFERENCES

Campbell, L. 1974. Theoretical implications of Kekchi phonology. *International Journal of American Linguistics* 40:269–278.

Campbell, L. 1976. Kekchi linguistic acculturation: Cognitive approach. In M. McClaran, ed., *Mayan Linguistics*, Vol. 1, 90–99. UCLA: American Indian Studies Center.

Campbell, L. 1977. Generative phonology versus Finnish phonology: Retrospect and prospect. In R. Harms & F. Karttunen, eds., *Texas Linguistic Forum*, Vol. 5, 21–58. Austin: University of Texas.

Campbell, L. 1980. The psychological and sociological reality of Finnish vowel harmony. In R. Vago, ed., *Issues in vowel harmony*, 245–270. Amsterdam: John Benjamins.

Campbell, L. 1981. Generative phonology and Finnish, theoretical contributions. In D. L. Goyvaerts, ed., *Phonology in the 1980's*, 147–182. Ghent: E. Story Scientia.

Hale, K. 1973. Deep-surface canonical disparities in relation to analysis and change: An Australian example. In T. Sebeok, ed., *Current trends in linguistics, Vol. 11: Diachronic, areal, and typological linguistics*, 401–458. The Hague: Mouton.

Hooper, J. 1975. The archisegment in natural generative phonology. *Language* 51:536–560.

Kiparsky, P. 1971. Historical linguistics. In W. O. Dingwall, ed., *A survey of linguistic science*, 576–649. College Park: University of Maryland.

Sapir, E. 1949. The psychological reality of phonemes. In D. Mandelbaum, ed., *Selected writings of Edward Sapir*, 46–60. Berkeley: University of California Press.

Sherzer, J. 1970. Talking backwards in Cuna: The sociological reality of phonological descriptions. *Southwest Journal of Anthropology* 26:343–353.

10

Word Games: Some Implications for Analysis of Tone and Other Phonological Constructs

JEAN-MARIE HOMBERT

INTRODUCTION

Word games have always been of interest to linguists because they represent an unusual sociocultural use of language. Nevertheless, from the very first articles on this phenomenon it has been recognized that word games can also assist the linguist in the task of discovering the structure of the language using them (see, e.g., Chao 1931, 1934; Conklin 1956, 1959; Haas 1957, 1969; Halle 1962; Burling 1970; Sherzer 1970, 1976; Bamgbose 1970; Laycock 1972; Hombert 1973; Surintramont 1973; Price & Price 1976). This latter aspect of word games received renewed attention in the late 1960s due to the greater interest in "psychologically real" accounts of language structure (Chomsky & Halle 1968, p. viii).

In this chapter I discuss some cases where word games can shed light on problems of phonological description, especially as these involve the issue of whether tone should be given a segmental or suprasegmental representation.[1] The possibility of inventing word games where none previously

[1]This is an expanded and completely revised version of papers presented in 1973 at the Summer Linguistics Conference at University of California, Santa Cruz, and at the December Linguistic Society of America Annual Meeting in San Diego. Some of the data were also discussed in Hombert (1973).

175

existed, that is, using them to perform what might be considered controlled experiments, is also discussed as well as potential limitations of the data yielded by them.

WORD GAMES AND THE ANALYSIS
OF SEGMENTS AND SYLLABICITY

In this section I illustrate the use of a naturally occurring word game in Bakwiri (a Bantu language, Duala group, Guthrie's A. 22), a language spoken on the southern slopes of Mount Cameroun. The game consists of inverting the position of the two syllables in disyllabic words.

Syllable Structure

CANONICAL FORMS OF SYLLABLES

Word games can help to define the canonical syllable structure used by a language. Given words of the sort in (1), one might wonder whether they should be syllabified as in the third or the fourth columns (where '$' indicates syllable boundary).[2]

(1) a. *mɔkɔ* 'plantain' *mɔ$kɔ*   or   *mɔk$ɔ*
     b. *iŋɔ*   'throat'   *i$ŋɔ*   or   *iŋ$ɔ*

These words are transformed by the word game as shown in (2).

(2) a. *mɔkɔ*   >   *kɔmɔ*
     b. *iŋɔ*   >   *ŋɔʔi*

Considering these data, the Bakwiri syllable structure should be analyzed as (C)V or, as seen later, (C)V(V). Of course, this conclusion is based on the assumption that it is the syllables that are manipulated by the word game. If we do not make this assumption, we can at least conclude that (C)V sequences form some kind of psychologically accessible chunk in the language.

It is interesting to notice the appearance of the glottal stop in *ŋɔʔi*. In Bakwiri, glottal stops occur only before a vowel in word-initial position such that the phonetic form of the original is [ʔiŋɔ]. These may escape the notice of the fieldworker whose native language makes glottal stops nonphonemic in this position, but they become obvious when the syllables are reversed in

---

[2]In this chapter the phonetic transcription follows the conventions of the International Phonetic Association. Tone is marked in three ways: with diacritics [´ ` ^ ˇ ¯] (signifying high, low, falling, rising, and mid tones, respectively); with the Chao tone letters (Chao 1930); and, where these prove inadequate, with parametric drawings of the pitch curve enclosed in square brackets. > is to be read "is transformed by the word game into."

the word game—yet another one of its uses for the phonologist. (This analysis is complicated by the fact that although the sequence [ɔí] does occur in the language, like other VV sequences, even with dissimilar V's, it seems to constitute a single syllable, as discussed below. Thus the glottal stop between the vowels in the transformed version might serve to preserve the disyllabic character of the word and as such could be inserted rather than lexical.)

THE ANALYSIS OF CLUSTERS

The only consonant clusters occurring in Bakwiri consist of nasals followed by homorganic voiced stops. This restricted distribution suggests that these clusters are phonological units. Their behavior in the word game confirms this analysis as shown in (3), where they are not broken up.

(3) a. *kómbà*   >   *mbákò*   'to take care of'
     b. *kóndì*   >   *ndíkò*   'rice'
     c. *záŋgò*   >   *ŋgózà*   'father'

Glides

One of the problems in the analysis of Bakwiri is establishing whether words such as those in (4) contain intervocalic glides or not.

(4) a. *lìjé*   or   *lìé*   'stone'
     b. *lówá*   or   *lóá*   'excrement'
     c. *tèjí*   or   *tèí*   'small'
     d. *mbówà*   or   *mbóà*   'village'

Phonetically, some sort of glide is present in all cases but one could argue that they are purely surface-level phenomena, that is, an automatic transition element: [j] after front vowels and [w] after back vowels. The word game provides a way to decide this issue, as shown in (5). Since the glide shows up in the transformation of (5a) and (5b), it is presumably not simply a surface-level element but is present at a deeper level.

(5) a. *lìjé*   >   *jèlí*
     b. *lówá*   >   *wáló*
     c. *tèjí*   >   *tèjí*
     d. *mbówà*   >   *mbówà*

On the other hand, the fact that (5c) and (5d) fail to undergo any transformation suggests that they are monosyllabic and that the glides that are heard are indeed transition elements. (Other phonological data reinforce this analysis. For example, the plural form of (5a) is [màjé] where the glide appears in a form and in an environment where it is less likely to be confused as a transitional element.)

Vowel Length

When a Bakwiri word with a long vowel is transformed by the word game, a curious thing happens, as shown in (6): The length is not transposed; it remains in the same place, even if it falls on different vowel quality.

(6)   a.   *lùùŋgá*   >   *ŋgàà́lú*   'stomach'
      b.   *zééjá*   >   *jáázé*   'burn'
      c.   *é zèè*   >   *zéʔèè*   'it is not'

When a long or double vowel is formed by two different vowels, the native speaker was sometimes unable to apply the word game but in other cases gave forms such as that in (7), where the double vowels do move but still leave length behind.

(7)   *lìòβá*   >   *βàà̀líó*   'door'

The problem encountered by the native speaker in such cases can have two origins. Either it can be a difficulty in replacing a sequence of two different vowels by a sequence of two identical vowels, or, more probably, the speaker feels he is violating the length pattern of the word by putting a double vowel in a position where there was a single vowel before the transformation. These data seem to suggest that in Bakwiri the length pattern is a property of the whole word and consequently is not dependent on the segment(s) to which it is originally assigned. The same kind of pattern is reported by Conklin (1956, 1959) for word games in Tagalog and Hanunóo as shown in (8a) and and (8b), respectively, and in Sanga (8c) as reported by Coupez (1969).

(8)   a.   *dooti*   >   *diito*
      b.   *buuŋa*   >   *ŋaabu*
      c.   *nkàɔ́mbɔ̀*   >   *mbɔ̀ɔ́nkà*

TONE

The Segmental or Suprasegmental Status of Tone

An issue which has been hotly debated in modern phonological literature on tone is whether tone should be represented as a segmental or suprasegmental entity. Schachter and Fromkin (1968), Maddieson (1971), Fromkin (1972), and Woo (1972) argue for segmental representation. Pike (1948) and McCawley (1970, 1978) view the syllable as the domain of tone. Welmers (1962) claims that tone should be regarded as a feature of the morpheme in Kpelle. Edmondson and Bendor-Samuel (1966) present evidence for regarding the phonological word as the tone-bearing unit in Etung. More recent studies on a number of languages, generally African, have presented the same view: Elimelech (1974) on Kru; Leben (1973) on Mende, Bambara, Maninka, and Hausa; Mazaudon (1972) on Tamang (a language of Nepal); and Goldsmith (1976) on Igbo. (See also Anderson 1978; Leben 1978; Goldsmith 1979.)

One argument for tone as a feature of the word in some of these languages is that the shape of the attested tone patterns is not dependent on the number of vowels or syllables a word has. For example, (9) exemplifies the entire inventory of tone patterns for monosyllabic and disyllabic words in Kru. Quite transparently, the disyllabic tone patterns are just expanded versions of the permissible tone patterns for monosyllabic words.[3]

(9) Monosyllabic   Disyllabic

    a.   *bá* [⎺]   'pepper'   *númó* [⎺ ⎺]   'wine'

    b.   *kɔ̀* [__]   'rice'   *tàpὲ* [__ __]   'cup'

    c.   *jǔ* [⁓]   'child'   *kélĕ* [— ⁓]   'inside'

    d.   *sû* [⁓]   'chicken'   *kítâ* [— ⁓]   'coconut'

That is, there are just four tone patterns, and these are mapped onto the phonological word as the tone-bearing units permit.

The Behavior of Tone in Bakwiri Word Games

As the reader has no doubt already noticed from many of the examples cited, the tone pattern of disyllabic words in Bakwiri is not affected by the word game transformation. These patterns are shown in a systematic fashion in (10).

(10)   a. *mɔ̀kɔ̀*   >   *kɔ̀mɔ̀*   'plantain'

      b. *kʷélí*   >   *líkʷé*   'death'

      c. *mɔ̀kɔ́*   >   *kɔ̀mɔ́*   'one person'

      d. *kʷélì*   >   *líkʷὲ*   'falling'

As was true for the length pattern of words, speakers abstract the tone pattern as a property of the whole word, that is, without a particular tone being attached to a particular syllable or segment. This suggests that in Bakwiri tone is a suprasegmental feature.

It is interesting to note that in Thai and Burmese word games, reported by Haas (1969), the above pattern does not occur. In word games which consist of interchanging the finals (or 'rhyme') or two successive syllables, the tones move with the transposed segments, as shown in (11a) for Thai and (11b) for Burmese, respectively.[4]

---

[3]This is not the case for all Kru dialects (W. Welmers, personal communication).

[4]According to J. Gandour (personal communication), dialect-specific and even speaker-specific variation occurs with respect to treatment of tone in the Thai word game.

(11) a. *kôn jàj*   >   *kàj jôn*   'big bottom'
     b. *mí bòw*   >   *mòw bí*   'fire place'

This suggests that in these languages tone may best be analyzed as a segmental feature.

Invented Word Games

In order to explore further this difference between speakers of different tone languages in their ability (or readiness) to separate tone from the syllable and segments on which it is normally realized, I attempted to use the same word-game technique with speakers of other tone languages. Since other linguistic communities or individual speakers of those communities may not know the kinds of word games required, I invented two word games which I refer to as WG1 and WG2; the transformation(s) of disyllabic words in these games are defined in (12). Simply stated, WG1 transposes the rhymes of successive syllables, like the Thai and Burmese games discussed above; WG2 is the same as the Bakwiri game in transposing successive syllables.

(12) WG1: $C_1 V_1 C_2 V_2$ > $C_1 V_2 C_2 V_1$
       WG2: $C_1 V_1 C_2 V_2$ > $C_2 V_2 C_1 V_1$

Using invented word games brings this technique more into the mold of what is commonly considered an experiment in the sense that the phonologist creates the circumstances under which the hypothesis-testing observations may be made (see Ohala, 1975). Except for the nature of the response elicited, the overall format of the method to be described is not unlike the concept formation technique discussed by Jaeger (this volume).

If they did not already know these word games, I taught them to speakers of Bakwiri, Dschang (a Bamileke language spoken in Cameroun), Kru (spoken in Liberia and Sierre Leone), Mandarin, Cantonese, Taiwanese, and Thai. The first three are referred to as 'the African tone languages' and the latter four as the 'the Asian tone languages.' There was one speaker of each language except for Cantonese and Taiwanese, which had two each. To train subjects in these games, I used only simple syllable structure (CV, not CVV or CVC) and words having identical tones on both syllables. When subjects showed mastery of the manipulations required on these simple words, I then gave them the disyllabic words of interest (occasionally with more complex syllable structure than CV) to transform in the same way.

In general, the results from WG2 were quite consistent for speakers of both the African and the Asian tone languages (data from the Taiwanese speakers are discussed separately below). As exemplified in (13), the tone pattern was left unchanged by speakers of the African tone languages.

(13) a. Bakwiri $k^w\acute{e}l\grave{\imath}$ > $l\acute{\imath}k^w\grave{e}$ 'falling'
      b. Dschang $\grave{a}k^w\bar{e}$ > $k^w\grave{e}\bar{a}$ 'bone'
      c. Kru $t\acute{u}w\hat{e}$ > $w\acute{e}t\hat{u}$ 'axe'

But apart from very rare exceptions which are discussed below, the tones were moved with the syllables by the speakers of the Asian tone languages; examples are given in (14).

(14) a. Thai p^hu ⟍ $ji\eta$ ⟍   > $ji\eta$ ⟍ p^hu ⟍   'woman'
      b. Cantonese $f\mathfrak{o}\eta$ ⟍ pin ⊣   > pin ⊣ $f\mathfrak{o}\eta$ ⟍   'convenient'
      c. Mandarin $t\mathvarphi'i$ ⟍ ma ⟍   > ma ⟍ $t\mathvarphi'i$ ⟍   'at least'

The treatment of words under WG1 was also consistent for the speakers of the African tone languages: the tones, again, were not moved when the vowels were interchanged. Examples are given in (15); see (13) for glosses.

(15) a. $k^w\acute{e}l\grave{\imath}$ > $k^w\acute{\imath}l\grave{e}$
      b. $\grave{a}k^w\bar{e}$ > $\grave{e}k^w\bar{a}$
      c. $t\acute{u}w\hat{e}$ > $t\acute{e}w\hat{u}$

However, the behavior of the speakers of the Asian languages was not so straightforward as it was for WG2. In Thai, the great majority of the forms elicited (70%) shifted tone with the shifted segments as exemplified in (16a), but for the rest, the tone remained in place as shown in (16b). (It should be recalled that this type of word game already has some currency among Thai speakers.)

(16) a. p^hu ⟍ $ji\eta$ ⟍   > $p^hi\eta$ ⟍ ju ⟍
      b. nam ⟍ nom ⊣   > nom ⟍ nam ⊣

With Cantonese, half of the responses (from the two subjects) moved the tone and half did not as exemplifed in (17a) and (17b).

(17) a. $f\mathfrak{o}\eta$ ⟍ pin ⊣   > fin ⊣ $p\mathfrak{o}\eta$ ⟍   'convenient'
      b. $ha\mathrm{:}m$ ⟍ $t\int\mathfrak{o}i$ ⊣   > $h\mathfrak{o}i$ ⟍ $t\int a\mathrm{:}m$ ⊣   'salted vegetables'

For Mandarin the tone pattern was almost always left unchanged when manipulated by WG1; in a very few cases the tones were shifted; (18) is an example of the dominant pattern.

(18) $t\mathvarphi'i$ ⟍ ma ⟍   > $t\mathvarphi'a$ ⟍ mi ⟍   'at least'

The different treatment of tone under WG1 and WG2 by the speakers of the Asian tone languages is puzzling, and I have no definitive explanation for it. One possibility is that since in these tone languages tone does seem to be tied to the segments on which it sits (as demonstrated by the consistent results from WG2), somehow the tone is also associated with the initial consonant whether syllabic or not, and when subjects are required by the word game to break up the initial and rhyme part of the syllable they sometimes keep the tone with this initial consonant and sometimes with the rhyme.

The different behavior of the speakers of the Asian and the African tone languages with these word games might be attributed not to inherent differences in the relation between tone and the syllables or segments on which they are realized but rather to the fact that in these Asian languages words tend to be monosyllabic as opposed to the polysyllabic tendency in the African languages. Speakers of the African languages might also shift tone if the transposed units were whole words. In order to try to control for this difference I included three types of disyllabic compounds in the items to be transposed by the speakers of the Asian tone languages: one set was compounds of two clearly distinct words, as in (19), a second set contained compounds which were "felt" to be single words, as in (20), and a third set consisted of artificial compounds of words which made very little sense together, as in (21). It was expected that if monosyllabism of words influenced speakers' behavior in the word games, then the first and the third sets would show a greater tendency to shift tones with syllables or segments than would the second set. As it happened, the first and second sets were treated uniformly in that tones were moved with the syllables and segments they were imposed on; some items from the third set, unexpectedly, were the only exceptions to this tendency during WG2.

(19)   a. Thai   *mai* ⌐ *ju* ⌐
       b. Cantonese   *maːu* ⌐ *mei* ⌐
       c. Mandarin   *hei* ⌐ *gou* ⌐

(20)   a. Thai   *pʰu* ⌐ *jiŋ* ⌐
       b. Cantonese   *maː* ⌐ *lau* ⌐
       c. Mandarin   *huo* ⌐ *tʂ'e* ⌐

(21)   a. Cantonese   *maːu* ⌐ *fuŋ* ⌐
       b. Mandarin   *huo* ⌐ *tʂu* ⌐

These studies with invented word games represent a very preliminary effort. Nevertheless, the largely consistent behavior of the speakers with WG2 suggests that the psychological representation of tone may be different for speakers of the African and the Asian tone languages. The speakers of the African tone languages never shifted tone when the syllables were interchanged, whereas the speakers of the Asian tone languages exhibited variable behavior on this point. Although it is possible that a contributory cause of this difference between the two language groups is the dominant monosyllabism of the words or morphemes in the Asian tone languages as opposed to the polysyllabic character of words or morphemes in the African tone languages, this does not seem to explain all the differences. I conclude, then, that there is strong evidence that the word is the tone-bearing unit in the African tone languages but that, tentatively, tone may be a feature on a smaller unit in the Asian tone languages. Further investigations with more speakers are needed.

LEVEL OF APPLICATION OF WORD GAME RULES

When word games are used by linguists as a method of gaining insight into the native speaker's psychological representation of words, it is very important to know at what level the word-game rules apply, that is, whether at the surface phonetic level or at deeper, possibly lexical levels. Obviously, the import of the resulting data will be different if the game operates on the surface level rather than on deeper levels. If the word-game rules interact with other productive phonological rules, it is sometimes possible to determine the level of their application. This is the case when the above word games apply to Taiwanese compounds which are subject to tone sandhi. If we consider only the nonchecked tones, Taiwanese has five tones, listed on the left in (22). When two monosyllabic words form a compound, the first tone is changed into its sandhi form, listed on the right in (22). The tone of the second word is left unchanged.

(22)   high level   ˥ > ˧
       high falling ˥˩ > ˥
       mid   ˧ > ˨
       low falling   ˨˩ > ˥˩
       mid rising   ˧˥ > ˧

Examples of how WG2 operated on three Taiwanese compounds also subject to tone sandhi are shown in (23), (24), and (25). In each case (a) presents the lexical tonal representation (that is, the underlying form) in slashes and the normal phonetic form due to tone sandhi in square brackets, (b) gives the form after WG2 is applied, and (c) gives the presumed order in which tone-sandhi (TS) and the word-game rule apply such that (b) could be derived from the underlying form in (a).

(23)   a. /i ˨˩ su ˨˩/ [i ˥˩ su ˨˩] 'meaning'
       b. su ˨˩ i ˥˩
       c. / ˨˩ ˨˩ / ---(TS)---> ˥˩ ˨˩ ---(WG2)---> [˨˩ ˥˩]
(24)   a. /hue ˧ lui ˨˩/ [hue ˨˩ lui ˨˩] 'flower'
       b. lui ˥ hue ˧
       c. /˥ ˥˩/ ---(TS)---> ˧ ˥˩ ---(WG2)---> ˥˩ ˧ ---(TS)---> [˥ ˧]

(25) a. /ku ⌐ tshu ⌐/ [ku ⌐ tshu ⌐] 'old house'
      b. tshu ⌐ ku ⌐
      c. /⌐ ⌐/ ---(WG2)---> ⌐ ⌐ ---(TS)---> [⌐ ⌐]

Unexpectedly, the order of application of word-game rule and tone-sandhi rules were quite variable: tone sandhi first then word game in (23) and (24), but in (24) tone sandhi applied a second time. In (25), however, the word game applied before the tone sandhi. (See also the different results obtained by Hsieh, 1970, and Liao, 1972, in their tests of the productivity of these tone-sandhi rules on neologisms.) Whatever the reasons for this behavior, the point is that it is possible to tell the relative level at which the word-game rules apply.

CONCLUSION

I have attempted to show that word games, naturally occurring or invented, can be used to gain insight into the psychological representation of a language's phonology. This is illustrated by clarifying the structure and representation of syllable structure, glides, vowel length, and tone in Bakwiri and other languages. One of the more significant findings is that tone is a feature of the word, not the syllable or segment, in three African tone languages studied. It is tentatively concluded that this is not true in some Asian tone languages examined.

Naturally, information derived from word games is most valuable when one obtains consistent responses from many speakers and comparable results from different languages (which was not always the case in this study). The results of this study, though tentative, demonstrate that larger, more elaborate studies using this technique are worth the effort.

ACKNOWLEDGMENTS

Some of the experimental work reported here was done at the Phonology Laboratory, University of California, Berkeley, and was supported in part by the National Science Foundation.

I am deeply grateful to my informants for their great patience and willingness to subject their linguistic knowledge to my investigation and experimentation. I also thank Steve Baron, Bill Ewan, Larry Hyman, Hector Javkin, Boyd Michailovsky, John Ohala, and the members of the tone seminar at UCLA for their valuable comments on earlier versions of this paper. Thanks also to Baruch Elimelech and Martine Mazaudon for the use of their data on Kru and Tamang, respectively. I take responsibility for the content of the chapter.

REFERENCES

Anderson, S. R. 1978. Tone features. In V. A. Fromkin, ed., *Tone: A linguistic survey*, 133–175. New York: Academic Press.

Bamgbose, A. 1970. Word play in Yoruba poetry. *International Journal of American Linguistics* 36:110–116.

Burling, R. 1970. *Man's many voices*. New York: Rinehart & Winston.

Chao, Y. R. 1930. A system of tone letters. *Le Maître Phonétique* 45:24–27.

Chao, Y. R. 1931. Eight varieties of secret language based on the principle of Fanch'ieh. *Bulletin of the Institute of History and Philology* (Academia Sinica) 2:310–354.

Chao, Y. R. 1934. The non-uniqueness of phonemic solutions of phonetic systems. *Bulletin of the Institute of History and Philology* (Academia Sinica) 4:363–397.

Chomsky, N., & M. Halle. 1968., *The sound pattern of English*. New York: Harper & Row.

Conklin, H. C. 1956. Tagalog speech disguise. *Language* 32:136–139.

Conklin, H. C. 1959. Linguistic play in its cultural context. *Language* 35:631–636.

Coupez, A. 1969. Une leçon de linguistique. *Africa-Tervuren* 15:1–5.

Edmondson, T., & J. T. Bendor-Samuel. 1966. Tone patterns in Etung. *Journal of African Languages* 5:1–6.

Elimelech, B. 1974. On the reality of underlying contour tones *(Working Papers in Linguistics* 27), 74–83. University of California at Los Angeles.

Fromkin, V. 1972. Tone features and tone rules. *Studies in African Linguistics* 3:47–76.

Goldsmith, J. 1976. Autosegmental phonology. Bloomington: Indiana University Linguistics Club.

Goldsmith, J. 1979. The aims of autosegmental phonology. In D. A. Dinnsen, ed., *Current approaches to phonology theory*, 202–222. Bloomington: Indiana University Press.

Haas, M. R. 1957. Thai word games. *Journal of American Folklore* 70:173–175.

Haas, M. R. 1969. Burmese disguised speech. *Bulletin of the Institute of History and Philology* (Academia Sinica) 39:277–285.

Halle, M. 1962. Phonology in generative grammar. *Word* 18:54–72.

Hombert, J.-M. (1973). Speaking backwards in Bakwiri. *Studies in African Linguistics* 4:227–236.

Hsieh, H.-T. 1970. The psychological reality of tone sandhi rules in Taiwanese. *Papers from Regional Meeting of the Chicago Linguistic Society* 6:489–503.

Jaeger, J. J. 1980. Testing the psychological reality of phonemes. *Language & Speech* 23:233–253.

Laycock, D. 1972. *Towards a typology of ludlings, or play-languages* (Linguistic Communications, Working Papers of the Linguistic Society of Australia, Monash University) 6:61–113.

Leben, W. 1973. The role of tone in segmental phonology. In L. M. Hyman, ed., *Consonant types and tone*, 115–149. Southern California Occasional Papers in Linguistics 1.

Leben, W. 1978. The representation of tone. In V. A. Fromkin, ed., *Tone: A linguistic survey*, 177–219. New York: Academic Press.

Liao, C. C. 1972. The psychological reality of tone sandhi rules in Taiwanese revisited. May 1972 *Monthly Internal Memorandum*, Phonology Laboratory, University of California, Berkeley, 24–30.

Maddieson, I. 1971. The inventory of features. In *Tone in generative phonology* Research notes, vol. 3, nos. 2 & 3, 3–18. University of Ibadan.

Mazaudon, M. 1972. Consonantal mutation and tonal split in six Himalayan dialects of Tibeto-Burmese. Paper presented at International Seminar on Anthropological Linguistics, Patiala, Punjab, 11–14 October 1972.

McCawley, J. 1970. Some tonal systems that come close to being pitch accent systems but don't quite make it. *Papers from the Regional Meeting of the Chicago Linguistic Society* 6:526-532.

McCawley, J. 1978. What is a tone language? In V. A. Fromkin, ed., *Tone: A linguistic survey*, 113-131. New York: Academic Press.

Ohala, M. 1975. Nasals and nasalization in Hindi. In C. A. Ferguson, L. M. Hyman, & J. J. Ohala, eds., *Nasalfest. Papers from a symposium on nasals and nasalization*, 317-332. Language Universals Project, Stanford University.

Pike, K. 1948. *Tone languages*. Ann Arbor: University of Michigan Press.

Price, R., & S. Price. 1976. Secret play languages in Saramaka: Linguistic disguise in a Caribbean creole. In B. Kirshenblatt-Gimblett, ed., *Speech play*, 37-50. Philadelphia: University of Pennsylvania Press.

Schachter, P., & V. Fromkin. 1968. *A phonology of Akan: Akuapem, Asante, and Fante* (Working Papers in Phonetics 9). University of California at Los Angeles.

Sherzer, J. 1970. Talking backwards in Cuna: The sociological reality of phonological descriptions. *Southwestern Journal of Anthropology* 26:343-353.

Sherzer, J. 1976. Play languages: Implications for (socio)linguistics. In B. Kirshenblatt-Gimblett, ed., *Speech play*, 19-36. Philadelphia: University of Pennsylvania Press.

Surintramont, A. 1973. Some aspects of underlying syllable structure in Thai: Evidence from Khampnuan—a Thai word game. *Studies in the Linguistic Sciences* 3:121-142.

Welmers, W. 1962. The phonology of Kpelle. *Journal of African Languages* 1:69-93.

Woo, N. 1972. *Prosody and phonology*. Bloomington: Indiana University Linguistics Club.

11

Experimental Phonology
at the University of Alberta

BRUCE L. DERWING
TERRANCE M. NEAREY

INTRODUCTION

Experimental linguistics—or psycholinguistics, as it is more commonly but somewhat misleadingly known (Derwing 1973:301–307)—is the study of the linguistic knowledge and abilities of speakers of human languages. It is distinct from more traditional descriptive or structural linguistic inquiry, both in its philosophical orientation and in its methodology. To begin with, experimental linguistics recognizes that language is not a natural object like a tree, stone, or chemical element but is rather a second-order product of human beings, created primarily for purposes of intersubjective communication. While this product can be described in many different ways, the only structure it really has is that which is put there by speakers or interpreted as being there by hearers; anything else is the result of purely arbitrary and artifactual analysis of regularities exhibited by (transcribed) utterances.[1]

Since the truth to be discovered is not physical in character but rather psychological and sociological, that is, psychological constructs shared by many,

[1]It is important to recognize that it is these transcriptions that are analyzed in descriptive linguistics, not the physical utterances per se. Clearly, the physical speech event or acoustic waveform, that is, the "stimulus object" of Kac (1980) has no linguistic structure whatsoever: Even discrete phones represent interpretations of the speech signal, not physical realities analogous to light waves or geometric configurations.

187

it follows that a large assortment of psychological tests is required in order to discover it. The task of psycholinguistics is thus not to take the findings of purely descriptive linguistics for granted and to show how the proposed structures, representations, and rules are learned and used by speakers (Rommetveit 1979:17) but rather to ascertain whether these proposed entities have any psychological validity in the first place. This dictates that the methodology of the discipline must be largely experimental in character. (See Derwing 1980a, 1980b, and Prideaux 1980a, 1980b, for further discussion of these basic issues.)

Experimental phonology, then, is merely that branch of psycholinguistics that is concerned with the formulation and testing of theories of linguistic knowledge and abilities involving learned or perceived sound structure. This includes such things as perceived sound units (e.g., phones, phonemes, lexical representations) and a variety of types of sound-based generalizations or rules (e.g., phonotactic, lexical, and morphophonemic, following the taxonomy of Derwing and Baker 1977; see also Linell 1979:Ch. 10).[2]

The division of labor is, of course, arbitrary; what is important is the recognition of the essential psychological nature of the enterprise and the resulting need for controlled experimental procedures in order to expose alternative theories or speculations to critical empirical tests.

EARLY STUDIES ON RULE PRODUCTIVITY

A program of experimental phonology began at the University of Alberta in 1970. Derwing had just completed his Indiana University dissertation (later published as Derwing 1973) and was convinced that some kind of experimental work would have to be done in order to resolve the important theoretical controversies in linguistics. Nevertheless, it was still far from clear what specific directions the Alberta research effort would take. The first steps, in fact, were taken by a graduate student as the result of a detailed assessment of the strengths and weaknesses of Berko's influential, but fragmentary, 1958 study of the acquisition of English morphology. This work, which eventually appeared as Innes (1974), extended the range of investigation from

---

[2]As employed here, the term 'experimental phonology' denotes the experimental psychological investigation of the units and concepts of formal phonological and morphophonemic analysis in linguistics. It excludes research in the far better established tradition of experimental phonetics. For some details of experimental phonetic research at Alberta, see Nearey and Hogan (this volume). Information on experimental research at Alberta in the areas of syntax, semantics, and pragmatics can be found in Prideaux, Derwing, and Baker (1980), Derwing and Baker (1978), and Derwing (1979).

Berko's original small handful of plural forms to at least the full set of final single-phoneme stem types. Innes also greatly expanded the age range of her subjects in the hope of identifying some clear developmental effects. The renewed attention given to the old problem of English pluralization yielded some new insights which served to direct the next phase of research.

It was recognized, for example, that there was quite a variety of ways of describing spoken English plural forms—all of them equally correct as far as the relevant linguistic or internal data were concerned and thus with no empirical grounds available for choosing among them. Moreover, this case served as an example, in miniature, of a much more general non-uniqueness problem which seemed to beset all of descriptive or structural linguistics, from Saussure straight through to the post-Chomskyan era. Yet a Chomsky-inspired solution did at least suggest itself: If the alternative linguistic theories could be viewed not merely as theories of forms, but rather as theories of the knowledge underlying speakers' ability to produce and comprehend forms, then a whole new range of ways of evaluating them opened up. Some analyses which were perfectly consistent with internal distributional data might well prove to be at odds with new kinds of psychological or external data indicative of what speakers actually know.[3]

This program of research immediately faced a number of problems, the most immediate of which was the question of what particular psychological claims, if any, were actually entailed by any given linguistic analysis. Very few linguistic analyses have ever been formulated in psychological terms (Derwing 1980a). What could it possibly mean psychologically, for example, to say that a particular linguistic form, say a plural form, was derived from some abstract underlying representation by the application of various rules ordered in a generative grammar (but not ordered in real time [Cook 1974])? This interpretation problem would have to be dealt with before any meaningful experiments could be carried out, since it would be impossible to decide what kind of test was appropriate until the nature of the claim to be tested was clear. On this point, as well, the English plurals seemed to provide a

[3]This and what is to follow should serve to correct the misimpression of Fromkin (1980: 200) that Derwing "seems to reject . . . the difference between linguistic knowledge and linguistic behavior". All of the experiments to be described here are concerned ultimately with questions of linguistic knowledge as opposed to questions of how that knowledge is put to use. What Derwing does reject, of course, is the view that linguistic competence can be established on the basis of purely formal, non-empirical, criteria which are devoid of any external psychological support, as in the work of Chomsky. Such competence has no valid pretense to represent knowledge in any familiar or meaningful sense and can only be declared so "by definition," as in Valian (1976). The crucial question, then, is not whether knowledge exists as distinct from behavior—Who but the most radical of behaviorists would doubt it?—but rather how this knowledge is to be discovered.

good basis for launching an experimental study, since for some of the alternative analyses the psychological interpretation seemed straightforward and the choice of tests clear.[4] The next couple of years were spent collecting data in face-to-face sessions with numerous children in local elementary schools and preschool daycare centers.

As a consequence of this research program we can now confidently affirm, on the basis of substantial empirical evidence, that quite a range of theories about the English speaker's pluralization capacities are inadequate, if not entirely wrong. First, as Berko's pioneering work had already demonstrated, we found that English speakers do not merely learn a long list of plural forms when they learn to pluralize; they also learn some broader generalizations or rules which enable them to pluralize forms not previously encountered. Second, we now also know something about the nature of the particular rules involved (which Berko's research could not tell us). Specifically, these rules (1) are largely phonologically conditioned, (2) do not, in general, take into account the stem-internal vowel (as might be expected if they were based on analogy and the template on which new forms were based was the rhyme of the stem), but rather only the final segment or consonant cluster, and (3) are based on some kind of feature analysis of the stem-final segment. All of these points, of course, have long been thought to be true by most linguists who have addressed the problem, but these opinions were supported almost exclusively by formal, distributional evidence, and *a priori* arguments (Halle 1964; Anderson 1974). Now they are buttressed by experimental evidence.

We do not yet know, however, whether the more general rules of voicing assimilation and vowel insertion are also learned and play a role in a speaker's pluralization behavior, nor do we have any idea whether such things as morpheme-invariant underlying forms are learned or used by linguistically naive speakers (however, reports of some preliminary attempts at addressing these issues follow).

It is possible and, in fact, quite necessary to subject these and all experiments to criticism. Kiparsky and Menn (1977), for example, suggested that all Berko-type experiments are invalidated by the strangeness of the contrived experimental situation—in Berko's case, getting children to form the plurals of names of imaginary animals presented through pictures. To test this, Rollins (1980) repeated the Berko experiment under conditions similar to her original study and also under more natural conditions, using stuffed animals and eliciting the desired plural forms from subjects in conversational or play

---

[4]The full details of the alternate analyses, interpretations, and the choice of tests was first developed by Derwing in papers presented to the Indiana University Linguistics Club in 1973 and at Reed College and the University of Toronto in 1974 and published in Derwing (1979, 1980b), and Derwing and Baker (1977, 1979, 1980).

situations. Subjects' responses were virtually identical under both conditions, with age being the only significant variable. Older children and adults are more likely to recognize that the nonsense stems used in such studies are not real words in their language and so seem to give somewhat less consistent responses than do young children (see also Haber 1975; Derwing & Baker 1977: p. 96, note 15).[5]

MORPHEME RECOGNITION STUDIES

Our research on the pluralization question was interrupted by the problem of how to test the various base-form analyses. Since we had no idea how to test for knowledge of a base form in any direct way, a more circuitous route was explored. As anticipated by Derwing (1973:Ch. 4) and developed by Derwing and Baker (1977), the rationale for this experimental approach can be briefly outlined as follows:

1. Base forms have been posited by phonologists for several cases of morphological alternation of which the English plural is just one example.
2. In all such cases, however, the descriptive strategy has been essentially the same, namely, to account for morpheme variants (allomorphs) as environmentally determined or rule-governed manifestations of a single, more abstract, underlying representation.
3. Such an analytic strategy only makes sense if the morpheme variants in question can all be presumed to share a common meaningful unit, that is, a morpheme. (Thus few synchronic analysts would be likely to relate such forms as *suppose* and *suppository*, to borrow an example from A.S. Abramson.)
4. Thus, tests designed to assess the ability of linguistically untrained English speakers to recognize morpheme identity might at least delimit the range of circumstances under which a base–form analysis is even feasible.

Work along these lines was begun in 1974 and the first results reported in Derwing (1976).

If the descriptive linguistic accounts had any merit, the two variables of phonetic and semantic similarity clearly ought to play a crucial role in permitting native speakers to recognize the same morpheme in different words

---

[5]Parallel research was conducted on other English inflections, and the productivity of a variety of English derivational processes along with some painstaking studies on the possible role of frequency of occurrence and other variables in determining the results obtained. Only a fraction of these research findings have been reported in print; see Derwing (1977, 1979), Derwing and Baker (1974, 1976, 1979, 1980).

(Derwing 1973). It ought to be relatively easy to recognize a common morpheme in word pairs like *teacher* and *teach*, which are presumably very similar in both meaning and sound, but less easy to do this for words showing
somewhat less similarity in one or both of these dimensions, for example,
awful–awe, handkerchief–hand, fabulous–fable. The first stage of this
research thus required the collection of some empirical estimates of similarity in both of these dimensions for a suitable representative sample of word
pairs and speakers. This was accomplished by means of a straightforward
set of rating studies involving large samples ($n > 100$) of linguistically naive
adult native speakers as subjects. From the results of the initial rating experiments, 50 word pairs were selected to represent the full range of variation
in both dimensions. These pairs were then used in a further series of studies
to assess the ability of other groups of linguistically untrained speakers to
recognize morphemes. Of the four experimental techniques employed in this
latter effort, the following three produced an acceptable degree of cross-
methodological covariance (with correlations ranging from .81 to .88 across
the 50 items):[6]

1. A "comes-from" test, in which subjects judge whether one word in
   each pair, presumably the morphologically more complex word, for
   example, *teacher*, comes from the other, usually the shorter, morphologically simple, word, for example, *teach*.
2. A recall test, in which the same subjects judge whether they have ever
   previously thought about the possibility of such a relationship between
   the words.
3. A meaning-unit test, in which two other groups of subjects are asked,
   in effect, to break the words down into their constituent morphemes.

Since this third study has not been previously reported, a brief summary
of the experimental procedure is provided here. Subjects, all undergraduate
university students newly registered in introductory linguistics courses at
Alberta, were told that they would be asked to identify the meaning units
which make up a small set of English words. They were then given the example
of the word *cats*, which was said to consist of two such units, the first being
cat (meaning 'cat') and the second, *s* (meaning 'plural' or more than one').
Subjects gave their responses on an answer sheet by placing a slash between
the units involved and by giving the meanings of each unit in spaces provided.
Ten other examples were analyzed in like manner (*played, player, winner,
heater, football, sadly, smoky, happy, unhappily,* and *banana*), noting that the
placement of the slash in *winner* was not completely clear (either *win/ner* or

---

[6]The method that failed is discussed in Derwing (1976) together with full details of the
comes-from and recall tests, which are only briefly described here.

winn/er) and that *happy* and *banana* were probably best not broken up at all. The subjects were then asked to analyze the remaining 50 words in an analogous way, as they thought appropriate.

The primary data from these three experiments are summarized in Table 11.1. The responses in the comes-from test were defined as follows:

4   no doubt about it (the percentage of such responses is recorded in Table 11.1 as " % yes")
3   probably
2   can't decide
1   probably not
0   no way (= "% no")

On the recall test, the responses were limited to 1 = yes (recorded in the table as "% yes"), 2 = not sure, and 0 = no ("% no"). Only the percentage of target-word identifications is recorded from the meaning-unit test.

The table demonstrates that the results converge substantially across all three of the experimental tasks, suggesting that a common task-independent phenomenon is being tapped. However, there are also some important (but not unexpected) differences in the absolute scores achieved from one task to another (the % yes scores on the recall test are quite consistently lower than those on the comes-from test. A few of the items stand out as anomalies: The word pairs *skinny–skin, handkerchief–hand, necklace–lace, breakfast–break* (and to some extent *rubber–rub* and *bashful-bash*) achieve much higher ratings on the third test than on either of the first two, quite possibly due to orthographic influence.

All three studies nonetheless reinforce the overall impression of a critical region for morpheme recognition as determined by the two variables of semantic and phonetic similarity. This is shown in Figure 11.1 for the results of the meaning-unit test, where the item numbers show the location of each pair in the two-dimensional space and the size of the circle around these numbers reflects the proportion of correct responses. (Table 11.1 shows the correspondence between the numbers and the individual word pairs.) In this figure the radius of each circle is proportional to the %All response for each item except when this is less than 15% (to retain legibility). For the sake of comparison, the reader should know that items 17 and 19 exhibit nearly the maximum dimensions (their %All scores were 97 and 96, respectively) and item 28 shows nearly half the maximum dimension (its %All score was 53). The results for item 20 (*lousy–louse*) show clear evidence of the influence of uncontrolled variables.

Notice that only a small minority of subjects provided correct reponses for items lying outside the area defined by a semantic similarity rating ≥ 2.0

Table 11.1

Results of Morpheme Recognition Studies

Word pairs	Comes-from test			Recall test			Meaning-unit test		
	Mean	% Yes	% No	Mean	% Yes	% No	% 1979 (n = 43)	% 1978 (n = 34)	% all (n = 77)
1. eraser–erase	3.94	94	0	3.35	75	8	86	76	82
2. teacher–teach	3.97	97	0	3.11	72	17	100	100	100
3. doggie–dog	3.88	92	0	2.89	55	21	65	79	71
4. dirty–dirt	3.95	95	0	2.98	68	18	100	97	99
5. quietly–quiet	3.97	97	0	3.11	72	17	100	100	100
6. messenger–message	3.72	77	8	2.49	52	28	70	74	72
7. strawberry–berry	3.20	65	1	2.92	60	14	65	53	60
8. hungry–hunger	3.80	85	0	3.35	78	11	63	53	58
9. lawyer–law	3.91	91	0	3.60	86	9	91	94	92
10. shepherd–sheep	3.69	72	5	3.20	77	17	67	50	60
11. numerous–number	3.43	66	6	2.28	41	28	63	50	57
12. kitty–cat	2.54	20	6	1.94	34	37	12	21	16
13. puppy–dog	0.93	1	41	.80	11	71	0	6	3
14. wilderness–wild	3.80	80	0	3.20	71	11	77	82	79
15. handle–hand	3.45	54	1	1.78	23	34	46	59	58
16. cookie–cook	2.91	18	0	1.38	21	52	33	32	32
17. wonderful–wonder	3.88	91	0	3.32	75	9	95	100	97
18. cupboard–cup	3.45	55	3	2.89	63	18	86	85	86
19. birdhouse–bird	3.85	88	0	2.68	55	21	100	91	96
20. lousy–louse	3.34	52	3	2.46	54	31	60	68	64
21. month–moon	3.54	65	1	2.74	61	25	7	3	5
22. holiday–holy	3.48	58	0	2.40	49	29	65	71	67
23. heavy–heave	2.48	11	3	.71	6	71	21	15	18
24. barber–beard	2.37	28	12	1.41	25	54	14	6	10

25. weather-wind	1.35	1	11	.61	6	75	0	0	0
26. precious-price	2.69	21	3	1.11	12	57	7	6	6
27. sweater-sweat	2.26	15	8	1.38	23	54	44	53	48
28. slipper-slip	2.86	26	3	1.45	20	48	56	50	53
29. skinny-skin	2.97	37	5	2.00	40	40	81	85	83
30. handkerchief-hand	3.18	46	3	2.46	51	28	91	85	88
31. necklace-lace	2.58	20	9	1.35	23	55	86	79	83
32. awful-awe	3.15	54	3	2.43	54	32	51	41	47
33. breakfast-break	3.26	58	3	2.92	69	23	84	82	83
34. spider-spin	2.06	9	8	.46	6	83	2	0	1
35. fabulous-fable	2.51	20	6	.83	17	75	21	9	16
36. Halloween-Holy	2.72	43	15	2.58	58	29	7	12	9
37. feather-fly	1.23	3	25	.52	6	80	0	0	0
38. timid-tame	2.45	14	3	.80	9	69	0	0	0
39. liver-live	1.55	11	18	.86	14	74	12	12	12
40. buggy-bug	1.77	14	21	1.05	15	63	28	18	23
41. eerie-ear	.85	9	41	.40	5	85	0	0	0
42. Friday-fry	.95	5	49	1.51	28	52	12	3	8
43. rubber-rub	1.63	6	15	.92	12	66	28	26	27
44. bashful-bash	.75	1	55	.43	5	83	19	38	27
45. gypsy-Egyptian	1.66	12	21	.55	12	85	0	3	1
46. cranberry-crane	.78	1	43	.25	5	92	2	0	1
47. hideous-hide	2.45	17	6	.89	12	68	19	32	25
48. ladder-lean	1.26	8	17	.21	0	94	0	0	0
49. carpenter-wagon	.38	1	75	.12	1	95	0	0	0
50. muggy-mist	1.63	5	14	.52	11	85	0	0	0

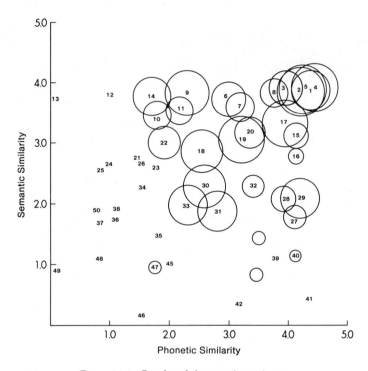

Figure 11.1   Results of the meaning-unit test.

and a phonetic similarity rating ≥ about 1.6. This confirms the finding established earlier on the basis of the other two tests (Derwing & Baker 1979). There are some items falling well within this range, however, for which the response scores are surprisingly low; items 15 (*handle–hand*) and 16 (*cookie–cook*) stand out in this respect. This indicates that variables other than those explicitly investigated here must play a role in this kind of task; the following are plausible candidates: (1) The type of construction involved, for example, noun compounds such as *birdhouse*, which are influenced by sound and meaning similarity in a different way from deverbative constructions such as *teacher*; (2) the frequency either of the members of the word pair or of the type of construction; (3) ambiguity, for example, the possibility of either a nominal of adjectival interpretation for the word *buggy*; (4) orthographic interference; and (5) subject variables, such as amount of formal education and verbal ability. Further research is underway to clarify the role of these and possibly other factors which complicate the interpretation of the experimental results.

STUDIES ON THE PSYCHOLOGICAL REALITY
OF THE PHONEME

An unexpected by-product of the research just described was an idea about how to construct a test to evaluate alternative phonemic analyses of English words. The germ of the idea came from Vitz and Winkler (1973; hereafter V&W), who attempted to devise an algorithm for predicting subjects' "judged similarity in sound" among various English words pronounced in citation form. Taking a standard phonemic analysis, they found that they were able to account for a substantial portion of the variation in such scores by means of the simple procedure of counting the phonemes in common between two words (see V&W for details), and they even achieved slightly better results when they treated entire consonant clusters as equivalent in weight to single vowels. Adopting V&W's phonemicizations and counting procedures, Derwing (1976) found that their results were replicated almost perfectly in the set of phonetic similarity ratings that had been gathered for the word pairs in his morpheme-recognition studies. Although at first the relative success achieved by such a simple algorithm seemed rather surprising, there was some theoretical basis to expect findings of the sort obtained by V&W. If, after all, speakers are supposed to be insensitive to the predictable phonetic variations manifested in their language, then a phonemic representation, which is an attempt to abstract away from precisely this kind of variation, ought to provide a good prediction of the judgements these speakers make about similarity in sound between utterances in their language. Furthermore, if the boundaries between phonemes are also more or less categorical ("all or none"), then a simple count of the shared phonemes between two forms ought to provide a perfectly adequate basis for this kind of prediction, since all phonemes would presumably be judged as equidistant from each other. If this is accepted, then given two alternative phonemicizations for the same two words, for example, *pain* and *pen:* /peyn/ versus /pen/ or /pen/ versus /pɛn/, the one which best predicts the judged "sound similarity" by native speakers ought to be the preferred analysis. For example, by V&W's simple phoneme count these two words would be ¾ similar under the former analysis but ⅔ similar under the latter.

There are, however, two obvious problems with this line of reasoning: (1) It is pure theory, not empirically supported, and, in fact, there is considerable experimental evidence that subjects can under certain circumstances compare phonemes on a gradient (see Ingram, 1980, and references cited therein). (2) The proper measure for predicting similarity in sound, even if it does partly involve counting shared phonemes, may be more complex that V&W

proposed due to the relatively narrow range of stimuli they actually investigated.

The attempt to solve these problems was a collaborative effort between the two present authors, who conducted a number of pilot studies in order to refine the V&W measure so that it could be used to test alternative phonemic analyses. These studies showed that the presence of the same phoneme in two strings consistently yielded increased judged similarity in control (i.e., clear) cases. Thus, a pair like *gill* and *grill* would always be rated closer than a pair like *gill* and *spill*.

This technique can be used to clarify how allophones are assigned to phonemes. Consider, for example, some of the stop allophones in English. Traditionally, stop consonants have been recognized as having three allophones: (1) voiceless aspirated as in *pill*, (2) voiceless unaspirated as in *spill*, and (3) voiced as in *bill*, where allophone (2) is in complementary distribution with both (1) and (3). Experimental research has shown that allophone (3) in *bill* is only rarely voiced during its closure in initial position in English and that it is, in fact, frequently very similar to voiceless unaspirates in other languages, at least from the point of view of voice onset time. Furthermore, perceptual experiments indicate that when the /s/ is gated from words like *spill*, English listeners identify the remainder as *bill*. From the point of view of phonetic similarity, therefore, there is some reason to link allophones (2) and (3) rather than (2) and (1), as is done in most standard phonemic analyses. Do the results of phoneme similarity judgments support this latter analysis?

Table 11.2 shows the results of a study of this sort. (Results of a pilot study on the same stimuli are presented in Nearey, 1981.) Pairs of words were recorded by J. T. Hogan, a Canadian phonetician, with each pair repeated twice. They were played over a loudspeaker in an ordinary classroom to 39 linguistically naive university students who were Canadian-born native speakers of English. In order not to draw listeners' attention to the focus of the test, the 7 word pairs of interest were embedded in a list of 120 pairs. Previous experiments we had run showed that subjects found greater similarity between pairs differing in [pʰ]–[sp] than those in [b]–[sp], in accord with traditional phonemicizations. However, orthographic interference is an important source of artifacts in all phonological experiments involving literate subjects. Indeed, V&W found some evidence of such interference in one of their experiments. The present experiment was designed to control for this, at least in part. The first two sets in Table 11.2 provide spelling support for a closer link between [pʰ]–[sp] types, whereas the next three sets do not. The sixth pair gives ambiguous spelling support (*cool–school* share *c*, while *ghoul–school* share *h*). The last pair involves only nonsense words.

All of the mean similarity judgments are higher for the [pʰ]–[sp] type than for the [b]–[sp] type. Both of the spelling-supported pairs (1 and 2) are sig-

Table 11.2

Similarity Judgments for Stop Allophones

Stimulus pairs	Mean	Difference mean	SD
Spelling supported			
1. pill–spill bill–spill	6.000 5.256	0.744***	1.141
2. skill–kill skill–gill	6.359 5.820	0.539*	1.603
Nonsupported			
3. skull–cull skull–gull	6.103 5.821	0.282	1.234
4. skein–cane skein–gain	6.026 5.513	0.513**	1.211
5. cot–squat got–squat	5.154 5.077	0.077	1.285
Other			
6. cool–school ghoul–school	5.974 5.590	0.385**	0.990
7. /spIf–pIf/ /spIf–bIf/	6.333 5.897	0.436*	1.231

*p < .05   **p < .01   ***p < .001

nificantly different at the .05 level but only one of the three not having spelling support (3, 4, and 5) is. The two remaining pairs are significantly different in the predicted direction. However, the small magnitude of the differences in the nonsupported sets suggests some degree of orthographic influence. Further testing with nonliterate subjects might be helpful.

On the whole, however, we are very encouraged by the results from these string similarity experiments and we believe that the technique has great potential as a probe in exploring phonological questions. Derwing (1976) provides evidence that orthography is at least not an overwhelming source of interference in these experiments, since partial correlation analysis of orthographic versus phoneme-based similarity metrics shows that orthographic similarity is only weakly correlated with listeners' similarity judgements ($r = .34$) when phoneme similarity is controlled for, whereas the phoneme-based measure of similarity is still quite highly correlated with subjects' judgments even after controlling for orthographic similarity ($r = .63$). (Both partial correlations were significant, however.)[7] Furthermore, the word list used in this latter study was subsequently presented auditorily to another group of subjects with the result that the responses correlated highly ($r = .97$) with responses obtained by orthographic presentation.

Results which also show that speakers' phonological judgments correspond well with some traditional phonemic analyses have been obtained by Jaeger (1980, this volume), using both classical conditioning and the concept formation paradigm. (See Derwing 1973:316–32 for a detailed account of this second type of experiment, adapted for various kinds of linguistic stimuli.)

FURTHER ATTEMPTS TO TEST PHONEMIC ANALYSES

We attempted further experiments designed to test certain alternative phonemic analyses, for example, those concerned with the classic issue of the status of /ŋ/ in English, but these have not yielded clear results. It seemed to us that a refinement of the V&W measures of similarity might help to shed light on these issues. V&W explored a number of possible minor refinements for their measure: (1) There may be a 'rhyme' effect whereby words that were identical at the end are judged more similar than those identical at the beginning. (2) There should perhaps be a differential weighting of syllable parts, with the vowel counting more than the consonants. (3) A multivalued, feature-based, measure of similarity for nonidentical segments may improve the measure.

V&W's implementation of (3) gave negative results. They tried an arbitrary feature system adapted from Chomsky and Halle (1968, henceforth SPE). In these comparisons, they assigned a value of 1.0 for identical phonemes in a pair, 0.5 for those differing by one feature, and 0 for those differing by more than one feature. They found that predictions of similarity derived in this way were less accurate than those not taking account of features.

In our own attempts at such refinements we have concentrated our attention on measuring the similarity of consonants.[8] It is apparent that certain

---

[7]In a study specifically designed to assess the role of orthography in phonological judgments, Dow (1980) asked subjects to indicate the number of speech sounds in a list of 120 mono- and disyllabic words. Responses correlated highly (.92) with the number of phonemes as determined by a traditional phonemic analysis, counting all vowels, diphthongs, and syllabic resonants as single segments. This strengthens the view that intuitive notions of 'speech sound' as well as 'similarity in sound' are based on something very close to the traditional phonemic representation.

[8]Nevertheless, pilot studies indicate that a feature analysis would also help the comparison of vowels. The difference between long (tense) and short (lax) vowels appears to be most salient, while within the long and short sets dissimilarity is related to the distances the vowels exhibit on an F_1 versus F_2 plot.

consonantal features, such as manner, are generally more salient (that is, contribute more to making two consonants seem dissimilar) than others, such as place and voicing. In the experiment to be described, particular combinations of feature differences among initial and final consonants were analyzed, specifically, (1) voicing in stops (V), (2) place in nonvoiced stops (Pn), (3) place in voiced stops (Pv), (4) voicing and place in stops (VP), (5) manner (stops vs. fricatives) (M), and (6) voice, place, and manner (VPM). These were studied in both initial (I) and final (F) position. The words used and their scores are presented in Table 11.3.

Since subjects varied somewhat in their use of the scales, we normalized the scores by transforming them to z-scores. These averaged standard scores are also given in Table 11.3. In general, there appears to be a good deal of consistency in the responses to the items on the test. The mean standardized score for each of the groups is plotted in Figure 11.2.

According to V&W's measure, all of these groups should have the same score since they all share two of three phonemes. However, a one-way analysis of variance reveals highly significant differences among these groups ($F(11,444) = 20.5$, $p < .0001$). The boxes in Figure 11.2 enclose means that are not significantly different (according to a Newman-Keuls a posteriori test), that is, those means not enclosed in boxes are significantly different at the .05 level or less. Tukey's more conservative "honestly significant difference" test also showed many of the group comparisons to be significantly different. However, among initials, only the difference between IV and IVPM reached the .05 level.

A number of patterns are evident from this analysis. First, differences involving manner of articulation are generally more important than those involving place or voicing. Second, differences in final consonants are more important than those among initials. Indeed, the relatively small differences that exist in the initials would suggest that V&W's unit-difference algorithm should work quite well for initials—but less well for finals. (This conclusion received further support from another pilot test as well.) Third, even though the differences in initials are small, the feature analysis that would apply best to them is similar to that for the finals. It would be premature to eliminate a feature-based element from the metric. However, the relative magnitudes of the differences in features are less than the effect of having any phonemic difference at all. That is, apparently there is a bigger difference between a 0 and 1 feature dissimilarity than between a 1 and 2 or more feature dissimilarity. This tendency may be observed by examining the change in the raw similarity scores as feature mismatches are incorporated in the same position within the syllable. Consider IV and FV items (those with voicing differences in initial and final positions, respectively), which have overall average ratings of 6.38 and 6.32 (where the nominal maximum rating—which should

Table 11.3
Similarity Judgments for Selected Feature Comparisons

Type	Pair	Raw mean ($n = 39$)	Raw SD ($n = 39$)	Mean Z	Standard Z	Average Z
Initial voice (IV)	pɪt–bɪt	6.308	1.673	.479	.562	.520
	tɪp–dɪp	6.333	1.752	.504	.696	
	kɔt–gɔt	6.513	1.760	.577	.605	
Final voice (FV)	pɪp–pɪb	6.410	1.499	.540	.633	.489
	pɪt–pɪd	6.410	1.650	.546	.649	
	pɪk–pɪg	6.128	1.720	.382	.663	
Initial place non-voiced (IPN)	pɔp–tɔp	6.282	1.297	.447	.479	.310
	pɔp–kɔp	6.000	1.469	.265	.702	
	kɔp–tɔp	5.846	1.755	.219	.590	
Initial place voiced (IPV)	bɔp–dɔp	6.205	1.852	.445	.816	.380
	bɔp–gɔp	6.026	1.386	.297	.541	
	gɔp–dɔp	6.237	1.441	.399	.517	
Final place nonvoiced (FPN)	pɔp–pɔt	6.564	1.392	.617	.539	.491
	pɔp–pɔk	6.333	1.840	.485	.769	
	pɔk–pɔt	6.026	1.755	.371	.540	
Final place voiced (FVV)	pɔb–pɔd	6.000	1.606	.331	.545	.297
	pɔg–pɔd	5.923	1.421	.264	.478	
Initial manner (IM)	pɪt–fɪt	5.795	1.809	.197	.560	.223
	tæp–sæp	5.641	1.423	.063	.680	
	bæt–væt	6.231	1.495	.409	.617	
Final manner (FM)	kæp–kæf	5.923	1.345	.287	.556	-.208
	kɪt–kɪs	5.282	1.468	-.101	.529	
	bʌd–bʌz	5.051	1.716	-.249	.633	

Category	Pair				
Initial voice & place (IVP)	pɛt–gɛt	5.897	1.552	.214	.568	
	pɔt–dɔt	6.128	1.740	.354	.728	.251
	tɔt–gɔt	5.872	1.361	.184	.617	
Final voice & place (FVP)	pɪg–pɪp	5.103	1.971	−.184	.841	
	tɔd–tɔp	5.410	1.601	.044	.530	−.104
	tæk–tæd	5.051	1.572	−.173	.533	
Initial voice, place & manner (IVPM)	bɪt–sɪt	6.000	1.606	.258	.632	
	kæt–væt	5.718	1.731	.124	.660	.218
	pɪp–zɪp	5.769	1.724	.146	.589	
Final voice, place & manner (FVPM)	gæg–gæs	5.222	1.922	−.481	.595	
	hæk–hæv	4.256	1.312	−.604	.468	−.481
	hɪp–hɪz	4.795	1.637	−.356	.500	

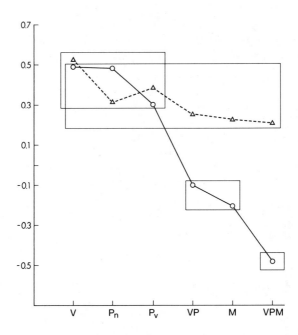

Figure 11.2 Results of the similarity judgment experiment comparing consonants in initial (Δ) and final (○) positions; data points are mean z-scores of different conditions.

have been assigned to identical items—could be 9.0). If place differences are added to these (in the IVP and FVP items), the means are reduced to 5.97 and 5.19. But additional data (not reflected in these tables) show that if voicing differences alone are manifested in different positions, the raw score goes down to 4.54 (/pit/–/bid/ = 4.26; /tip/–/dib/ = 4.82), which is even lower than the values for three-feature mismatches in either initial or final positions, as shown by the means for the IVPM and FVPM items, which are 5.83 and 4.76. Thus a voicing mismatch in both initial and final position has a greater effect on the similarity rating than do voicing, place, and manner mismatches in a single position in the syllable. While the number of features that disagree has some effect, the location of the mismatches, as well as the particular features involved, must also be considered. All of these findings suggest that V&W's holistic phonemic approach must be amended somewhat, although the relatively high sensitivity of similarity judgments to the difference between a perfect feature match on a segment and even a one-feature difference would justify the continued use of their technique in many areas of experimental phonology, particularly where only gross measurements are required. Further research is needed to determine the level (phonological vs. phonetic) at which subjects are operating when making these judgments.

EXPERIMENTS ON PHONOLOGICAL RULES

Another series of experiments conducted in our department has been concerned with the question of whether (or when) a putative phonological or morphological rule expresses a true generalization, that is, one which is psychologically real. In his 1976 doctoral dissertation, for example, Cena used a paired-associate learning task to assess the psychological reality of the vowel alternations embodied in the vowel shift analysis of SPE. His experiments, which are described in condensed form in Cena (1978), show that (1) it is easier for subjects to learn pairs of nonsense items that show the correct English vowel alternations than those that do not, and (2) the attested English alternations interfere with the learning of non-English vowel alternations. Thus, as an example of (2), subjects who were taught a pair like /ɪnsayp/–/ɪnsɛpɪti/ tended to "correct" the latter to /ɪnsɪpɪti/ in the recall phase. Other experiments (Moskowitz 1973; Myerson 1976) have also provided support for the psychological reality of at least some of the same vowel-shift alternations.

Some experiments indicate, however, that there are important differences between fully productive, relatively shallow rules such as those involved in English plural formation and minor rules such as vowel shift which apply to a more restricted set of lexical items. Indeed, there is some doubt as to whether such minor rules are really learned as rules at all.

When Steinberg and Krohn (1975) in their experiment required subjects to add derivational suffixes such as -*ic* or -*ity* to stems on which they do not ordinarily occur, for example, *snide,* they were generally unable to provide the predicted vowel-shifted form spontaneously. Such behavior contrasts sharply with the correct and unhesitating responses typically provided in the novel pluralization task described earlier and thus points to important differences in the two cases.

A further, more subtle, difference should also be mentioned. McCawley (1979) points out that some of the subjects' responses in Cena's experiment differ from those predicted by the SPE version of vowel shift. Cena himself indicated that the vowel alternation /ʌ–aw/ behaved differently from the others: It was both more difficult to learn and was less likely to interfere with the learning of arbitrary non-English alternations. In fact, even the formally unrelated /ɔ–aw/ alternation showed a stronger influence than /ʌ–aw/, in that it was both more easily learned and interfered more with learning other alternations. McCawley believes that this provides evidence for the 'individuation' (as opposed to 'generalization') of the vowel-shift alternations. The /ʌ–aw/ alternation in English is extremely rare, yet formally, in the SPE account of the vowel shift, it is treated as completely parallel to the considerably more frequent /ɪ–ay/ alternation, as in *divinity–divine.* In

Cena's experiment, the latter alternation had a considerable influence on subjects' learning patterns while the former did not. But to exclude /ʌ-aw/ from the SPE vowel shift rules would require a formally unmotivated complication of the analysis and thus undermine it seriously.[9]

The extent to which frequency of occurrence of a certain subpart of a given alternation determines speakers' ability to process it may provide evidence on whether the alternation represents a generalization they have made or not. Derwing (1979) found the frequency of occurrence of a particular stem ending had very little influence on children's ability to pluralize nonsense stems. For example, it made little difference whether the stems ended in the very frequent /i/ or the relatively infrequent /ɔ/, in the frequent sibilant consonants /s/ or /ǰ/ or the very rare /ž/. However, when results for irregular English plurals were studied, frequency was highly predictive of order of difficulty. In fact, the frequency was completely predictive of order of difficulty when the effect of competing regular patterns was controlled for (see also Derwing & Baker 1979). If, therefore, the learning of the English vowel shift alternations proceeds on a piecemeal basis as the data above suggest, it would seem to parallel the irregular plurals rather than the regular ones. Thus, the best vowel shift analysis should have more the properties of a complex list rather than the form of a simple set of broad generalizations. Research is continuing on the question of the precise psychological status of such alternation patterns.

Finally, we have begun a new series of productivity studies designed to show whether or not rules such as voicing assimilation and vowel insertion or deletion are learned by speakers who have mastered such processes as the formation of English plurals, and noun possessives. Briefly, in these studies we teach subjects stems which are the names for imaginary mature and healthy (pink) animals (also presented through pictures). We then teach novel suffixes, for example, /-ž/ or /-g/, which when attached to the stems designate immature (blue) or sickly (yellow) counterparts of the same animals. Once subjects learn to attach these suffixes to stems ending in the voiced non-sibilant and nonvelar consonants (e.g., /zebž/, an immature /zeb/, or /ɛvg/, a sickly /ɛv/), they are required to add the suffixes to stems ending in consonants excluded from the training session. In this case the question is, are /-ž/ and /-g/ automatically devoiced to /-š/ and /-k/, respectively, when first attached to voiceless stems like /ayp/ or /plərf/, as would be expected from speakers

---

[9]Jaeger (1984) offers another analysis of the problem with the [ʌ-aw] alternation. Results from her concept-formation experiment indicate that subjects' awareness of the vowel-shift alternations are based on their knowledge of spelling, in particular the sounds associated with the five vowel letters *a, e, i, o, u* when "long" or "short." In the case of *u*, this would dictate the alternation [ju] (or [u])-[ʌ], not [aw]-[ʌ]. This conclusion is further buttressed by Wang (1985) in a broader based study.

who know a general voicing-assimilation rule for obstruent clusters? And is the reduced vowel /ə/ or /I/ inserted when /-ž/ is attached to a stem with a sibilant at the end, like /swərǰ/, and when /-g/ is attached to a stem ending in a velar, such as /drɔyg/, as would be expected from speakers who know a general vowel-insertion rule of the kind usually proposed for English plural or past tense formation? Or, alternatively, is the vowel instead deleted by another group of subjects, in the complementary phonological environments, if they are taught that the basic forms of the suffixes are /-əz/ and /-əg/? (See Derwing 1980b, pp. 87-93, for details of the proposed rules and relevant environments.)

Preliminary results indicate that most subjects use the voicing-assimilation rule spontaneously and consistently in all of the appropriate environments, while the vowel–insertion or –deletion rule is almost never used. While much larger subject samples and stricter controls should be employed before these findings can be taken seriously, the tentative conclusion to be drawn is that, of the proposed rules, only voicing assimilation seems to be a genuine part of speakers' grammar. (See Derwing & Baker 1980: 260–261, for discussion of a plausible theory that would be consistent with these findings.)

CONCLUSION

It is clear from the foregoing as well as from accounts of experimental phonological investigations elsewhere that only a small fraction of the questions which occupy phonologists have yet been studied experimentally and, of these, few could be said to have been given confident answers. In part this is a consequence of the relative newness of the experimental approach in phonology—the methods are still in need of much refinement—but more important, it is due to the fact that so few linguists have been inclined to devote their energies to this method of evaluating phonological claims. We suppose that one reason for this latter condition is that there has been scant encouragement for this type of work, no doubt due in part to widespread unawareness of the need for external validation. More understandable are views like those of Ladefoged and Traill (1980) who readily identify with the problem yet despair of experimental solutions in the face of many obvious technical and practical difficulties. We are less pessimistic; in fact, we are greatly encouraged by the amount of progress already achieved by so few in so short a span of time. We fully believe that if enough phonologists apply their considerable energies and imagination to these problems, there is no limit to the range of phonological issues that can be resolved by means of a thoroughgoing experimental approach. In the long run, in fact, there is no viable alternative.

REFERENCES

Anderson, S. R. 1974. *The organization of phonology*. New York: Academic Press.

Berko, J. 1958. The child's learning of English morphology. *Word* 14:150-177.

Cena, R. M. 1976. An experimental investigation of vowel alternation in English. Ph.D diss. University of Alberta, Edmonton.

Cena, R. M. 1978. *When is a phonological generalization psychologically real?* Bloomington, IN: Indiana University Linguistics Club.

Chomsky, N., & M. Halle. 1968. *The sound pattern of English*. New York: Harper & Row.

Cook, V. J. 1974. Is explanatory adequacy adequate? *Linguistics:* 133, 21-31.

Derwing, B. L. 1973. *Transformational grammar as a theory of language acquisition: A study in the empirical, conceptual and methodological foundations of contemporary linguistics*. London: Cambridge University Press.

Derwing, B. L. 1976. Morpheme recognition and the learning of rules for derivational morphology. *The Canadian Journal of Linguistics* 21:38-66.

Derwing, B. L. 1977. *The acquisition of English morphology*. Final report to the Canada Council, Leave Fellowship No. 451-77502.

Derwing, B. L. 1979. Psycholinguistic evidence and linguistic theory. In G. D. Prideaux, ed., *Perspectives in experimental linguistics,* 113-138 Amsterdam: John Benjamins.

Derwing, B. L. 1980a. Against autonomous linguistics. In T. Perry, ed., *Evidence and argumentation in linguistics,* 163-189. Berlin: de Gruyter.

Derwing, B. L. 1980b. English pluralization: A testing ground for rule evaluation. In G. D. Prideaux, B. L. Derwing, & W. J. Baker, eds., *Experimental linguistics: Integration of theories and applications,* 81-112. Ghent: E. Story-Scientia.

Derwing, B. L., & W. J. Baker. 1974. *Rule learning and the English inflections*. Final report to the Canada Council, File No. S72-0332.

Derwing, B. L., & W. J. Baker. 1976. *On the learning of English morphological rules*. Final report to the Canada Council, File No. S73-0387.

Derwing, B. L., & W. J. Baker. 1977. The psychological basis for morphological rules. In J. Macnamara, ed., *Language learning and thought,* 85-110. New York: Academic Press.

Derwing, B. L., & W. J. Baker. 1978. On the re-integration of linguistics and psychology. In R.N. Campbell & P. T., Smith, eds., *Recent advances in the psychology of language. Part B: Formal and experimental approaches,* 193-218. New York: Plenum Press.

Derwing, B. L., & W. J. Baker. 1979. Recent research on the acquisition of English morphology. In P. J. Fletcher & M. Garman, eds., *Language acquisition: Studies in first language development,* 209-223. Cambridge: Cambridge University Press.

Derwing, B.L., & W. J. Baker. 1980. Rule learning and the English inflections (with special emphasis on the plural). In G. D. Prideaux, B. L. Derwing, & W. J. Baker, eds., *Experimental linguistics: Integration of theories and applications,* 247-272. Ghent: E. Story-Scientia.

Dow, M. L. 1980. On the role of orthography in experimental phonology. M.Sc. thesis, University of Alberta, Edmonton.

Fromkin, V. A. (1980). The psychological reality of phonological descriptions. In E. Fischer-Jørgensen, & N. Thorsen, eds., *Proceeding of the Ninth International Congress of Phonetic Sciences* (Vol. 3), 195-202. University of Copenhagen.

Haber, L. 1975. The muzzy theory. *Papers from the Regional Meeting of the Chicago Linguistic Society,* 11:240-256.

Halle, M. 1964. On the bases of phonology. In J. A. Fodor & J. J. Katz, eds., *The structure of language: Readings in the philosophy of language,* 324-333. Englewood Cliffs, NJ: Prentice-Hall.

Ingram, J. C. L. 1980. Perceptual dimensions of phonemic recognition. In G. D. Prideaux, B. L. Derwing, & W. J. Baker, eds., *Experimental linguistics: Integration of theories and applications,* 273-291. Ghent: E. Story-Scientia.

Innes, S. J. 1974. Developmental aspects of plural formation in English. M.Sc. thesis, University of Alberta, Edmonton.

Jaeger, J. J. 1980. Testing the psychological reality of phonemes. *Language & Speech* 23:233-253.

Jaeger, J. J. 1984. Assessing the psychological status of the Vowel Shift Rule. *Journal of Psycholinguistic Research* 13:13-36.

Kac, M. B. 1980. In defense of autonomous linguistics. *Lingua* 50:242-245.

Kiparsky, P., & L. Menn. 1977. On the acquisition of phonology. In J. Macnamara, ed., *Language learning and thought,* 47-78. New York: Academic Press.

Ladefoged, P., & Traill, T. 1980. *The phonetic inadequacy of phonological specifications of clicks* (Working Papers in Phonetics 49), 1-27. University of California at Los Angeles.

Linnel, P. 1979. *Psychological reality in phonology: A theoretical study.* Cambridge: Cambridge University Press.

McCawley, J. D. 1979. Remarks on Cena's vowel shift experiment. In P. R. Clyne, W. F. Hanks, & C. L. Hofbauer, eds., *The elements: A parasession on linguistic units and levels,* 110-118. Chicago: Chicago Linguistic Society.

Moskowitz, B. A. 1973. On the status of vowel shift in English. In T. E. Moore, ed., *Cognitive development and the acquisition of language,* 223-260. New York: Academic Press.

Myerson, R. F. 1976. A study of children's knowledge of certain word formation rules and the relationship of this knowledge to various forms of reading achievement. Ph.D. diss., Harvard University.

Nearey, T. M. 1981. The psychological reality of phonological representations: Experimental evidence. In T. Myers, J. Laver, & J. Anderson, eds., *The cognitive representation of speech,* 359-369. North-Holland: Amsterdam.

Prideaux, G. D. 1980a. In rejection of autonomous linguistics. *Lingua* 50:245-247.

Prideaux, G. D. 1980b. Review of M. B. Kac, *Corepresentation of grammatical structure. Lingua* 50:171-178.

Prideaux, G. D., B. L. Derwing, & W. J. Baker, eds., 1980. *Experimental linguistics: Intergration of theories and applications.* Ghent: E. Story-Scientia.

Rollins, W. C. 1980. Laboratory vs. "free" testing situations in language acquisition research. B.Sc. honours thesis, University of Alberta, Edmonton.

Rommetveit, R. 1979. Deep structure of sentences versus message structure: Some critical remarks on current paradigms and suggestions for an alternative approach. In R. Rommetveit & R. Blakar, eds., *Studies of language, thought and verbal communication,* 17-34. New York: Academic Press.

Steinberg, D. D., & R. Krohn. 1975. The psychological reality of Chomsky and Halle's vowel shift rule. In E. F. K. Koerner, ed., *The transformational-generative paradigm and modern linguistic theory,* 233-259. Amsterdam: John Benjamins.

Valian, V. 1976. The relationship between competence and performance: A theoretical review. *CUNYForum* 1:64-101.

Vitz, P.C., & B. S. Winkler. 1973. Predicting the judged 'similarity of sound' of English words. *Journal of Verbal Learning & Verbal Behavior* 12:373-388.

Wang, H. S. 1985. On the productivity of vowel shift alternations in English: An experimental study. Ph.D. diss., University of Alberta, Edmonton.

12

Concept Formation as a Tool for Linguistic Research

JERI J. JAEGER

INTRODUCTION

Concept Formation

A language is a system of categories. This unsurprising fact is due to the nature of language users: human beings who deal with the world by mentally categorizing and organizing it as much as possible (Boas 1911:20–21; Sapir 1921: Ch. 1). Linguists regularly make claims, covertly or overtly, about the organization, stucture, and content of speakers' linguistic categorizations; such concepts as 'phoneme,' 'morpheme,' 'word,' and 'sentence' are, in fact, theories about what units count as being 'the same' in speakers' conceptualizations. However, such theories have rarely been rigorously tested.

This chapter presents an attempt at developing the methodology for testing such claims, using the concept formation (CF) experimental paradigm, which is a standard tool of psychological research (see Bruner, Goodnow, & Austin 1956; Deese & Hulse 1967: Ch. 12; Dominowski 1970).[1] In the discussion below I first describe the mechanics of the CF technique and then present the results of two experiments in which the CF design was used to assess the categorical nature of several linguistic phenomena.

---

[1]The concept formation technique has been applied previously to other linguistic questions; see, for example, Baker, Prideaux, and Derwing (1973), Moskowitz (1973).

211

Overview of the Experimental Paradigm

METHODOLOGY

In the version of the CF experiment I am concerned with, Ss are taught to form some category by being presented with positive and negative exemplars of that category; they demonstrate that they have formed the category by correctly sorting new tokens into positive and negative instances. The parameters of the categories thus formed can be further explored by asking Ss to make decisions on unclear cases. There are three basic types of questions that can be asked using the CF techniques: (1) What is the psychological status of the categories thus formed? (2) What are the composition and internal structure of specific categories? (3) What are the (taxonomic or hierarchic) interrelations among different categories?

THE PSYCHOLOGICAL STATUS OF THE CATEGORIES TESTED

In most CF experiments, the fact that a S can form a particular category is usually taken to imply that either that category preexisted in the S's mind or that at least the components or attributes of that category preexisted. For example, if Ss are asked to form a category 'large red octagons' (the shape of stop signs), it is reasonable to assume that for those Ss who are automobile drivers, this will be a preestablished category; however, if Ss are asked to form the category 'large red rectangles,' it is more likely that they have no such preexisting category and that their performance would be based on their knowledge of the concepts 'large,' 'red,' and 'rectangle.' There are several ways in which the psychological preexistence of categories can be inferred from Ss' behavior in CF experiments.

First, there should be some correlation between the ease with which a category is formed and whether it was known previously to Ss. Brown (1956) demonstrated this clearly by teaching two groups of Ss, speakers of English and speakers of Navaho, to sort color chips into four categories, the (nonsense-word) names of which differed both by vowel quality and by vowel length (*ma, ma:, mo, mo:*). While the Navaho speakers, for whom vowel length is distinctive, all sorted the chips correctly on the first try, the English speakers all ignored the vowel length and divided the chips into two categories with names differentiated only by vowel quality. When told this was incorrect, they all eventually discerned the vowel length difference, but it was clearly an unnatural categorization for them. Similarly, Ohala (1983) taught two groups of English-speaking Ss two opposing phonemic categorizations: one was taught to group the [k] in *school* with [kʰ] as in *cool*, and the other with [g,g] as in *good, ago*. The first group formed the category easily, but many Ss in the second group could not form it at all, and those who did reported it as a disjunctive category: '[gə] sounds, and the [kʰə] sound after s'. It could be concluded from this that [k,kʰ] is more likely to be a preestablished grouping for these Ss than is [k,g̦,g,].[2] Second, the way Ss generalize a category to stimuli differing from those used to exemplify it can reveal something about its possible prior existence in the minds of Ss. If Ss quickly and consistently include in the category certain tokens which differ qualitatively from those taught as being positive instances, then this could be a reflection of a previously existing category which contains a broader range of members than those presented as positive instances. This pattern of performance is evident in the experiments discussed below.

THE INTERNAL COMPOSITION AND
STRUCTURE OF CATEGORIES

Rosch and her associates (Rosch 1973, 1978; Mervis & Rosch 1981) have demonstrated that natural categories are generally not strictly binary, in the sense that an item either is a member of that category or is not, and all members are equally good instances of the category. Instead, natural categories have a complex internal structure which includes prototypical members (those with the most typical confluence of attributes, which are the most different from prototypical members of other categories at the same taxonomic level) and more peripheral members (which have a less typical set of attributes and may be considered members of more than one catgegory at the same taxonomic level). In other words, the boundaries of natural categories are somewhat fuzzy. In categorization experiments, prototypical members of a category are more rapidly identified as members of that category than are peripheral members, and there is more consistency in the categorization of prototypical members both by individual Ss and across Ss (Rosch 1978). Therefore, in CF experiments both the reaction times and the response patterns of Ss give evidence about the internal structure of categories.

THE EXTERNAL STRUCTURE OF CATEGORIES

Categories are interrelated in a hierarchically arranged taxonomic structure, so that any particular object can be categorized at a number of different levels of abstraction. Categories formed at some levels of abstraction are more salient or accessible to consciousness than others (Brown & Lenneberg 1954; Brown & McNeill 1966; Deese & Hulse 1967: 433ff.; Rosch 1978; MacKay 1978). Rosch (Rosch, Mervis, Gray, Johnson, & Boyes-Braem 1976)

---

[2]The phonemic classification of the velar segment after [s] in words such as *school* is a classic problem; see Bloomfield (1933:80,99), Bloch & Trager (1942:44), Jakobson, Fant, and Halle (1951:36–38), Lotz, Abramson and Gerstman, Ingemann, and Nemser (1960), Reeds and Wang (1961), Davidsen-Nielsen (1974), Fink (1974), and Hooper (1976:21). Phonetically, this segment is more similar to word-initial /g/ than to word-initial /k/.

has presented evidence that for every object there is one particular level of categorization which is the most salient or basic; this 'basic level' of categorization depends on both physical and functional attributes and reflects the level of abstraction at which human beings most frequently interact with the object. So, for example, there exist a number of objects which have four metal legs, a plastic seat, and a metal and plastic back, which can be sat upon. The basic level of categorization for this object is 'chair'; superordinate categorizations include 'furniture' and 'thing', while subordinate classifications include 'kitchen chair'. Since basic-level categories are more accessible than either superordinate- or subordinate-level categories, Ss in CF experiments can form basic-level categories more rapidly and with more consistency across Ss than they can categories at other levels of abstraction. Likewise they can make decisions about the categorization of particular objects most rapidly and consistently when they are asked to sort them into basic-level categories.

THE CONCEPT-FORMATION TECHNIQUE

As with any experimental technique, the kinds of variation in design are limited only by the imagination or resources of the experimenter. The CF experiments described here represent only a few of the designs possible.

A Sample Experiment

There are four major components to these CF experiments: the instructions, the learning session, the test session, and the post-experimental interview. The instructions direct Ss' attention to the relevant attributes of the stimuli while allowing them to form the category without any explicit verbal explanation from E of what the category includes. During the learning session, Ss are exposed to positive and negative instances of the category and are given feedback as to the status of each token. They form the category by abstracting the properties common to the positive tokens but missing from the negative tokens. In the test session, Ss categorize tokens representing new cases which are ambiguous and potentially members of the category. In the interview, Ss are asked to name the category and discuss their decision-making strategies. The following sample experimental session illustrates the basic components of the CF paradigm, and is the basis for the discussion to follow.

The S is seated in a quiet room, and E reads the following instructions aloud:

> This is an experiment designed to help us learn something about the way
> the English language works. You will be listening to a series of spoken

English words. Some of these words will contain *a certain sound*, and others will not contain this sound. After each word there will be a three-second pause, then the voice on the tape will tell you whether the word you just heard had the sound or not. It will say "yes" if the word had the sound and "no" if did not. Your job is to figure out what the sound is that the 'yes' words have in common, that the 'no' words don't have. After you have some idea what the sound is, you should respond by saying "yes" or "no" during the pause after each word, before the voice on the tape says the correct answer. You will know that you have figured out the correct sound when your responses always match those of the voice on the tape. Remember that you are listening for some sound that all the 'yes' words have in common that the 'no' words don't have.

The S then hears the following list of words:

1. kind	yes		8. kiss	yes		15. key	yes
2. left	no		9. knit	no		16. acclaim	yes
3. clear	yes		10. recruit	yes		17. choose	no
4. because	yes		11. great	no		18. crow	yes
5. star	no		12. children	no		19. knife	no
6. chrome	yes		13. choir	yes		20. science	no
7. gift	no		14. candy	yes			

If the S responds correctly on some preestablished number of words, E then administers the test session, after giving these instructions:

Now I'm going to give you a test. You will hear a list of 20 words, and you should answer just as you have been doing; the sound you will be listening for is the same one you have just figured out. However, in the test you will not be told if your answer is correct or not. You will only hear the word and the three seconds of silence, then the next word, and so on. You should just continue answering as accurately as possible, based on the sound you have just figured out.

The S then hears the following words, with no reinforcing answers (the words in parentheses identify the functions of the tokens for the reader's sake).

1. penny	(no)		11. Christmas	(yes)
2. chest	(no)		12. meeting	(no)
3. climb	(yes)		13. keen	(yes)
4. skin	(TEST)		14. scare	(TEST)
5. queen	(CONTROL)		15. guide	(no)
6. partition	(no)		16. knothole	(no)
7. raccoon	(yes)		17. sequester	(CONTROL)
8. greedy	(no)		18. ascend	(no)
9. quiche	(CONTROL)		19. except	(TEST)
10. bookshelf	(TEST)		20. cherries	(no)

How do Ss respond to these words? If they say "yes" to *queen* and *sequester,* which contain the aspirated [kʰ] which they were trained to respond to (but spelled with a letter they have not yet been exposed to), then we know they have formed the category and can apply it to new cases correctly (for reasons detailed below). If they say "yes" to words such as *scare* and *bookshelf,* they are following a phoneme-like classification. If they reject *except* or include *knothole,* they are making use of the spelling of the words. If they include *greedy* or reject everything but aspirated [kʰ], then they have categorized the sounds in a way which does not coincide with traditional phonemic analyses of English.

It can be seen from this example that, while the CF experiment is a relatively simple one, it may be designed to reveal a great deal about how linguistically naive speakers classify the elements of their language.

Motivation of the Design

INSTRUCTIONS

The instructions must direct Ss' attention to the relevant aspects of the stimuli without giving too much or too little information. If too much information is given, Ss may base their responses on E's implied category rather than on their own intuitive classifications. If too little information is given, Ss may either be unable to form any category at all, or may form as incorrect category which they will stubbornly try to apply.

In the above experiment, the concept to be tested was the phoneme /k/. The S was told to listen for "a certain sound"; this leaves Ss free to define for themselves what constitutes the notion of 'a sound' and which aspect(s) of the sounds of the words occurs in all positive tokens. Telling them to listen for "a [kʰə] sound" would be too much information, as it might lead Ss to reject any unaspirated [k]; instructing them that "some of these words have something in common" would be giving them too little information and would send them in pursuit of similarities in meaning, spelling, stress, or whatever notion happened to strike them first.

The more complicated a category is, the more detailed the instructions need to be; this is demonstrated in the discussion of the [voice] experiment below. If a group of Ss is participating in a series of CF experiments, the instructions should be as similar as possible throughout.

THE LEARNING SESSION

The learning session is designed to teach Ss the concept by presenting them with tokens which exemplify the concept and tokens which do not.'Positive tokens' should be chosen which contain the range of features included in the concept, excluding those to be tested. 'Negative tokens' should include all possible interfering factors which are to be excluded from the concept, as well as non-interfering (i.e., 'neutral') words. For example, in the learning session of the sample experiment presented above, the choice of words was motivated as follows: The 11 positive tokens all contain aspirated [kʰ]; there are instances of initial and medial [kʰ]; all possible spellings except one are represented (*q* was reserved to serve as a control in the test session; see below). [kʰ] appears before several different vowels; there are clusters as well as single-consonant initials. Negative tokens include words spelled with *k, c, ch,* which are not pronounced as a velar stop, and the contrasting velar stop /g/. (Although the words are presented orally, various spellings are represented in case Ss refer to mental images of the written word.) The S is thus taught to discriminate [kʰ] from phonetically and orthographically similar segments; a wide range of acceptable manifestations of the correct sound is presented in the positive tokens.

THE TEST SESSION

In general, the test session includes tokens of the types presented in the learning session as well as test tokens and, optionally, control tokens. 'Control tokens' are words whose category membership (or lack of it) is clear but which contain some attribute not yet encountered by the S. These control tokens are checks on the possibility that a S may have formed a category different from that intended by E, or may even have just memorized the members of the category taught in the learning session. If Ss respond incorrectly to control words, then their responses to test words are of questionable value, since it is not clear what category they have actually formed. Responses to control tokens are generalized responses and are typically weaker than responses to tokens of the types taught as belonging (or not belonging) to the category in the learning session; that is, they induce more errors, longer reaction times, and so on.

In the sample experiment, no tokens of [kʰ] spelled *q* were presented in the learning session, but they were included in the test session as positive controls. If Ss responded "yes" to these tokens, then they had correctly formed the category being taught; "no" probably indicated that Ss had formed their category based on spelling rather than sound.

'Test tokens' are the tokens whose category membership is in question. Ss are given the opportunity to extend to these unclear cases the category which they have been taught. As noted above, Ss' inclusion or exclusion of the test words in the target category gives information about both the structure and composition of the category and its reality or previous existence. As responses to test words are also generalized responses, they are weaker than those to words of the type presented in the learning session and are comparable in this respect to responses to the control tokens. In the sample experiment, the test words are those containing the unaspirated velar stop after initial [s], and medial unreleased [k°]; Ss' inclusion of these tokens in the category indicates that the S is responding on the basis of a phoneme-like classification, as noted earlier.

In the test session, Ss are not given feedback as to the correctness of their responses to either the test words or the control words, since it is Ss' unguided responses to these words which are of interest. However, feedback may or may not be given following words of the type presented in the learning session, depending on the difficulty of the concept. In the test session of the sample experiment no feedback was given; this works well when the concept is relatively simple and it is unlikely that Ss will have trouble transferring it (i.e., remembering it) from the learning to the test session. However, if the concept is relatively difficult, the break between learning and test session and lack of reinforcement in the test session may cause Ss to forget what criteria they were previously using to guide their responses, and their responses in the test session may become increasingly random. Therefore, with more difficult concepts a better method is to give all the instructions at the beginning of the learning session, and then switch to the test session (with no break in continuity) as soon as the S has reached criterion; in the test session some percentage of the responses to tokens which are neither control nor test items can continue to be reinforced.[3]

Interpretation of the Data

There are four kinds of data obtainable during the CF experiment which yield useful information: number of trials to criterion, proportion of positive to negative responses to different token types, reaction times, and ability to name the category.

TRIALS TO CRITERION

In the experiments discussed below, the criterion '15 trials in a row with two or fewer errors' was used. This criterion was chosen partly because it was felt that Ss should hear at least this many tokens to be assured of having been exposed to the full range of positive exemplars. Further, it is extremely unlikely that a S could respond correctly this many times by chance ($p = .004$, one-tailed binomial test). The number of trials to criterion can be adjusted to the difficulty of the task; however, when a series of experiments is being performed using the same Ss, the criterion should be held constant throughout

[3]This variation in the design was suggested to me by Saul Sternberg.

so that this measure can be compared among the different tasks. Variations in number of trials to criterion would indicate that some concepts are more difficult to form than others (assuming Ss have equal opportunity to learn them) and can provide evidence as to the relative degree of accessibility of different linguistic categories.

If trials to criterion across several experiments are to be compared, the order of presentation of positive and negative tokens should be the same in all experiments. However, even when this order is constant, different types of concepts differ inherently in the amount of information contained in each token. In a binary set, a positive token contains exactly as much information as a negative token, and relatively few tokens (minimally, two) may be enough to clarify the category. In a concept such as the phoneme /k/, positive tokens contain more information than negative tokens; however, a single positive token is not enough to clarify the category but only begins to narrow down the possibilities (see Dominowski 1970: 162ff.). These inherent differences must be taken into account when comparisons of the learnability of different categories are made.

POSITIVE VERSUS NEGATIVE RESPONSES

In the learning session, the pattern of errors in positive and negative responses can give evidence about the internal structure of the category, that is, which members are relatively easy to categorize (i.e., are more prototypical members of the category) and which are more difficult to discriminate and categorize (i.e., more peripheral members). In the test session, of course, the positive and negative responses to the test words indicate whether Ss are including them in the category or not.

REACTION TIMES

The time it takes a S to respond affirmatively or negatively to each word can be measured and reaction times (RTs) to different conditions compared. Longer RTs can indicate more complex processing (Friedman 1968; Fry 1970); because of this, Ss who develop a more complex decision-making strategy would be expected to have consistently longer RTs than Ss who develop a simpler strategy. Further, longer RTs can indicate less confidence in one's responses; thus, positive tokens which consistently elicit long RTs are probably less central examples of the category, and negative tokens which elicit long RTs probably have some salient attribute in common with the positive tokens. RTs to test words are generalized responses and so may be longer than RTs to words taught as having a particular category membership; they are more comparable to RTs to control words.

Interpreting RTs is problematic for a number of reasons. Responding positively and responding negatively are different kinds of cognitive tasks and take differing amounts of time to perform. Complications arise if the information allowing the S to make the decision occurs at different places in words. For example, in the word *cool*, Ss have enough information to make the decision that they have heard a /k/ after the burst of the [kʰ]; but in *plain* they have enough information to decide that they have not heard a /k/ only at the end of the word. RTs measured from these differing points in words show large systematic differences, due to the fact that different amounts of the word remain to be processed when the response is initiated. Further, it seems to take differing amounts of time to answer correctly as opposed to making an error (see Jaeger 1980a for a more detailed discussion of the problems involved in assessing RTs). For these reasons, in the experiments to be reported here, RTs have only been compared for like tokens (e.g., all non-/k/ words) within a single experiment (not across experiments).

ABILITY TO NAME CATEGORY

Brown and Lenneberg (1954) have developed the notion of 'codability,' which has proven useful for explicating the category-naming behavior of Ss in these CF experiments (see also Chafe 1977). According to Brown and Lenneberg, a category which is higher on the availability-to-consciousness hierarchy will be more codable, in the sense that (1) it will be named with a single word or with very few words, (2) Ss will respond rapidly when asked to name it, (3) Ss will agree among themselves as to the correct name of the category, and (4) a single S will be consistent in the name he or she gives the category at different times.

In the experiments discussed here, evidence was gathered on the first and third of these points. Further, it was hypothesized that naming ability would be correlated with Ss' ability to remember the concept and transfer it to the test session. However, it should be noted that Ss can form and correctly apply a concept without being able to name it or even explain on what basis they are making categorizations (Deese & Hulse 1967: 416). Such concepts are probably extremely low in the accessibility hierarchy.

The name a S gives to a concept is usually related to the categorization strategy the S is using; it is also often reflected in the errors the S makes. For example, in the sample experiment, Ss who named the category 'words with a [kʰə] sound' would probably also report that they were either listening for the target sound in each token or repeating the words to themselves to see if they "felt" the sound; they would respond rapidly and would err on the phonetically similar /g/. Ss who named the concept 'words with hard *c*' would probably also report spelling words to themselves or visualizing the spelling; they would have longer RTs since visualizing spelling is a more complex processing strategy than listening for sounds; and they would err on words with 'silent *k*'.

EXPERIMENT 1: AUTOMATED CONCEPT FORMATION

Method

The first CF experiment to be discussed here tested the concept 'the phoneme /k/' as described in the sample experiment above. However, in this experiment, Ss were trained to make rapid decisions about the categorization of each word and to indicate their choices by pushing a button rather than giving verbal responses (see Jaeger 1980a, 1980b, for details). Ss were seated in a sound-treated room in front of a panel which contained two lights, red and green, and a box which contained two contract-switch buttons, also red and green. Ss heard a list of words over headphones. They were instructed that after each word they should quickly indicate whether it was part of the category (by pressing the green button) or not (by pressing the red button). If they responded incorrectly or if they failed to respond quickly enough, the lights would come on indicating the correct response (green for 'category' and red for 'non-category'); the lights were timed to allow the Ss a response interval which was randomly distributed in a Gaussian fashion, mean = 1500 msec, SD = 150 msec. In this way the lights both signaled the time limit for responding and provided the feedback which permitted Ss to learn the category. During the test session, the green light was disconnected and the red light served only as a timing device; there was no feedback as to correct or incorrect responses.

The stimulus tapes were designed similarly to those in the sample experiment, except that there were no control words included in the design. The learning session contained 61 words; it was designed to gradually teach the concept 'words containing [k^h].' It included 32 [k^h] words intermixed with 29 other words introduced in the following order: words 1–18: neutral words; words 19–31: spelling interferences; words 32–48: other velars; words 49–61: all types of words. The test session contained 40 words, randomly intermixed, including 13 [k^h] words, 12 words with phonetic or orthographic interferences, 6 neutral words, and 5 test words: 3 containing initial [sk], and 2 with final [k°].

There were nine Ss, native speakers of English, all of whom were linguistically naive and over 18 years of age. They were instructed to listen for "a certain sound" and to respond as rapidly as possible. All Ss heard all the words, so that a large number of responses to all types of words would be available for evaluation. Ss' positive or negative responses and RTs were recorded. A small laboratory computer ran the experiment; it turned on the lights and recorded Ss' responses.

Results

All nine Ss reached criterion (15 tokens in a row with 2 or fewer errors) in an average of 19 trials (range 15–32, $SD = 5$). Average RTs and positive responses for all Ss are shown in Tables 12.1–12.3.

In the learning session, variations in RT to the [k^h] words due to variations in spelling or variations in sound were nonsignificant: spelling, $F(3,225) = .969$, p > .25; sound, $F(3,225) = .561$, $p > .50$.[4] However, there were significantly more negative responses made to [k^h] words spelled with q than to [k^h] words spelled with either k or ch: comparing percent positive responses, $F(3,24) = 3.826$, $p = .023$; k versus q and ch versus q, $t(8) = 2.940$, two-tailed $p < .02$. That the interference was caused by the spelling and not the phonetic environment (i.e., [k^hw]) is shown by the fact that a comparison of percent positive responses grouped along the phonetic dimension reveals no significant differences ($F(3,24) = 2.138, p > .10$). The two types of non-/k/ words which caused some interference are words with spelled k (e.g., *kneel*), which have long RTs, and words with phonetic [tʃ] spelled ch, with 22% errors. These both indicate some orthographic interference, and the latter probably some phonetic interference as well.

The test words containing initial [sk] and final [k°] were clearly being categorized with the [k^h] words; a comparison of the percent positive responses of each S to these three types of words in the test session shows that there were no significant differences: $F(2,16) = 3.469, p > .05$. The slightly weaker response to the final [k°] is probably due to its position in the word, since Ss had not been hearing words where the crucial segment was word final and were often answering before the word was completed. The difference between RTs to the [sk] words and to [k^h] words in the test session was significant ($t(8) = 1.89, p < .05$); note that it is predicted that generalized responses will be weaker (in this case will take longer) than responses to stimuli learned as being part of the category.[5]

---

[4]For all the analyses of variance in which RT scores were compared, a two-way factorial design was used; F scores for treatments (word types), blocks (individual Ss), and treatments by blocks were calculated. For the analyses of variance in which the percent correct scores of each S were compared across several treatments, a one-way randomized blocks design was used; see Matheson, Bruce, and Beauchamp (1978: Ch. 20).

[5]It is possible that the longer RTs to [sk] clusters is partially due to the position of the target segment in the word. Warren (1971) found that RTs for identifying plosives were considerably longer when the target was the second or third segment in a word than when it was the first segment.

Table 12.1

Results of Experiment 1: [kʰ] words

[kʰ] words grouped by spelling			[kʰ] words grouped by phonetics		
Letter	Reaction time[a]	% Positive	Phone	Reaction time[a]	% Positive
Learning session					
k	754	100	[kʰV]	730	99
c	712	97	[kʰl]	748	98
ch	765	100	[kʰr]	712	96
q	737	89	[kʰw]	737	89
Test session					
k	679	100	[kʰV]	697	100
c	680	99	[kʰl]	694	100
q	681	100	[kʰr]	597	94
			[kʰw]	681	100

[a]In msec, measured from burst of the [kʰ].

Table 12.2

Results of Experiment 1: Non-/k/ Words, Learning and Test Sessions Combined

Type of word	Reaction time[a]	% Positive
/g/	456	2
kn-[n]	504	7
c-[s]	423	4
ch-[tʃ]	391	22
sc-[s]	338	0
other	420	1

[a]Measured from end of word.

Table 12.3

Results of Experiment 1: Test Words

Type of word	Reaction time	% Positive
[sk]	746[a]	93
[k°]	523[b]	78

[a]Measured from burst of [k].
[b]Measured from end of word.

All nine Ss were able to name the category. Six Ss gave it a phonetic-based name (e.g., "words with [kʰ]" or "[kʰə]"); these Ss rarely made orthographic errors and answered quite rapidly. Three Ss gave the concept an orthographic-based name (e.g., "hard c"); these Ss accounted for 100% of the errors on 'silent-k' words, they also had longer RTs.

Discussion

This experiment provides evidence supporting the existence and categorical nature of phonemes and particularly supports the analysis that in English the [k] after initial [s] belongs to the /k/ phoneme. Some interference from spelling in this experiment indicates that the most convincing data on the question of the psychological status of phonemic groupings would have to come from either speakers of unwritten languages or illiterate speakers of written languages. However, it may be that for speakers of written languages, orthography partially shapes their phonemic categorizations, so that an analysis which takes orthography into account may in fact be the psychologically real one (for similar arguments referring to other phonological phenomena, see Michaels 1979; Skousen 1979; Jaeger 1984). Actually this may be putting more emphasis on orthographic factors than necessary. Read (1971), who studied the spontaneous spellings of preliterate English-speaking children who made up spellings for words based on the names of the letters, found that the children always spelled the stops after initial [s] with the letter for the voiceless phoneme; for example: *STRT* 'start', *SKEEIG* 'skiing'. This indicates that the phonetic quality of these phones is the more important factor involved in their phonemicization. Possible explanations include (1) speakers expect consonant clusters to have the same voicing, so identify the second sound in an [sC] cluster as the voiceless phoneme; and (2) speakers expect medial voiced stop phonemes to be phonetically voiced.

In general, this experimental design proved to be quite successful, highly controllable, and potentially flexible. One drawback of this method, however, is that given current technological constraints, it must be performed in a laboratory. If one wanted to perform these sorts of experiments with speakers from a broad range of languages, including unwritten languages, it would clearly be more useful to have a design which could be used in the field, away from the laboratory. There was some concern that a design which would be appropriate in the field could not elicit as rapid responses from Ss as the laboratory-based design and therefore might provide less useful results, as it would allow a more considered, conscious decision in which first impressions might be overruled. But for the sake of physical flexibility, the following set of experiments was tried.

EXPERIMENT 2: VERBAL-RESPONSE CONCEPT FORMATION

Method

There were two major innovations in this set of experiments: (1) the experiment was run without the use of the computer or any other equipment besides the tape recorder; (2) four different linguistic question were probed, and all Ss participated in all four parts.

The stimulus tapes were constructed in the same manner as the sample experiment. During the learning phase, a short tone occurred approximately 500 msec before each word; the word was followed by three seconds of silence, then the correct response was spoken; 2 seconds of silence followed, and then the tone signaled the beginning of the next trial. During the test phase there was a tone, the word, 3 seconds of silence, and the tone preceding the next trial.

Eighteen linguistically naive native speakers of English between the ages of 18 and 35 served as Ss. Ss sat in a sound-treated room and listened to the words over headphones. Separate instructions were given at the beginning of each section of the experiment, although the basic format remained the same throughout. Ss were told to listen to the words and when they had some idea of what the correct concept was to say "yes" or "no" out loud during the three-second pause after each word. E sat in a different room, out of sight of the S; she monitored and tabulated Ss' positive and negative responses.[6] Once a S reached criterion (as above), E informed the S that the test was beginning and moved to the test portion of the tape. [7] All Ss heard the entire test session.

The Four Target Categories

NOUNS VERSUS VERBS

The purpose of the first section was to teach Ss how to perform the task with a relatively easy concept; in this way trials to criterion of the other sections could be compared without interference from factors involved in learning the task.

The concept was 'nouns'; all tokens were either nouns or verbs. There was

[6]RTs were not recorded, but they could be retrieved by recording the stimulus words and the Ss' responses on tape and then measuring the interval between the two.

[7]In the laboratory, using two tape recorders makes the experiment run more smoothly, as the learning sessions can be on one recorder and the test sessions on the other. However, in the field it is undoubtedly more practical to use just one recorder.

only a learning session. There were 70 words, 35 nouns and 35 verbs, all 2 syllables, half with initial stress and half with final stress, evenly distributed between nouns and verbs. An attempt was made to balance the words for abstractness. This design rules out Ss' reliance on the phonological form of the word or some semantic factor other than noun or verb as the basis of categorization decisions. Ss were told, "The thing the 'correct' words have in common has to do with their part of speech."

THE PHONEME /k/

This part was essentially like the other /k/ experiments described above, except that in this case the test words consisted of initial [sk] words and words with medial [k°] instead of final [k°] (in order to minimize the problem of the position of the test segment in the word). Also, the word list was organized so that Ss heard examples of all [kʰ] and non-[k] word types throughout the entire tape, intermixed quasi-randomly (with examples of all these word types occurring in the first 20 words).

AFFRICATES: UNITS OR CLUSTERS?

The linguistic question probed in this section was whether the affricates [tʃ] and [dʒ] in English are considered to be one segment or two. This is, of course, a classic question, and arguments for both sides have tended to revolve around such things as how affricates pattern (i.e., whether they contrast with clusters or single phonemes), pattern symmetry, syllable structure, and phonetics (see, e.g., Bloomfield 1933:120; Trager & Bloch 1941:229; Bloch & Trager 1942: 49; Hockett 1955:164; Chomsky & Halle 1968:318ff.) However, their psychological representation for linguistically naive speakers is what was being tested here.

The correct concept was 'words which begin with two consonant sounds.' The learning session consisted of 70 words, 35 with initial clusters (e.g., [sp, bl, fr]) spelled with two or three letters (e.g., *steak, school, sphere*) and 35 words with initial single consonants spelled with one or two letters (e.g., *dog, thin, gnome, knife, psalm, sheet*). The test session consisted of 40 words: 16 with clusters (of the type learned as category members in the learning session); 16 nonclusters (the type learned as noncategory); 2 control words beginning with *wh* pronounced [h] (i.e., 2 letters but a noncluster); 6 test words, 3 beginning with the affricate [tʃ] spelled *ch* (*chew, chain, cheat*) and 3 beginning with the affricate [dʒ] spelled *j* or *g* (*jail, joke, gyp*). Ss were told that the concept "has to do with how many consonant sounds are at the beginning of the word."

THE FEATURE [VOICE]

The linguistic question being probed in this section had to do with the voicing status of the stops /b, d, g/ in English. Research has shown that voiced stops in English are normally voiceless in word-initial position (Lisker & Abramson 1964) and that they are fully voiced only intervocalically. But they are traditionally termed 'voiced' by linguists for the sake of pattern symmetry and for historical reasons. Some linguists use this designation without comment (e.g., Sapir 1921: 45–50; Hockett 1955:27); others note the voiceless variation and use the features 'fortis–lenis' or 'tense–lax' to further clarify the differences between the 'voiced and voiceless' stops (e.g., Bloomfield 1933:97–99; Jakobson, Fant, & Halle 1951: 36–39; Chomsky & Halle 1968:176; 324–327). There are two potential ways of testing whether there is psychological support for calling /b,d,g/ 'voiced': (1) testing whether naive speakers categorize these phonemes with /z, ð, l, m/ and other fully voiced consonants, and (2) testing whether they categorize the relationship between words such as *pie–buy*, which is phonetically one of presence or absence of aspiration, as the same as the relationship between words such as *fat–vat,* which is in fact one of voicing.

For this section of the experiment, then, there were two different formats, with 8 Ss participating in one and 10 in the other. In the first format, the concept was '(minimal) pairs of words which differ by at least voicing.' The learning session consisted of 90 minimal pairs with the differing phoneme either initial or medial. Forty-five pairs were of the type *mail–sail,* which exhibit a voicing contrast, and 45 were of the type *they–lay* or *tan–fan,* which do not. The contrasting phonemes used in the learning session were: voiceless /p, t, k, f, θ, s, h/, and voiced /v, ð, ʒ, m, n, l, r, w, j/. The test session consisted of 42 pairs: 12 pairs of the type learned as being positive instances of the category, 12 learned as negative instances, 9 pairs containing the control phonemes /ʃ/ and /z/, and 9 test pairs of the type *bone–cone,* in which each 'voiced' stop was paired with each voiceless (aspirated) stop.

Ss were instructed that in the category pairs there was 'a certain relationship' between the differing sounds which did not occur in the noncategory pairs. They were directed to practice isolating the differing segments and repeat them to themselves. They were also given a detailed example with a relationship similar to the type in the target concept: nasal/non-nasal initial consonants.

The second format taught the concept 'words which start with a voiced consonant'; words were heard singly rather than in pairs. The learning session consisted of 80 words, 40 beginning with the voiced segments /v, ð, z, m, n, r, w, j/, and 40 beginning with the voiceless /p, t, k, f, θ, s, h/.

The test session consisted of 43 words: 14 learned as category, 14 learned as noncategory, 6 words with control phonemes /ʃ/ and /l/, and 9 test words, 3 each beginning with /b, d, g/. Ss were told that the concept had to do with the way the first sounds in the words were pronounced. They were instructed to isolate the first sound, say it aloud, and listen to its quality.

In both of the voicing experiments, Ss were told that they could ask to have the tape stopped at any time to either ask questions or terminate the experiment. This was done in order to help alleviate the frustration which this task seemed to provoke.

Results

TRIALS TO CRITERION

All Ss reached criterion in the first three parts of the experiment (see Table 12.4). However, results in part 4 were much less uniform. Of the eight Ss with the word-pairs format, only four reached criterion; two of these requested and were given help by E during the learning session (in the form of more practice isolating and repeating the contrasting sounds). One S who reached criterion did not form the category correctly (as seen by random answers during the test); one S who did not reach criterion but seemed to have formed the category correctly was given the test and performed correctly on most of the learned and control pairs. Of the 10 Ss with the single-word format, 5 formed the category, 3 with help.

The average number of trials to criterion for all parts of the experiment is also shown in Table 12.4. The figures for the first three parts show little variation: noun–verb = 21, /k/ = 19, and affricates = 23. An analysis of variance of individual trials to criterion showed that the differences among these three categories were not significant: ($F(2,34) = 1.283$, $p > .25$). However, the average trials to criterion for the fourth part, [voice], were much higher, with an average of 54 for the word-pairs format and 44 for the single-words format. This fourth category was clearly considerably more difficult for Ss to learn than any of the first three.

POSITIVE VERSUS NEGATIVE RESPONSES

NOUNS VERSUS VERBS. Positive versus negative responses for the category 'noun' revealed that the more abstract nouns were more difficult for Ss to categorize than those which named some visualizable object; the nouns which received the largest number of incorrect rejections were *essence, advice, theory, virtue*. Further, it appeared that the more concrete verbs received the most incorrect postitive responses: *injure, wrestle, withdraw*. The fact that many Ss were using the strategy of trying to visualize the 'person, place, or thing' the noun names probably accounts for these errors.

Table 12.4

Experiment 2: Subjects and Trials to Criterion

				Trials to criterion		
Experiment	Number of subjects	Number formed category	% formed category	Mean	SD	Range
Noun–verb	18	18	100	21	5.0	17–32
/k/	18	18	100	19	2.5	16–27
Affricates	18	18	100	23	11.0	16–60
Voice						
word pairs	8	4	50	54	12.5	44–68
single words	10	5	50	44	21.5	28–73

PHONEME /k/. The pattern of positive and negative responses to the various token types in the learning session of the /k/ experiment was extremely similar to that obtained in the /k/ experiment presented above; the [kʰ] words spelled with *q* had significantly more rejections than did other [kʰ] words, and the [tʃ] *ch* words proved to cause the most interference from the negative tokens. The results for the test session are presented in Table 12.5. It is quite clear that the test words were being categorized with the [kʰ] words rather than with the non-/k/ words. An analysis of variance of the individual Ss' percent positive responses to [kʰ] versus [sk] versus [k°] words showed that some of the differences were significant ($F(2,30) = 4.814$, $p < .025$); the one significantly different pair was [kʰ] versus [k°] ($t(15) = 3.017$, one-tailed $p < .025$). There was no difference, however, between responses to the two types of test words ($t(15) = .970$, two-tailed $p > .20$).

AFFRICATES. In the learning session of part 3, the experiment dealing with affricates, Ss showed little variation in responses to different types of positive tokens (words with initial consonant clusters). However, negative tokens (words beginning with single consonants) spelled with two letters had considerably more incorrect positive responses than those spelled with one

Table 12.5

Experiment 2, /k/: Responses to All Word Types, Test Session

Word type	Positive responses	Negative responses	N	% positive responses	% negative responses
[kʰ]	218	6	224	97	3
[#sk]	56	8	64	88	12
[-k°-]	40	8	48	83	17
Non-/k/	5	229	304	2	98

Table 12.6

Experiment 2, Affricates: Responses to All Word Types, Test Session

Word type	Positive responses	Negative responses	N	% positive responses	% negative responses
Clusters	273	15	288	95	5
Nonclusters	5	283	288	5	98
Control: *wh* [h]	1	35	36	3	97
[tʃ]	3	51	54	6	94
[dʒ]	0	54	54	0	100

letter, again indicating some spelling interference. Responses to all word types in the test session are shown in Table 12.6. The test words (affricates) were overwhelmingly excluded from the category, as were the control words. An analysis of variance comparing individuals' percent negative responses to the test words, the control-negative words, and the learned-negative words showed that there were no differences among rates of rejection of these words: $(F(2,34) = 1.882, p > .10)$.

THE FEATURE [VOICE]. In the single-word format of the [voice] category, Ss' positive and negative responses indicated that the category they were forming was not unidimensional, based soley on the presence or absence of vocal-fold vibrations, but that it also depended on attributes such as continuancy and noisiness. The tokens considered to be the most prototypical members of the category were the voiced, nonturbulent continuants (nasals and liquids), whereas the noncontinuants (glides) and the voiced fricatives were considered more peripheral members, eliciting more negative responses. Likewise, the voiceless stops (noisy, noncontinuants) received no incorrect inclusions in the category, but the voiceless fricatives (continuants) were erroneously included in the category 18% of the time. Responses in the format using word pairs followed the same pattern, in that positive pairs (i.e., minimal pairs differing in at least voicing) which had the same continuancy and noisiness received the most incorrect rejections from the category, and the optimally correct pair was considered to be a voiceless stop versus a voiced sonorant.

Table 12.7 shows responses to all word types in the test session of the [voice] single-words format experiment. Individual Ss either completely accepted or completely rejected all the test words, resulting in an approximately 50–50% split of positive and negative responses overall. Ss' responses to test words depended partly on how much consideration they gave to the continuancy factor and whether or not they were repeating the sounds to themselves as voiced or voiceless. Nevertheless, it was quite clear that a number of Ss were responding to the actual phonetic voicelessness of these sounds.

Table 12.7

Experiment 2, [voice], Single-Words Format: Responses to All Word Types, Test Session[a]

Word type	Positive responses	Negative responses	N	% positive responses	% negative responses
[+ voice]	60	10	70	86	14
[− voice]	7	63	70	10	90
[l] (control)	12	3	15	80	20
[ʃ] (control)	1	14	15	7	93
[b, d, g]	21	24	45	47	53

[a]Five subjects.

Table 12.8, which shows the results for the test session of the word-pairs format, provides an interesting contrast to Table 12.7. Here it is clear that Ss recognized the phonological parallel between such pairs as /p–b, k–g/ and /f–v, s–z/, as Ss included the test pairs in the 'voiced–voiceless' category 89% of the time, slightly more often than even the control–positive pairs. Moreover, the difference between responses to learned-positive pairs and test pairs was not significant ($t(3) = .813$, one-tailed $p > .10$).

ABILITY TO NAME CATEGORY

NOUNS VERSUS VERBS.   In part 1, all Ss said the correct category was 'a noun'. Strategies for deciding if a token belonged to the category or not ranged from putting the word in a syntactic context (e.g., in the frame 'a/an _____'), to trying to visualize the 'person, place, or thing' which the noun named. As noted above, Ss made more errors on abstract nouns than on any other word type; neither strategy seemed to cause Ss to make fewer errors. Ss with the fewest trials to criterion reported noticing that all words were either a noun or a verb and eliminating verbs as well as identifying nouns.

Table 12.8

Experiment 2, [voice], Word-Pairs Format: Responses to All Word Types, Test Session[a]

Type of word pair	# positive responses	# negative responses	# No response	N	% positive responses	% negative responses
Learned-positive	45	1	2	48	94	2
Learned-negative	10	34	4	48	21	71
Control-positive	14	1	1	16	88	6
Control-negative	1	19	0	20	4	95
Test	32	4	0	36	89	11

[a]Four subjects.

PHONEME /k/.   In part 2, there were the same two basic category names and strategies for inclusion or exclusion as in the earlier experiment; 12 Ss gave phonetic-based names (one of whom rejected all but aspirated [kʰ] words from the category), while 6 gave orthographic-based names. The 6 Ss who relied on spelling accounted for 61.5% of all the negative responses to test words; 5 out of the 6 rejected the test word *except* on the basis of the letter *x*.

AFFRICATES.   In part 3, all 18 Ss reported the category as 'words which begin with 2 consonant sounds'. Most Ss reported relying purely on sound, since spelling either confused them or was of no help; only one S reported visualizing the spelling. Several Ss differentiated clusters spelled with two letters (e.g., *sp*) from single sounds spelled with two letters (e.g., *sh*[ʃ]), by saying that in the latter the "two sounds are run together," or "the second sound is not emphasized," clearly spelling-based statements. But most Ss reported either only listening for the "separate sounds" or repeating words to themselves to see how many "gestures" or "movements" they produced before the first vowel.

THE FEATURE [VOICE].   Ss differed greatly in the names which they gave the category in part four and tended to give lengthy descriptions rather than a single name; in other words, this category was the least codable. Of the nine Ss who formed the category correctly, two mentioned the term 'voice'; others described it as "a growl versus a sharper tone," "an oscillation versus air just coming out," "a vibration in my ears," "a rumble in your throat before it came out," "a vibrating sound versus more air." So although some Ss were paying attention to the continuancy factor, the voicing factor was the more salient, and all Ss referred to it when naming the category. Clearly there was no possible reliance on spelling; most Ss reported just repeating the segments in question to see if they produced, felt, or heard the "rumble." One telling point was that if Ss repeated the initial sounds in the test words as fully voiced, they answered positively. When a S gave a negative answer to a /b, d, g/ word, she or he had usually repeated the segment as voiceless.

Discussion

CHANGES IN EXPERIMENTAL DESIGN

The innovations in the format seem successful and useful. With the tape recorder as the only necessary piece of equipment, the experiment can be designed and implemented much more flexibly and rapidly. It had been predicted that allowing Ss more time to respond might be a drawback in that it would give them time for more considered, conscious decisions which might overrule first judgements. This did in fact seem to occur, and manifested itself in more interference from orthography and slightly weaker responses to test words. Possibly slightly less response time should be allowed in the test session for the simpler concepts, although this would presumably not be a major problem when working in field situations with nonliterate Ss, for example.

THE FOUR LINGUISTIC QUESTIONS

Since the notions 'noun' and 'verb' are taught in school, this experiment gives little information as to linguistically naive speakers' intuitive semantic categorizations. Experiments of this type might be quite interesting, however, if performed with nonliterate Ss, especially speakers of an unwritten language.

The second part of the experiment gives further support for the theory of the phoneme and the categorization of the velar segment after initial [s] with the /k/ phoneme.

The third part of the experiment gives evidence that Ss consider the affricates to be one sound. Orthographic considerations mitigate this evidence somewhat in two ways: (1) Many single phonemes usually spelled with two letters are of the type C + *h*, and in fact there are no C *h* combinations that are pronounced as two sounds in English. Since *ch* [tʃ] fits this model, it is not clear whether Ss were following the orthographic pattern or answering by considering the sounds of the words. (2) There are no initial single letters which stand for two phonemes, so that Ss had no model for calling *j* or *g* [dʒ] two sounds. Further investigation of this problem calls for using words with medial or final affricates with more varied spellings, for example, *kitchen, badge, box* (see Ehri 1984).

Results of the fourth part indicated that the categorization of the word initial /b, d, g/ as voiced or voiceless is not straightforward, since the category [voice] is not strictly a binary category for most speakers but is multidimensional and depends on the attributes of voicing, continuancy, and noisiness (see Jaeger & Ohala 1984, for further discussion). Both phonetic and phonological factors were involved in Ss' categorization judgments: the single-words format encouraged phonetically based judgments while the word-pairs format encouraged phonological judgments.

COMPARISON OF THE FOUR CATEGORIES

It is clear that the first three categories were much easier to form and apply than the fourth, [voice]. It is not at all surprising that a (learned) semantic category and (letter-sized) phonological segments are more readily discerned and consciously manipulated than a particular component or feature of a segment. What might be considered surprising is that Ss had such great difficulties with the [voice] feature, especially given the importance of the voiced–voiceless contrast in phonological systems universally. However, it has been reported in several studies that when Ss are asked to consciously manipulate featural distinctions, [voice] has very little effect on their behavior and thus is shown to be one of the least accessible features (Shepard 1972; LaRiviere, Winitz, Reeds, & Herriman 1974; Ingram 1980). It is quite likely that in experiments of this sort, Ss are operating in a primarily articulatory mode, and since the articulatory correlates of the voicing distinction are not very obvious kinesthetically, it is rather difficult for Ss to become aware of them; this would also account for the interference from the continuancy feature, which is quite salient articulatorily.

A possible explanation for the differences in Ss' responses to the phonemic versus featural units lies in the notion of 'basic levels' discussed above. In both types of experiments, Ss were directed to pay attention to speech sounds. It is likely that the activities through which literate speakers most often consciously interact with speech sounds are reading and writing. Therefore, for speakers of a language written with an alphabet, a phoneme-size unit is the basic level of categorization for speech sounds, whereas syllables, for example, comprise units of sound larger than the optimal size for conceptualization, and the featural components of a segment are in some sense smaller (more fine grained) than the optimal size. Since basic-level categories are the most accessible to consciousness and are those which are the most uniform across members of a community, this would explain why Ss found the phoneme-based categories easier to form than the featural categories, and why there was more agreement as to categorization of the test sounds and more agreement as to the name given the category (i.e., higher codability). Further evidence for this claim comes from an experiment similar to the /k/ experiment reported here, in which Japanese speakers' awareness of their phoneme /t/ was explored (Jaeger 1980a). The Japanese Ss had much difficulty forming and manipulating this category and in general behaved toward it much like the English speakers did toward the featural category. It could be hypothesized that for Japanese speakers the syllabic writing system has caused the syllable to be the basic level of categorization of speech sounds. It appears, then, that for literate speakers, orthography has a fundamental effect on the arrangement of the classification hierarchy of speech sounds.

CONCLUSIONS

The Experimental Design

The CF experimental paradigm has shown itself to be extremely appropriate for testing a wide range of linguistic claims. It yields useful information not only about the psychological validity of certain linguistic concepts but also about their internal and external structure. It appears that the design which forced rapid responses is more reliable for gathering information about questions for which there could be some interference from orthography. The design which allows longer response times works better for more difficult questions and those which have no possible orthographic interference (e.g., features); it can be easily adapted for work in the field.

Other Linguistic Questions

One obvious extension of the current experiments would be to look at the same types of questions (e.g., the phoneme) in languages with varying writing systems (e.g., Thai final stops, Japanese /t/) or in unwritten languages. Another possibility is to use nonsense words with English speakers, although the value of this is unclear, since it has been shown (Jaeger 1984) that Ss usually impute somewhat predictable spellings to nonsense words.

The experimental paradigm could further be used to look at such questions as the reality and binariness of a number of phonetic features (as reported in Jaeger 1980a; Jaeger & Ohala 1984), various posited rules (e.g., the Vowel Shift Rule, Jaeger 1984), and also problems with larger units (e.g., morphological or semantic). We are currently looking into several of these problems, and in so doing we hope to further demonstrate the versatility and usefulness of the concept-formation experimental paradigm in linguistic research.

ACKNOWLEDGMENTS

I gratefully acknowledge the help of the following people in designing, implementing, and interpreting these experiments: Hector Javkin, Haruko Kawasaki, Steve Palmer, Steve Pearson, Robert Van Valin, James Wright, Karl Zimmer, and especially John Ohala. Rich Janda gave me helpful comments on an earlier draft of this paper. This research was partly funded by a grant from the Graduate Division and a Regents' Graduate Fellowship, both of the University of California, Berkeley.

REFERENCES

Baker, W. J., G. C. Prideaux, & B. L. Derwing. 1973. Grammatical properties of sentences as a basis for concept formation. *Journal of Psycholinguistic Research* 2:210–220.
Bloch, B., & G. L. Trager. 1942. *Outline of linguistic analysis.* Baltimore: Linguistic Society of America.
Bloomfield, L. 1933. *Language.* New York: Holt, Rinehart & Winston.
Boas, F. 1911. Introduction. *Handbook of American Indian Languages.* Bulletin 40, Pt 1. Bureau of American Ethnology. Washington, D. C.: Government Printing Office. (Reprinted in 1966. P. Holder, ed., Lincoln: University of Nebraska Press.)

Brown, R. W. 1956. Language and categories. Appendix to J. S. Bruner, J. J. Goodnow, & G. A. Austin, *A study of thinking*, 247–312. New York: Wiley.

Brown, R. W., & E. Lenneberg. 1954. A study in language and cognition. *Journal of Abnormal & Social Psychology* 49:454–462.

Brown, R. W., & D. McNeill. 1966. The 'tip of the tongue' phenomenon. *Journal of Verbal Learning & Verbal Behavior* 5:325–337.

Bruner, J. S., J. J. Goodnow, & G. A. Austin. 1956. *A study of thinking*. New York: Wiley.

Chafe, W. L. 1977. Creativity in verbalization and its implications for the nature of stored knowledge. In R. Freedle, ed., *Discourse production and comprehension*, 41–55. Norwood, NJ: Ablex.

Chomsky, N., & M. Halle. 1968. *The sound pattern of English*. New York: Harper & Row.

Davidsen-Nielsen, N. 1974. Syllabification in English words with medial *sp, st, sk*. *Journal of Phonetics* 2:15–45.

Deese, J., & S. Hulse. 1967. *The psychology of learning* (3rd ed.). New York: McGraw-Hill.

Dominowski, R. L. 1970. Concept attainment. In M. H. Marx, ed., *Learning: Interactions*, 152–191. New York: Macmillan.

Ehri, L. C. 1984. How orthography alters spoken language competencies in children learning to read and spell. In J. Downing & R. Valtin, eds., *Language awareness and learning to read*, 119–147. New York: Springer Verlag.

Fink, R. 1974. Orthography and the perception of stops after *s*. *Language & Speech* 17:152–159.

Friedman, S. R. 1969. A developmental study of the relationship between reaction-time, instructions and concept learning. (Ph.D. diss., University of Louisville, 1968). *Dissertation Abstracts* 29 (8-B).3104.

Fry, D. B. 1970. Reaction time experiments in the study of speech processing. *Proceedings of the 6th International Congress of Phonetic Sciences* 337–346. Prague: Czechoslovak Academy of Science.

Hockett, C. F. 1955. A manual of phonology. *International Journal of American Linguistics* Memoir 11.

Hooper, J. 1976. *An introduction to natural generative phonology*. New York: Academic Press.

Ingram, J. C. L. 1980. Perceptual dimensions of phonemic recognition. In G. D. Prideaux, B. L. Derwing, & W. J. Baker, eds., *Experimental linguistics: Integration of theories and applications*, 273–291. Ghent: E. Story-Scientia.

Jaeger, J. J. 1980a. Categorization in phonology: An experimental approach. Ph.D. diss. University of California, Berkeley.

Jaeger, J. J. 1980b. Testing the psychological reality of phonemes. *Language & Speech* 23:233–253.

Jaeger, J. J. 1984. Assessing the psychological status of the Vowel Shift Rule. *Journal of Psycholinguistic Research* 13:13–36.

Jaeger, J. J., & J. J. Ohala. 1984. On the structure of phonetic categories. *Proceedings of the 10th Annual Meeting of the Berkeley Linguistics Society*, 15–26. Berkeley: Berkeley Linguistics Soc. (U. C. Berkeley)

Jakobson, R., G. Fant, & M. Halle. 1951. *Preliminaries to speech analysis: The distinctive features and their correlates*. Cambridge, MA: MIT Press.

LaRiviere, C., H. Winitz, J. Reeds, & E. Herriman. 1974. The conceptual reality of selected distinctive features. *Journal of Speech & Hearing Research* 17:122–133.

Lisker, L., & A. Abramson. 1964. A cross-language study of voicing of initial stops: Acoustic measurements. *Word* 20:384–422.

Lotz, J., A. Abramson, L. Gerstman, F. Ingemann, & H. Nemser. 1960. The perception of English stops by speakers of English, Spanish, Hungarian, and Thai: A tape-cutting experiment. *Language & Speech* 3:71–77.

MacKay, D. G. 1978. Speech errors inside the syllable. In A. Bell & J. B. Hooper, eds., *Syllables and segments*, 201–212. Amsterdam, North Holland.

Matheson, D., R. L. Bruce, & K. L. Beauchamp. 1978. *Experimental psychology: Research design and analysis* (3rd ed.). New York: Holt, Rinehart & Winston.

Mervis, C. B., & E. Rosch. 1981. Categorization of natural objects. In M. R. Rosenzweig & L. W. Porter, eds., *Annual Review of Psychology* 32:89–115.

Michaels, D. 1979. Spelling and the phonology of tense vowels. Paper presented at the Summer Meeting of the Linguistic Society of America, Salzburg.

Moskowitz, B. A. 1973. On the status of vowel shift in English. In T. Moore, ed., *Cognitive development and the acquisition of language*, 223–260. New York: Academic Press.

Ohala, J. J. 1983. The phonological end justifies any means. In S. Hattori & K. Inoue, eds., *Proceedings of the XIIIth International Congress of Linguists, Tokyo, 29 Aug.–4 Sept. 1982*, 232–243.

Read, C. 1971. Pre-school children's knowledge of English phonology. *Harvard Educational Review* 41:1–34.

Reeds, J. A., & W. S.-Y. Wang. 1961. The perception of stops after *s*. *Phonetica* 6:78–81.

Rosch, E. 1973. On the internal structure of perceptual and semantic categories. In T. E. Moore, ed., *Cognitive development and the acquisition of language*, 111–144. New York: Academic Press.

Rosch, E. 1978. Principles of categorization. In E. Rosch & B. B. Lloyd, eds., *Cognition and categorization*, 27–48. Hillsdale, NJ: Erlbaum.

Rosch, E., C. B. Mervis, W. D. Grey, D. M. Johnson, & P. Boyes-Braem. 1976. Basic objects in natural categories. *Cognitive Psychology* 8:382–439.

Sapir, E. 1921. *Language*. New York: Harcourt, Brace.

Shepard, R. N. 1972. Psychological representation of speech sounds. In E. E. David & P. B. Denes, eds., *Human communication: A unified view*, 67–113. New York: McGraw-Hill.

Skousen, R. 1979. English spelling and phonemic representation. Paper presented at the Winter Meeting of the Linguistics Society of America, Los Angeles.

Trager, G., & B. Bloch. 1941. The syllabic phonemes of English. *Language* 17:223–246.

Warren, R. M. 1971. Identification times for phonemic components of graded complexity and for spelling of speech. *Perception & Psychophysics* 9:345–349.

13

Testing Hypotheses Regarding the Psychological Manifestation of Morpheme Structure Constraints*

JOHN J. OHALA
MANJARI OHALA

INTRODUCTION

Linguists have for many decades recognized that not all possible sequences or types of sounds occur in the morphemes of any single language. These restrictions were called 'phonotactic' or 'distributional' constraints by the classical structuralists and 'morpheme structure' rules or conditions by generative phonologists. Although these constraints may originally have been conceived of as merely descriptive statements one could make about the sound pattern of the language, there is sufficient evidence now that native speakers are also aware of them, that is, that many of the constraints noted by linguists are psychologically real (Esper 1925; Greenberg & Jenkins 1964; Zimmer 1969; Fromkin 1971; Ohala 1972, 1983; Wright 1975).

It is of interest, then, to try to find out how these morpheme structure constraints (henceforth MSCs) are represented in speakers' heads and how they use them. This chapter reports some attempts to do this.

*This research was supported in part by the National Science Foundation and by the Committee on Research, University of California, Berkeley.

EXPERIMENTAL PHONOLOGY

PRIOR HYPOTHESES

There have been various proposals about the nature of MSCs, although often they have not been perfectly explicit. Thus in reviewing some of these claims we may inadvertently read into them certain details that were not intended. Also it is not always clear how much psychological reality various authors meant their proposals to have. In any case, our primary purpose is not to do battle with straw men but to attempt to show how it is possible to pit one reasonably explicit and superficially plausible hypothesis regarding MSCs against another and in that way to determine which has more empirical support as a model of how native speakers react to the phonetic shape of words.

Greenberg and Jenkins

Greenberg and Jenkins (1964) (hereafter G&J) offer one of the clearest statements regarding the psychological manifestation of MSCs; we call it the phoneme-substitution procedure. According to them, the degree of closeness of a given 'word' to the native pattern is inversely proportional to the number of zero-, one-, two-, and up to n-phoneme substitutions for the n original phonemes in the word which resulted in existing words in the language, as given in Table 13.1.

To find the distance from English of /klæb/, /klɛb/, and /zbyk/ using their phoneme substitution procedure, we first note that a zero phoneme substitution would not yield an existing word, as this would happen only if the word we start with were already an existing word, which none of these are. We next try changing single phonemes. If we change the first phoneme we can get /slæb/ from /klæb/ but cannot derive any existing words from /klɛb/ or /zbyk/.[1] Changing the second of the four phonemes also succeeds with /klæb/ but not the other two forms; and so on, for two, three, and finally four simultaneous phoneme substitutions, the latter type, of course, yielding an existing word for any sequence of four sounds. We then total the number of substitutions which give an existing word and subtract that from the number of possible substitutions plus one; this is 17 in the case of sequences of four phonemes. Thus /klæb/, /klɛb/, and /zbyk/ are predicted to be respectively 2, 5, and 15 units away from English on a 16-point scale. The

---

[1]The Oxford English Dictionary lists *bleb*, defining it as a smaller variety of *blob* and, in fact, this word is widely used today in microbiology. In all likelihood, though, this word is not in the lexicons of most speakers of English and so would not decrease the predicted difference between /klæb/ and /klɛb/. We made similar decisions about other potential phoneme substitutions for the words in Table 13.1 and others used in the experiments described later on, but we do not discuss them in detail here.

Table 13.1

Example of Greenberg and Jenkins' Phoneme-Substitution Method

	Word		
Type of substition	/klæb/	/klɛb/	/zbyk/
CCVC	—	—	—
C̲CVC	slab	—	—
CC̲VC	crab	—	—
CCV̲C	club	club	—
CCVC̲	clam	Clem	—
C̲CVC	stab	—	—
CC̲VC	crib	crib	—
CCV̲C	clip	clip	—
CC̲VC	slob	slob	—
CCV̲C	slam	phlegm	—
CCV̲C	cram	Kress	—
CCV̲C	grub	grub	creek
CCV̲C	cream	cream	—
CCV̲C	spat	bread	—
CC̲VC	flip	flip	—
C̲CVC	gruff	gruff	gruff
Total successful substitutions	15	12	2
(17 − total) = "distance" from English	2	5	15

only substitutions G&J allow in this procedure are consonant substitutions for consonants and vowels for vowels. They rule out vowels substituted for consonants and vice versa, and they rule out phoneme additions and deletions.

Early Generative Phonology

Proposals regarding MSCs in early generative phonology (hereafter EGP) (Halle 1959, 1962; Stanley 1967) seem to include the following claims:

1. The function of MSCs is to differentiate between existing or admissible phoneme sequences and inadmissible sequences, that is, a binary classification; or, under some interpretation, a ternary classification between existing words, accidental gaps, and inadmissible forms.

2. MSCs are stated in terms of features, not phonemes.

3. MSCs are separate from the lexical entries themselves and are presumably relatively small in number in comparison to the lexical entries. That is, they capture only rather broad generalizations, such as that in English a nasal consonant may be the second member of an initial cluster only if /s/ is the first, but they would not include such specific constraints as that /ɛ/ may not appear after the initial cluster /kl/ if /b/ follows it.

The Sound Pattern of English

In *The Sound Pattern of English* Chomsky and Halle (1968:417) (hereafter C&H) offer a rather explicit proposal regarding the form and function of MSCs. They claim that the degree of closeness to the native pattern of a given form is inversely proportional to the complexity of the rule—measured by counting the features mentioned in it—which would differentiate that form from all the entries in the regular (existing) lexicon. That is, one finds the simplest rule which would not change any entry in the regular lexicon but which would change an irregular or nonexisting form. One then counts the number of features utilized in this rule (which presumably need not incorporate any features which can be specified by universal marking conventions) and then takes the distance from the native pattern to be the reciprocal of this number. Note that the rule which should change a nonexisting form but no regular, existing form does not, unlike the G&J phoneme-substitution procedure, have to make an existing form out of the nonexisting form to which it applies. Some examples are given in Table 13.2. (a) Gives the rule offered by C&H as being the simplest one which differentiates /blɪk/ from all entries in the English lexicon. Since this form is at best an accidental gap in the English lexicon, the rule must be very specific and thus very complicated if it is to affect /blɪk/ but no regular English morpheme. The rule takes 17 features to state and is thus 1/17 or .059 units away from English on a scale that presumably runs from zero to .5. (b) Gives the much simpler rule which differentiates /bnɪk/ from the rest of the English lexicon, and (c) and (d) give the rules which we offer as differentiating the made-up forms /xlox/ and /xrit/, and /mløf/ and /spøf/, respectively, from the regular forms in English. Since these forms violate more fundamental English MSCs, fewer features are needed to state the rules which apply to them but to no regular English words.

THE CONFLICT BETWEEN THE HYPOTHESES

There are a variety of quite opposite claims made by these models.

Both the G&J and the C&H models predict that speakers are capable of making scalar judgments on the degree to which a given form adheres to the pattern of their native language. The EGP model, however, predicts that speakers could make only ternary distinctions. G&J's experiments proved that subjects could make scalar judgments.[2]

G&J posit that, in making judgments about the well-formedness of spoken

[2]This might account for some results which seemed anomalous in a study by Ohala (1972, 1983). She asked Hindi-speaking subjects to categorize normal and rare Hindi words and made-up words as 'existing', 'possible but nonexisting', and 'not possible' for Hindi. In some cases they unexpectedly assigned what the linguist would consider 'accidental gaps' to the category 'not possible'. This may have happened because the three-way classification was too restrictive; more reasonable responses may have been obtained if they had been allowed to make scalar judgments.

Table 13.2

Examples of Chomsky and Halle's Algorithm for Measuring Degree of Distance from the Regular Lexicon[a]

(a) Minimal rule which differentiates /blIk/ from English lexicon

$$[+\text{cons}] \longrightarrow [-\text{lateral}] \;/\; [-\text{seg}] \begin{bmatrix} +\text{cons} \\ -\text{voc} \\ +\text{ant} \\ -\text{cor} \\ +\text{voice} \end{bmatrix} \underline{\quad} \begin{bmatrix} +\text{high} \\ -\text{back} \\ -\text{tense} \end{bmatrix} \begin{bmatrix} +\text{cons} \\ -\text{voc} \\ -\text{ant} \\ -\text{cor} \\ -\text{cont} \\ -\text{voice} \end{bmatrix}$$

Number of features required: 17
Distance from English: $1/17 = .059$ (min. $= 0$; max. $= .5$)

(b) Minimal rule which differentiates /bnIk/ from English lexicon

$$[+\text{cons}] \longrightarrow [-\text{nasal}] \;/\; [-\text{seg}] \begin{bmatrix} +\text{cons} \\ -\text{cont} \end{bmatrix} \underline{\quad}$$

Number of features required: 5
Distance from English: $1/5 = .2$

(c) Minimal rule which differentiates /xlox/ and /xrit/ from English lexicon

$$\begin{bmatrix} +\text{cons} \\ +\text{cont} \end{bmatrix} \longrightarrow [-\text{back}]$$

Number of features required: 3
Distance from English: $1/3 = .33$

(d) Minimal rule which differentiates /mløf/ and /spøf/ from English lexicon

$$\begin{bmatrix} +\text{syllabic} \\ -\text{back} \end{bmatrix} \longrightarrow [-\text{round}]$$

Number of features required: 3
Distance from English: $1/3 = .33$

[a]Chomsky & Halle, 1968:417.

forms, speakers refer to the existing words in the lexicon; except for the phoneme-substitution procedure itself, they need not store lexicon independent rules. The EGP model seems to posit that speakers refer to independent rules, the MSCs.

Related to these two opposing details is that mentioned earlier, that is, whether speakers can detect deviations from only the most general patterns of the language or whether they can notice even the specific deviations. The EGP model would allow only the broad generalizations to be reflected in MSCs, whereas the G&J model, since it has the input forms compared to the entire list of existing morphemes, would permit deviations from even the most specific patterns to be detected. It was this difference between the G&J and the EGP model that we sought to test first. (Further conflicting predictions made by these models are addressed later.)

JOHN J. OHALA AND MANJARI OHALA

EXPERIMENT 1: G&J VERSUS EGP

To test these two models we constructed pairs of forms for which each model would give different predictions about the relative distance of each member of the pair from the English pattern. Table 13.3 gives five such word pairs. In the case of the first pair, /klɛb/ and /klæb/, we have already explained why the G&J model predicts the latter to be farther from English than the former (see Table 13.1). Presumably the EGP model would predict that they are both equally far from English since the rules that would differentiate them would be too specific (i.e., not general enough) to qualify as MSCs. The four word pairs /θlɛz/, /θlɛd/; /ʃriz/, /ʃrɪd/; /flʊt/, /flɪg/; /sθɛʃ/, /sθip/ would pattern like /klɛb/, /klæb/ as far as the two models' predictions are concerned, as indicated in the second and third columns of Table 13.3.

We then obtained native English speakers' subjective judgments on the 'distance' from the English pattern of these forms (and other filler items selected to range over the entire 16-point G&J scale). We did this in essentially the same way as G&J. The individual forms (i.e., not in pairs) were recorded using a high-quality system by a phonetically trained speaker (the first author) who spoke them in two different randomized orders. The tape was played to individual subjects (either over a loudspeaker in a sound-treated room or over high quality earphones), and they were asked to judge the "distance" of each form from English using an 11-point scale and to indicate their responses on an answer sheet. (G&J in their study used both an 11-point scale and the free-magnitude-estimation technique and found both of them to give the same results. We used an 11-point scale since it was simpler to explain to the subjects how to use it.) Instructions to the subjects, given ad lib, went approximately as follows:

> You will hear a list of words. Some will be English words, some have been obtained from languages close to English and some from languages quite unlike English. We want you to listen to each word and judge by how it sounds how far it is from the pattern of English words, using an 11-point scale. If it is an English word check '1' off on the answer sheet; if it is very far away from English mark '11' on the answer sheet. The closer to English you judge the word to be, the smaller should be the number you mark; the farther away the word is from the English, the larger should be the number you mark. Please try to use the entire 11-point scale.

Then a minute or so of the tape was played to familiarize the subjects with the format of the tape and to let them hear the type of words used. We answered any questions they had, and then the tape was started again from the beginning and the subjects gave their judgments on the words. Before the words were played to them in the second randomized order, the subjects

Table 13.3

Stimuli, Predictions, and Results of Experiment 1

Stimuli		Predictions		Results	
A	B	Greenberg & Jenkins	Early generative phonology	Order	Mean difference
klɛb	klæb	A > B	A = B	A > B	0.276
θlɛz	θled	A > B	A = B	A > B	1.557
ʃrɪz	ʃrɪd	A > B	A = B	B > A	0.107
flʊt	flɪg	A > B	A = B	B > A	0.550
sθɛʃ	sθip	A > B	A = B	A > B	1.483
Mean					0.532*

*p < .001.

were told that since they now had a better idea of the total range of variation of the word types they could, on this second run, change their ratings
of the words if they liked.

The subjects were adult speakers of English and were nonlinguists. We
obtained judgments from 21 subjects.

Some subjects failed to use the entire 11-point scale. To make their
responses comparable to the others' their ratings were normalized, that is,
the portion of the scale they did use was stretched linearly so that the extreme
scores equaled 1 and 11.

Although given a chance to change their scores on the second run of the
stimuli, our subjects, like those of G&J, gave ratings that were statistically
indistinguishable on both runs. (Although this was not our main concern,
it turned out that, in agreement with the original results reported by G&J,
there was a strong positive correlation for the entire body of stimuli between
the ratings obtained by the G&J algorithm and our subjects' ratings.)

In tabulating the results, it was the *difference* between the ratings given
to the two words of a pair on any single run (i.e., a given randomized order)
that was counted. For example, if one subject gave word A a rating of 5
and word B a rating of 7, then this would be counted the same as another
subject who gave the ratings 2 and 4, respectively, to the same words, since
in both cases their ratings of the two words differed by +2. As we were just
interested in whether or not one member of the pair was judged farther from
English than the other, a one-tailed *t*-test was performed to assess the significance of the difference, that is, whether the mean difference in scores
for all the pairs of interest was significantly distinct from zero.

The results are given in the rightmost columns of Table 13.3. In two of
the five pairs, namely /ʃriz/, /ʃrɪd/ and /flut/, /flɪg/, the difference in
scores was small and in the opposite direction of that predicted by G&J. In
the other three pairs the difference was in the direction they predicted. The
average difference for all five pairs was .532, which is highly significant
($p < .001$). It may be safe to conclude, then, that deviations from rather
narrow, quite particular, patterns in the language contribute to the perceived
distance of a word from the native pattern, as G&J predict.[3]

EXPERIMENT 2: G&J VERSUS C&H

Another point of difference between the models reviewed above is whether
subjects' decision on the degree of deviation from the native pattern is based
on only *part* of the form or the *whole* form. The C&H model, especially in

[3]Ohala (1972, 1983) found that her subjects not only gave evidence of knowing the MSCs
of Hindi but in some cases also the MSCs appropriate to different parts of the Hindi lexicon,
for example, the consonant clusters appropriate to English loanwords or words of Urdu origin.

the case of words violating very fundamental patterns, allows only the most serious violation, and then only one instance of it, to influence speakers' reaction to a form. For example, as given in 13.2d, even though there are two violations of English MSCs in /mløf/, namely, a bad initial cluster and a non-English segment /ø/, as opposed to only one violation in /spøf/, namely, the same non-English segment, according to the C&H model, both are equally far from the English pattern since they are both differentiated from existing English words by the same minimal rule, the one given in 13.2d. The G&J model, on the other hand, predicts that all parts of the word affect its judged deviation from the regular lexicon.

We used the same method as in Experiment 1 to test which of these two models better predicts subjects' behavior. The four word pairs used are given in Table 13.4 along with the predictions of how the members of each pair should be regarded by native speakers. In the case of the pair /sfub/, /sfɛt/ we assume, perhaps wrongly, that C&H would consider the initial /sf/ cluster as a deviation from the regular English pattern, in spite of the exceptional words *sphere*, *sphinx*, *sphincter*, and *sforzando*. In this experiment there were 11 subjects.

The results are given in the rightmost columns of Table 13.4. In all four word pairs, the difference in ratings is in the direction predicted by G&J and in three of these cases the difference is very large. The mean difference for the four pairs is 1.914, which is highly significant ($p \ll .001$). This seems to establish fairly conclusively that the whole word and not just part contributes to speakers' evaluation of it.

EXPERIMENT 3: JUDGMENTS ON PAIRED STIMULI

Although both Experiment 1 and Experiment 2 show highly significant results which enable us to evaluate competing hypotheses, the fact that two of the five pairs in Experiment 1 show a difference opposite to that of the group was disturbing. This could have arisen due to any one or a combination of several reasons. First, the G&J model could be inappropriate in very specific cases. Second, the experimental method itself could be deficient in that it permits a great deal of "noise," from, among other things, drift in subjects' frame of reference when making their judgments. To see whether distortions due to this second factor might be eliminated, we conducted a third experiment.

Since we were really interested in the difference, if any, which subjects perceived in the members of each pair with regard to their adherence to the native pattern, in Experiment 3 we presented the words in pairs and asked subjects to judge which member of each pair was closer to the native English pattern. In other respects, the methods used, for example, presentation over

Table 13.4

Stimuli, Predictions, and Results of Experiment 2

Stimuli		Predictions		Results	
A	B	Greenberg & Jenkins	Chomsky & Halle	Order	Difference
mlɔʒ	mlit	A > B	A = B	A > B	0.514
mløf	spøf	A > B	A = B	A > B	3.014
xlox	xrit	A > B	A = B	A > B	2.209
sfʊb	sfɛt	A > B	A = B	A > B	2.018
Mean					1.914*

*$p < .001$.

tape, the background of the subjects, and the words used, were the same as in Experiments 1 and 2. Sixteen subjects participated. The instructions given, ad lib, were approximately as follows:

> You will hear a list of pairs of words. Some will be from languages close to English and some from languages quite unlike English. We want you to listen to each pair and, based on how they sound, judge which member of each pair is closer to English and indicate your judgment on the answer sheet.

This method—obtaining judgments of paired items—should be a more accurate and sensitive way of getting the kind of data needed. Analogously, it is easier to judge which of two individuals is taller if they stand back to back than it is to judge the absolute height of individuals considered in isolation. (This was the method used by Zimmer in his 1969 study on Turkish MSCs.)

The results are presented in Tables 13.5 and 13.6. The trend of the data is similar to that from Experiments 1 and 2 except that this time all pairs show majority judgments in the direction predicted by the G&J model. The differences are again highly significant.

DISCUSSION

We believe that the results of these experiments suggest (although perhaps do not conclusively prove) that the speakers make reference to the words in the lexicon, not to lexicon-independent rules, when making judgments of the kind we required of them. If they used rules, these results suggest that they would have to incorporate implausibly fine detail on the sound pattern

Table 13.5

Stimuli and Results of Experiment 3: Greenberg & Jenkins versus Early Generative Phonology (see Table 13.3 for predictions of each model)

Stimuli		Number of subjects	
A	B	A closer to English	B close to English
klɛb	klæb	4	12
θlɛz	θlɛd	1	15
ʃriz	ʃrɪd	5	11
flʊt	flɪg	7	9
sθɛʃ	sθip	7	9
Total		24	56*

*$p < .001$.

Table 13.6

Stimuli and Results of Experiment 3: Greenberg and Jenkins versus Chomsky and Halle (see Table 13.4 for predictions of the two models)

Stimuli		No. subjects	
A	B	A closer to English	B closer to English
mlɔʒ	mlit	4	11[a]
mløf	spøf	1	15
xlox	xrit	5	11
sfʊb	sfɛt	1	15
Total		11	52*

[a]One of the 16 subjects gave no response.
*$p < .001$.

of the language. In general, then, our results give support to the G&J model.[4]

There are still many other details to test, of course—among others, whether the speaker operates with phonemes or features in comparing the target form with existing words. Relevant to this question is the research of Derwing and Nearey (this volume), who show that when subjects judge the phonetic similarity of pairs of forms, there is some evidence that a featural analysis is performed.

[4]Halle (personal communication, 1975) acknowledges that the proposals in *The Sound Pattern of English* on the quantification of morpheme well-formedness were tentative and incorrect to the extent that they did not predict /mløf/ to be further from English than /spøf/.

Another issue is whether, as G&J somewhat arbitrarily maintain, deletions and additions play no part in the transformation made in the comparison precedure. Implicitly, such operations are allowed by the algorithm of Vitz and Winkler (1973), which was offered as a model of how subjects compare the phonetic similarity of forms and which received some empirical support from their experiments as well as those of Derwing and Nearey. The resolution of this issue has potentially important implications for the interpretation of the results of an interesting experiment conducted by Pertz and Bever (1975). They investigated the awareness which monolingual speakers of English have of universal consonant-cluster patterns. They found that their subjects judged a word such as [ntel] to be more common in the world's languages than [nkel] (which, of course, is the case). They concluded that since neither of these clusters occurs in initial position in English and that since both words would be rated equally far from English using the G&J measure, including the prohibition on addition or deletion of phonemes, their subjects could not have used their knowledge of English in making their judgments. (Pertz and Bever concluded that the source of knowledge which subjects invoked in making these judgements must have been formed during language acquisition.) However, this conclusion, like ours, is only as good as the assumptions it is based on. If subjects can use something like the G&J measure but with addition or deletion of phonemes as part of the transformations permitted, then these initial clusters could become final or medial clusters. In that case the homorganic nasal + stop clusters would certainly be judged preferable or more common than the nonhomorganic clusters, since the former are also more common in English. The word *lintel* (top part of a doorway) might form the nearest match in that case, whereas there seems to be no comparably close match exhibiting the sequence [-nkel-]. Thus we do not necessarily have to assume that Pertz and Bever's subjects gave the responses they did from knowledge not based on the sound patterns in their mental lexicons of English.

Other factors deserve study, too. Does the number of existing word(s) that the input forms are transformed into or their frequency of occurrence influence speakers' judgments? Would sound sequences that are frequently or easily pronounced by English speakers, but are not necessarily lexical, be regarded by speakers as close to English? Would existing, though rare, clusters in common loan words still be judged far from English? As a preliminary answer to these last two questions, the results from G&J-type experiments done by our students (at Berkeley and San Jose) as class assignments have quite consistently given the result that forms like [θlæt] and [sræt] are rated by linguistically naive English speakers as being as close as or closer to the English pattern than a form like [sfæt], even though [sf-] clusters appear in existing English words—loans from Greek and Italian—as noted above.

Although [sr-] is not a normal cluster of English, according to most analyses, it does occur phonetically in the most common pronunciation of polysyllabic words such as *ceramic*, [sræmIk]. [θl-] is a well-known substitute for [sl-] in speech that attempts to imitate a lisp. (On the problem of accidental gaps in consonant clusters, see Fischer-Jørgensen, 1952.)

On the other hand, a pilot study by Larson (1982) showed that the predicted "Englishness" for most clusters by the G&J metric correlates (inversely) with their frequency of occurrence in the English lexicon (this is not the same thing as frequency of occurrence in running text or running speech). However, in the cases she examined where the two would give different predictions (for example, /glip/ and /trip/ would be equally close to the English pattern by the G&J metric—according to our analysis of Larson's stimuli—but /trip/ has a cluster that is more frequent in the lexicon), it turns out that frequency of occurrence is a better predictor of native speakers' ratings.

It would also be worth investigating the role that spelling might play in influencing speakers' judgments of the well-formedness of forms, that is, the extent to which their reactions are based on "graphotactic" rather than phonotactic patterns. In a preliminary study which addressed this question, Perucca-Ramirez (1982) found that six-year-old American children, though literate in a relatively small fraction of their aural vocabulary (and thus presumably less influenced by spelling), nevertheless treated made-up words virtually identically to adults in a G&J-type experiment.

CONCLUSION

We believe that the methods we report here, first applied to the study of phonological problems by G&J and by Zimmer, are capable of giving answers to these and additional questions regarding the psychological manifestation of MSCs. All that is really necessary to make this or any experimental technique useful is the formulation of hypotheses in a fashion that is explicit enough to render them testable.

REFERENCES

Chomsky, N., M. Halle. 1968. *The sound pattern of English*. New York: Harper & Row.

Esper, E. A. 1925. *A technique for the experimental investigation of associative interference in artificial linguistic material*. Language Monographs, no. 1.

Fischer-Jørgensen, E. 1952. On the definition of phoneme categories on a distributional basis. *Acta Linguistica Hafniensia* 8:8–39.

Fromkin, V. A. 1971. The non-anomalous nature of anomalous utterances. *Language* 47:27–52.

Greenberg, J. H., & J. J. Jenkins. 1964. Studies in the psychological correlates of the sound system of American English. *Word* 20:157-177.

Halle, M. 1959. *The sound pattern of Russian*. The Hague: Mouton.

Halle, M. 1962. Phonology in generative grammar. *Word* 18:54-72.

Larson, M. 1982. Referring to one's lexicon for judgments on morpheme structure constraints: Evidence from the issue of frequency. San Jose, CA. Ms.

Ohala, M. 1972. Topics in Hindi-Urdu phonology. Ph.D. diss. University of California, Los Angeles.

Ohala, M. 1983. *Aspects of Hindi phonology*. Delhi: Motilal Banarsidass.

Perucca-Ramirez, M. 1982. Experiment on morpheme structure conditions: Adult and child native-speaker intuition. San Jose, CA. Ms.

Pertz, D. L., & T. G. Bever. 1975. Sensitivity to phonological universals in children and adolescents. *Language* 51:149-162.

Stanley, R. 1967. Redundancy rules in phonology. *Language* 43:393-436.

Vitz, P. C., & B. S. Winkler. 1973. Predicting the judged 'similarity of sound' of English words. *Journal of Verbal Learning & Verbal Behavior* 12:373-388.

Wright, J. 1975. Nasal-stop assimilation: Testing the psychological reality of an English MSC. In C. A. Ferguson, L. M. Hyman, & J. J. Ohala, eds., *Nasalfest. Papers from a symposium on nasals and nasalization*, 389-397. Language Universals Project, Stanford University.

Zimmer, K. 1969. Psychological correlates of some Turkish morpheme structure conditions. *Language* 46:309-321.

14

Sound Change in Perception: An Experiment

TORE JANSON

INTRODUCTION

This chapter reports a successful attempt to trace an ongoing sound change through the use of listening tests given to people who belong to successive generations of users of the same dialect. The report is meant to provide a stimulus for using perception data in the study of sound variation and sound change, a technique which has so far been used very little. It is shown that even a slow, gradual change may be detected in this way.

The dialect chosen for investigation is the Swedish language as used in the Stockholm area. In an earlier study (Janson 1979) I found clear indications of a difference between older Stockholmers and teenagers in the perception of short front vowels. However, the previous experiment was not designed primarily to account for dialectal differences in the perception of vowel quality. Rather, the aim was to find out if there is an effect of perceptual compensation for short duration of vowels (which turned out to be the case). The discovery of a difference between generations was an unexpected additional finding.

Thus, it was decided to perform a new experiment aimed specifically at mapping differences in vowel-phoneme identification between different groups of Swedes. One phoneme boundary was selected for investigation, namely the one between /a:/ and /o:/. It has frequently been observed that the long /a:/ in the Stockholm dialect is backed in comparison with most

EXPERIMENTAL PHONOLOGY

other Swedish dialects. It has not been clear, however, whether this is the result of a completed change or represents a change still in progress. The immediate goal, then, was to clarify this issue.

METHODS

The method chosen to explore this question was to present Stockholmers of different generations with stimuli in the boundary region between the two phonemes and to let them identify these stimuli as either /a:/ or /o:/. If this revealed a systematic difference between the generations, it would indicate an ongoing shift of the phoneme boundary.

A listening test was prepared in the following manner. Stimuli consisted of short phrases of synthetic speech, representing the expressions *ett tag* [et:a:g] 'a while,' or *ett tåg* [et:o:g] 'a train.' The short vowel and the consonants were kept constant in all stimuli, while the long vowel was varied systematically in 20 steps.

The synthesized stimuli, which were produced on OVE 3 at the Royal Institute of Technology in Stockholm, approximated the voice of a male speaker of the Stockholm dialect. F_0 in the long vowel was 110 Hz. The higher formants had constant values, F_3 at 2475 Hz and F_4 at 3400 Hz. Thus, only F_1 and F_2 were varied. The extreme values for F_1 and F_2 were chosen to agree with mean values for productions of Stockholm [o:] and short [a], respectively . The remaining 18 values were located at equal distances along a line between the extreme values in a two-dimensional vowel space. The values were calculated to be equidistant according to the mel scale rather than the Hz scale. The F_1 and F_2 values in Hz and in mels are shown in Table 14.1.

For each of these 20 different stimuli, six tokens were produced. The resulting 120 tokens were recorded in randomized order on a test tape. The tokens were presented at intervals of about 3 seconds, with somewhat longer intervals (around 10 seconds) after each group of 10 tokens. The total play time of the tape was a little more than 8 minutes.

Subjects listened to this tape over headphones, usually from a portable tape recorder of good quality. They were asked to identify each token as either *ett tag* or *ett tåg* by filling in the letter *a* or *å* on an answer sheet. They were told to choose one of the alternatives even when they felt uncertain.

There were two groups of informants in this experiment, young Stockholmers (YS) and older Stockholmers (OS). The first group included 15 persons between 13 and 18 years of age. All were high school students who were born in the Stockholm area and had lived there since. The second group comprised 17 persons who were between 33 and 70 years of age, the mean age being

Table 14.1

Formant Values for Stimulus Vowels

Stimulus vowel	F_1		F_2	
	Hz	mels	Hz	mels
1	750	807	1250	1170
2	730	791	1220	1151
3	711	775	1191	1132
4	691	758	1162	1112
5	672	742	1134	1094
6	653	725	1106	1075
7	635	709	1078	1055
8	616	692	1051	1035
9	598	676	1024	1017
10	580	660	997	998
11	562	643	971	979
12	544	627	945	960
13	527	611	920	941
14	510	595	895	922
15	492	577	870	903
16	476	562	845	884
17	459	545	821	865
18	442	528	797	846
19	426	512	773	826
20	410	496	750	807

42. All had lived in Stockholm during their childhood and youth and all or most of the time after that. Information about the social background of the subjects is very incomplete, but almost all seem to belong to the middle class. There are no drastic phonetic differences in sociolects in the Stockholm area.

RESULTS AND DISCUSSION

Before the main findings of this study are presented, a few remarks should be made about the general nature of the responses. In the first place, the identification task was obviously not a very difficult one. The listeners were willing to give a verdict on all stimuli and they showed no signs of stress or fatigue. Further, they obviously perceived a fairly sharp phoneme boundary somewhere along the continuum represented by the 20 different stimulus types. For example, one typical subject reported the following number of identifications as *å* for the test vowels 1 through 20: 0,0,0,0,0,0,0,0,0,0,0,1,3, 5,6,6,6,6,6,6,6. That is, he identified all tokens of the first 10 vowels unequivocally as *a*, was hesitant about vowels 11, 12, and 13, and rated all tokens of vowels 14 through 20 as *â*. Thus, there is a region of uncertainty between the areas of positive identification. Given the fact that the test vowels were spaced only 25 mels apart in the vowel space, the range of uncertainty seems rather narrow. In our example, the width of the range is three stimulus vowels, corresponding to 75 mels. As a matter of fact, the distances may be regarded as being even smaller. Since the two varying formants are so close, it seems quite probable that the listener really perceives them as a unit (I owe this observation to Gunnar Fant, personal communication). If that were the case, the space between stimuli would be 18 mels rather than 25 mels.

The location of the phoneme boundary along the continuum varied greatly between subjects. Obviously, one of the reasons for this variation should be differences in the linguistic norms of the groups to which the listeners belong. This was what the study set out to test. But unfortunately, there are other reasons for variation, too. People are not just group members but individuals as well, with their own experiences, expectations, and habits. Thus, just as there are considerable differences between users of one dialect at the level of phonetic production, similar differences must be expected to exist in perception. And indeed they do exist, as is evident from this and similar tests. Further, there is also a certain amount of variation between the performance of one individual in the same test at different times, due to such factors as level of attention and fluctuations in the functioning of the perceptual mechanisms.

Thus, there is intra-individual variation, inter-individual variation, and inter-group variation. In this study, we are primarily interested in the third of these. The obvious way to investigate it is to make appropriate samples from the relevant groups and to compare mean values. It should be remembered that the variation within the groups is composed of both inter-individual and intra-individual variation. That is, observed differences between tests of informants in one group may depend both upon permanent differences in perception and upon random day-to-day fluctuations, and in this investigation, at least, these two are not separated. Thus, there is no way to tell how much variation should be attributed to each of the two. (For further discussion, see Janson 1981.)

The results of the tests are summarized in Figure 14.1, which shows the mean identification functions for both groups. As expected, both curves show crossovers of identification from one perceptual category to the other as the stimulus parameters change. As can be seen, the curves for the YS and the OS groups are close to each other, but still clearly apart in the central portion. The members of the YS group interpret a larger proportion of the stimuli as *a*, which means that the shift goes in the expected direction. Thus, the result does support the hypothesis that a gradual sound change is going on in the Stockholm dialect.

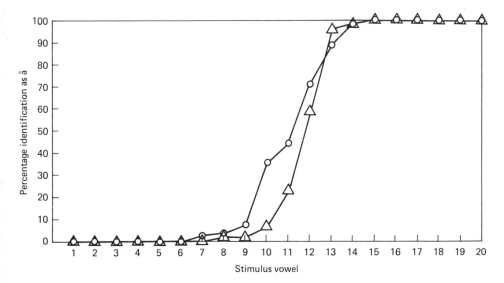

Figure 14.1   Identification of stimuli 1 through 20 as *å* by young Stockholmers (Δ) and older Stockholmers (○).

However, the difference between the two groups is very small, and this raises a number of questions. The first one is whether or not the difference is statistically significant. An affirmative answer can be given to this question. There are several possible ways of making a statistical comparison between the two groups. A very simple one is to note, for each test, the proportion of identifications as *å*. For example, if a person has identified 30 of the 120 tokens as *å*, the proportion *p* is .25. The *p* values for each group may be regarded as samples from the populations represented by the groups. For these samples, ordinary parametric tests can be used. Calculations show that the mean *p* value for the OS group is .476, with standard deviation .042, and the mean for the YS group is .440, with standard deviation .033. A *t*-test shows that the difference is significant at the .01 level ($p = .006$).

Another question which may be raised is whether the small difference between the groups really indicates a change in the dialect, or whether it might be just a reflection of some general difference in perception between young and old people. To check this, the test was also given to two groups of persons speaking another Swedish dialect, the one used by the Swedish minority in Finland. The first of these groups, OH, consisted of 19 inhabitants of Helsinki between 33 and 70 years, with the mean age of 49. All had the Swedish dialect of Finland as their mother tongue, but some had grown up outside the Helsinki area. The second group, YH, consisted of 15 school children from 10 to 12 years. The results for these two groups are shown in Figure

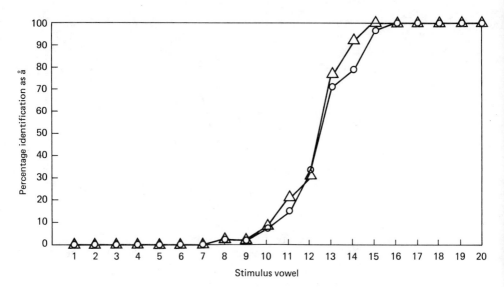

Figure 14.2 Identification of stimuli 1 through 20 as *å* by young (Δ) and older (○) persons from Helsinki.

14.2. As can be seen, the curves are almost identical. A *t*-test performed as above showed no significant difference between the groups.[1]

Thus, it seems that the difference between the two Stockholm groups is at least not caused by a general difference between young and old informants. Still there are other questions to be considered. An important one is the following: How great is this mean difference between young and old in Stockholm when compared to the variation within the groups, or to the region of uncertainty for each person?

The answer is that it is small in relation to both of these. First, the variation between individuals (which is really composed of intra-individual and inter-individual variation, as has been noted above) is so large that there is a considerable overlap in the two distributions of individual *p* values. As can be seen from the figures presented above, the difference between mean *p* values is .476 − .440 = .036. This is of the same magnitude as the standard deviations of the groups, which are .042 and .033, respectively. This means that if all individual *p* values for Stockholmers were plotted in one diagram

---

[1]There is a very strange thing about the Helsinki tests which cannot be fully discussed here, namely the location of the boundary. In the Helsinki dialect, the /a:/ is considerably more fronted than in the Stockholm dialect and the /o:/ is lower. Thus, one would certainly expect a larger number of identifications as *å* in Helsinki than in Stockholm. Instead, the reverse is the case. So far, I have not found any real explanation for this. It should be noted, though, that tests of four Finnish-speaking inhabitants of Helsinki gave results very similar to the ones for the Swedish-speaking people in the same city. I hope to return to this problem in the future.

without regard to age, it would not look like two distributions but rather like one with a barely perceptible dip in the center.

As for the region of uncertainty for each individual, it was shown above that it was three stimulus vowels, corresponding to 75 mels, for one typical informant. This is in fact exactly the mean value for all informants in the four groups. The p values can be given a very natural interpretation as points on the line in the vowel space. The distance between the two means of the groups, which is .036, corresponds to a distance of 18 mels. Thus, it is considerably smaller than the average region of uncertainty.

CONCLUSIONS

We have, then, a systematic difference in perception of the phoneme boundary between the two groups, but it is so small that, in practice, it will never show up as systematic misidentifications of phonemes between members of the groups, since differences in perception among individuals within the groups is a more important factor, and the sounds which might be interpreted in different ways by the two groups will at any rate belong to the region of uncertainty for individual listeners. It is of course tempting to believe that the situation at the perception end mirrors what is going on in production. That is, there may be statistically significant differences between old and young Stockholmers in the pronunciation of the long vowels, the young ones tending to back the /a:/ and perhaps the /o:/, too. But to work through the vast amount of production data necessary to establish significant figures for such minute differences between large groups of people would be a forbiddingly laborious task, even with the help of computerized spectrum analysis.

Thus, by studying perception and not production, we have found a way to discover even very slow and gradual sound change. As is well known, linguists up to the mid 1960s believed that virtually all sound change was indeed slow and gradual. We now know that this view is not correct, through the work of Weinreich, Labov, Wang, and others. But it is still quite possible, and indeed even probable, that a large part of all sound change is in fact slow and gradual (Labov 1981).[2] And for this type of change, linguists have for a long time accepted the view of earlier generations that direct observation is not possible. But it seems that Hockett (1965), Jespersen (1922:167), and the others were wrong. If changes are going on, they can be observed if the right technique is applied. In this chapter, one such technique has been demonstrated.

[2]For further discussion of the theoretical aspects of this experiment, see Janson 1983.

ACKNOWLEDGMENTS

The work presented in this chapter has been furthered by help from several people. Gunnar Fant at the Royal Institute of Technology in Stockholm made it possible for me to obtain synthesized stimuli, and Lennart Nord produced these stimuli from OVE 3. At the University of Stockholm, Björn Lindblom made valuable suggestions concerning the planning of the experiment, and Ronny Klingberg helped much with the technical equipment. In Helsinki, Mikael Reuter provided invaluable assistance by establishing contacts with all the informants I needed. And last but not least, my thanks to all the kind persons who willingly spent some of their time to perform a dull task.

REFERENCES

Hockett, C. F. 1965. Sound change. *Language* 41:185–204.
Janson, T. 1979. Vowel duration, vowel quality, and perceptual compensation. *Journal of Phonetics* 7:93–103.
Janson, T. 1981. Identical sounds and variable perception. In W. Dressler, O. Pfeiffer, & J. Rennison, eds., *Phonologica 1980* 215–221. Innsbruck: Institut für Sprachwissenschaft.
Janson, T. 1983. Sound change in perception and production. *Language* 59:18–34.
Jespersen, O. 1922. *Language*. London: Allen & Unwin.
Labov, W. 1981. Resolving the neogrammarian controversy. *Language* 57:267–308.

Subject Index*

A

Acquisition, 15, 82
Affricates, 10, 106, 112–113, 116, 226ff.
Air pressure, oral, 8, 127ff.
Analogy, 190
Analysis of variance, 7, 71–78, 222
Aspiration, 112–113, 150ff., 198–199, 212ff.
Assimilation, 46, 82ff., 207
Auditory processes, 7, 13, 18–20, 23ff., 82

B

Barks, 24
Base of articulation, 72, 76, 78
Borrowing, 164, 169

C

Categorization, 211–235
    models
        a posteriori probability, 145ff.
        normal *a posteriori* probability, 150ff.
        Thurstonian, 148ff.
Chomsky & Halle, *see* "Sound Pattern of English"
Cleft palate, 48, 95
Clicks, 112, 115
Comparative method, 10–11
Computer simulation, 19, 20–23, 29–34, 60–62
Concept Formation, 9–10, 206, 211–235
Confusion studies, 48–49, 54

Consonant clusters, 41, 120, 170–171, 177, 190, 240ff.; *see also* Phonotactics
Consonant/vowel ratio, 109
Contrast, 15, 28–36, 40, 47–50, 61–65, 84–87, 108, 115, 141–160
Critical band, 24, 47

D

Diachronic processes, *see* Sound change
Diphthongs, 36, 64, 106, 166–168
Discriminant function analysis, 147ff.
Dissimilation, 95
Distance metric, 19–21, 26–29, 42, 48

E

Ejectives, 8, 114, 116, 125–126, 130ff.
Electrical analogs of vocal tract, *see* Speech synthesis
External evidence, 164ff.

F

Features, 41, 190, 200–204, 227ff., 241
Fieldwork, 9–10, 127–138, 163–173, 176, 224, 235
Formalism, 4
Formant frequencies, 18ff., 49, 55–64, 69–77, 159, 254–256
Fricatives, 40, 110ff., 158–159
Functional load, 20
Fundamental frequency, 159

*When an entire chapter deals with a given topic, the page numbers of the *text* of the chapter are given, excluding Acknowledgments and References.

G

Generative grammar, 141, 163–164, 189, 241ff.
Glides, 177
Glottalized stops, 8, 125–138; *see also* Ejectives; Implosives
Greenberg & Jenkins model, 240ff.

H

Hearing, *see* Auditory processes
Historical change, *see* Sound change

I

Implicational hierarchies, 113ff., 126
Implosives, 8, 114, 125–126, 130ff.
INDSCAL, *see* Multidimensional scaling

L

Language change, *see* Sound change
Listener's expectations, 8, 19, 86–87

M

Markedness, 15–16, 242
Mel scale, 18, 21, 26, 56, 254–256, 259
Metrics, 164
Models, 4, 7
Morphemes, 107–108, 169–171, 191ff., 211
Morpheme structure constraints, conditions, *see* Phonotactics
Morphophonemes, 81, 143, 188
Multidimensional scaling, 50–57, 63, 71

N

Nasal consonants, 82ff., 110ff.
Nasalization, *see* Vowels, nasalized
Nasals, voiceless, 113
Natural generative phonology, 169
Natural phonology, 16
Normalization, 14, 31, 70–71, 78

O

Orthography, 164, 171, 196, 198–199, 206, 216–217, 220ff., 251

P

Palatography, 52–53
PARAFAC, *see* Multidimensional scaling
Perception, 8, 13, 17, 142ff., 253–259
Phonemes, 8, 10, 14, 106ff., 141ff., 188, 197ff., 211ff., 239ff., 253–259
Phonological inventories, 8, 105–122
Phonological rules, 9, 164ff., 188ff.
Phonotactics, 9–10, 81, 86–87, 95, 122, 169, 188, 239–251; *see also* Consonant clusters
Phons, 25
Pluralization, English, 189ff., 206–207
Principal components analysis, 58–60
Productivity, 191, 206
Prototypes, 213–214, 219
Psycholinguistic studies, 9–10, 187–207, 211–235, 239–251
Psychological mechanisms, 6
Psychological reality, 9–10, 163ff., 175ff., 188ff., 212ff., 239–251
Psychophysics, 7, 151

Q

Quantal theory of speech, 37

R

Reaction time, 213, 218–223
Rhyme (of syllable), 179, 200

S

Saussure, 81, 189
Scientific Revolution, 3
Secondary articulations, 117
Simplicity, 4
Sones, 24–26
Sound change, 6, 8, 10, 46, 81–87, 94, 116, 164, 253–259
"Sound Pattern of English," 15–16, 175, 200, 205–206, 227, 242ff.
Speech errors, 82, 164
Speech production, 13, 38–40, 150ff.
Speech recognition, automatic, 5
Speech synthesis, 5, 48–50, 60–61, 142ff., 254ff.
Spelling, *see* Orthography
Stanford Phonology Archive, 14, 96, 106

Stress, 106–107, 119
Structural linguistics, 189, 239
Surprasegmentals, 8, 118–122, 178ff.
Syllable, 83, 95, 120–121, 169, 176ff.

T

Tone, 9, 106–107, 119–121, 175ff.
Tone Sandhi, 183–184

U

Universals, phonetic and phonological, 6–8, 13–44, 46–47, 81–96, 105–122, 125–138, 250
UPSID, 8, 105–122

V

Voice onset time, 130, 142ff., 198
Vowel epenthesis, 165, 207
Vowel harmony, 107, 166, 168–169
Vowel length, 178, 212, 253
Vowel quality, 7, 69–78, 159–160, 253–259
Vowels, front rounded, 14–16, 28ff., 113, 166ff.
Vowel shift rule, 205–206, 235
Vowels, nasalized, 7–8, 40, 45–65, 81–96, 109
Vowel space, 13–42, 45–65, 259
Vowel systems, 7, 13–44, 45–65, 69–79, 109, 113, 159–160

W

Word games, 2, 9, 164ff., 175–184

Language Index

A

Akan, 82, 96, 113
Alabaman, 82, 96
Amahuaca, 31, 85, 96
Apinaye, 85, 96
Arabana-Wanganura, 112
Armenian, 82, 96
Asmat, 85n, 96, 108
Auca, 113
Australian, 112, 116
Awadhi, 82, 96
Azerbaijani, 82, 83, 96

B

Bakwiri, 176ff.
Bambara, 112, 179
Bashkir, 113
Beembe, 46, 47, 84, 96, 113
Bengali, 36, 63, 82, 83, 84, 96
Breton, 84, 96
Burmese, 84, 96, 179
Burushaski, 109

C

Cakchiquel, 129ff.
Cantonese, 85n, 96, 120, 121, 180–182
Capanahua, 83, 96
Carib, Island, 83, 84, 97
Caucasian, 109
Cayapa, 83, 96
Cham, 85n, 96
Chamorro, 31
Changsha, 84, 96
Chaozhou, 84, 85, 86, 96

C (continued)

Cheremis, 113
Chinatec, Quiotepec, 84, 97
Chinese, 40, 46, 84, 96
Chinese, Middle, 84, 85, 86
Chipewyan, 83, 97
Chontal, 83, 97

D

Dafla, 32
Dakota, 46, 47
Danish, 7, 76ff., 170ff.
Daribi, 109
Dayak, Land, 83, 97
Delaware, 83, 97
Diegueño, 85n, 97, 116
Dschang, 180–181
Dutch, 59–60, 70ff.

E

Ebrie, 46, 47
Efik, 113, 125
English, 7, 9, 63, 70ff., 83, 85n, 97, 142, 158, 188–207, 212ff., 240ff.
English, American, 48, 51ff., 87ff.
English, Canadian, 158–160
Etung, 178
Ewe, 83, 97, 113, 114

F

Fasu, 109
Finnish, 165–168, 170, 258n
French, 46, 48, 71, 84, 97
Fur, 112

G

Gã, 83, 97, 120, 121
Gbeya, 85, 97
Georgian, 83, 97
German, 48, 77ff.
Germanic, 76, 106
  East, 106
  North, 106
  West, 106
Goajiro, 83, 84, 97
Greek, 250
Greek, Modern, 83, 97
Greenlandic, 83, 97
Guarani, 83, 85, 95, 97
Gujarati, 63, 84, 97

H

Haida, 109
Hanunóo, 178
Hausa, 125, 179
Hawaiian, 108, 113, 120, 121
Higi, 120
Hindi, 63, 83, 84, 86, 97, 242n, 246n
Hopi, 113
Hupa, 83, 97, 113

I

Igbo, 113, 179
Ijo, 84, 97
Ila, 83, 97
Indo-European, 46
Irish, 116
Irish, Modern, 84, 97
Italian, 36, 71, 250

J

Japanese, 234–235
Jaqaru, 109
Javanese, 32
Jinan, 84, 96
Jukun, Takun, 84, 97
Jukun, Wukari, 85, 98

K

Kanuri, Yerwa, 83, 98

Kariera–Ngarluma, 112
Kashmiri, 83, 84, 97
K'ekchi, 128ff., 165, 168–171
Khalaj, 113
Khoisan, 107, 109
Kirghiz, 113
Korean, 85n, 97
Kpelle, 83, 85, 97, 178
Kru, 179, 179n, 180–181, 184
Kunjen, 83, 97
Kurux, 83, 84, 97
Kwa, 84n, 97

L

Latin, 84
Loma, 83, 97
Luo, 83, 97

M

Mabuiag, 116
Malagasy, 83, 97
Malay, 83, 97
Mandarin, 180–182
Maninka, 179
Mayan, 8, 125–138, 165, 171
Mazahua, 126
Mazatec, 83, 84, 97
Mende, 179
Mianka, 32
Mixtec, 83, 84, 97
Mongolian, 112
Mundari, 83, 97
Mura, 107

N

Nahuat, 83, 97
Nama, 83, 84, 97
Navaho, 83, 84, 97, 212
Nez Perce, 83, 97
Norwegian, 33
Nubian, Dongolese, 83, 97
Nupe, 84, 97
Nyangumata, 83, 97

O

Ojibwa, 83, 97

Ossetic, Western, 83, 98
Otomi, 85, 97
Ǫwǫn Afa, 84, 97

P

Paez, 83, 84, 97
Pawaian, 109
Picuris, 83, 95, 97
Pocomchi, 128ff.
Polish, 84
Polynesian, 109
Portuguese, 46, 47, 84, 84n, 97
Portuguese, Brazilian, 84, 96
Portuguese, Old, 84
Punjabi, 83, 84, 97

Q

Quechua, 120, 121
Quiche, 129ff.
Quichean, 8, 125–138

R

Rotokas, 107, 108, 118, 119n, 120, 121

S

Sanskrit, 84
Sentani, 83, 97
Shanghai, 84, 96
Shuangfeng, 84, 96
Sinhalese, 97
Siriono, 85, 97
Slavic, Common, 84, 97
Slavonic, Old Church, 84, 97
Slavonic, Pre-Old Church, 84
Somali, 83, 97
Songhai, 97
Spanish, 83, 97, 168–170
Spanish, Panamanian, 83, 97
Squamish, 31
Sundanese, 83, 97
Suzhou, 84, 96
Swahili, 83, 97
Swedish, 10, 38, 39, 40, 253–259

T

Tacana, 126
Tagalog, 83, 97, 113, 178
Taiwanese, 180–184
Taiyuan, 84, 96
Tamang, 179, 184
Tarascan, 114
Telefol, 85n, 97
Telugu, 83, 97
Tewa, 83, 84, 97
Thai, 83, 97, 120, 121, 142ff., 179n,
    180–182, 235
Ticuna, 83, 97
Tillamook, 83, 98
Tolowa, 83, 98
Tsou, 120, 121
Tunica, 83, 94, 98
Turkish, 32, 248
Tzeltal, 113
Tzutujil, 129ff.

V

Vietnamese, 120, 121, 126

W

Wichita, 112
Wolof, 83, 98, 113

X

Xiamen, 84, 84n, 85, 86, 96
Xian, 84, 97
!Xũ, 107

Y

Yangzhou, 84, 97
Yao, 83, 98
Yoruba, 64, 120, 121
Yuchi, 83, 84, 98

Z

Zulu, 83, 98
Zuni, 113